Praise for

THE TURNAROUND

"This is a true 'From Red to Black' story that every business executive should read and use as a reference manual to grow their business, improve their management skills, and increase the profits of their company. Bob Curry's first book, *From Red to Black,* was focused on improving the management's leadership skills, productive business operations, and hiring the best employees. Throughout *The Turnaround,* Bob's second book in the From Losses to Profits series, he has highlighted the 'Best Practices' that he used to grow the company's sales, improve the productivity of the management team, and take a company from losses to profits.

"This book is easy to read and makes a 'bookmark' obsolete. You will not be able to put this book down until you have read the last page. Keep a notebook close to record Bob's 'best business practices' while you read this book. Mark my words, you will read this book more than once . . . it is a great resource to learn more about how to make a business more profitable."

—Kathy Anthony, Vistage Florida Chair–
Executive Coach & Facilitator

"*The Turnaround* is brilliantly written by one of the best in his field, Robert Curry. This book is about an incredible turnaround of a distressed 48-million-dollar company that was headed for bankruptcy and how it grew to $130 million in sales and $4 million in profits in nine months. It is about growing sales and improving the management of a company to improve profits. A must-read for business executives and anyone looking to improve sales and profits."

—Dr. Joe Pace, Performance Psychologist and Chairman
of the Board–Global Education, The Pacific Institute

"Within the first few pages of this book, you'll realize Robert Curry is among the elite business turnaround experts in America. The book is very interesting because it tells the story about a company Bob took over and how he grew the company from $48 million and losing almost a million dollars in the prior year to $130 million in the first nine months, making the company very profitable.

"In this book, Mr. Curry describes the 'Best Practices' that were used to grow the business and to make the managers and employees accountable. This is definitely the type of book that once you start reading it, you cannot put it down until you finish the last chapter. Bob is the kind of guy you want on your team and with this recent book, *The Turnaround,* you can now have a peek into his million-dollar-business strategies."

—Shirley Solis, Peak Performance Coach and Family Catalyst

The TURNAROUND

TO PROFITS

FROM LOSSES

A True Story About ABC Computer Distributors and How They Went FROM **RED** TO **BLACK**

ROBERT S. CURRY
TURNAROUND SPECIALIST

RED TO
BLACK
BOOKS
FORT LAUDERDALE

Disclaimer: This book is designed to provide accurate and authoritative information regarding the subject matter covered. The publisher and author are not engaged in rendering legal advice or any other professional services to the reader. If legal advice or other assistance is required, the services of a competent professional should be sought. The reader should be aware that laws and rules applicable to their situation may differ from the information in this book. It is the responsibility of the reader to seek professional guidance whenever necessary. The author and publisher are not responsible for any adverse effects or consequences resulting from the use of the information in this book.

The Turnaround is based on a real client. However, actual names and identifying characteristics have not been used, and any resemblance to a specific individual or company is coincidental.

Published by:
Red to Black Books
Fort Lauderdale, Florida

Printed in the United States of America.

*To my wife, Esther Curry—
my best friend, partner, lover,
advisor, and supporter.*

CONTENTS

INTRODUCTION

"Leadership is a matter of having people look at you and gain confidence, seeing how you react. If you're in control, they're in control."

—Tom Landry, NFL Coach

I AM BOB CURRY, AN AUTHOR, BUSINESS TURNAROUND specialist, business coach, and motivational speaker. This book is a story about my first-ever turnaround engagement of a middle market company that had been in business for over ten years. The firm's financial institution hired me to salvage the company from filing bankruptcy. My job as the president/CEO of the organization was to improve the cash flow and profitability of the business. The engagement lasted a total of nine months.

During my twenty-year career of working with distressed companies and the owners of these businesses, I have experienced problems and issues with these organizations that I never learned about in any of my business textbooks in college. Each turnaround had its unique group of issues that caused the business to be unprofitable. It has not been the sole issue, but the one common problem of these distressed companies was poor leadership from the owners and management teams. My clients have ranged from a small hurricane shutter company with annual sales of $3.4 million (see my first book *From Red to Black—A Business Turnaround: The Matter of ABC Hurricane Shutters*) to a wholesale distributor with over $1 billion in annual sales. I have successfully worked on turning around

1

businesses in several industries, including service, distribution, manufacturing, wholesale, healthcare, and retail.

The goal of this book is to tell the story of ABC Computer Distributors to illustrate the problems that were causing this company to lose money. I will explain how we corrected the issues and made the company profitable again. This business was doing approximately $50 million in sales and had lost slightly less than $1 million in the prior twelve months before I joined the organization. This company had taken a steady downhill slide from being profitable to losing money during the preceding two years. There were a plethora of reasons why, but the main reason was that the owner and president of the company took his focus off the business. The owner of the company had a poor reputation with the customers, vendors, and employees. The company that financed ABC Computer Distributors was ready to shut the business down, liquidate the assets, and close the doors for good before I joined the organization.

I do not want to tell the results of the turnaround in the first couple of pages of the book, but I will share that you will be surprised at the material impact on the profitability that resulted when we upgraded the management team and implemented some "best practices" procedures in several areas of the business.

The company was at the breakeven point within one month of my engagement and very profitable within three months. ABC Computer Distributors was so successful that we sold the company at a premium nine months after I joined the organization. We returned 100 percent of the loan balance to the financing company, distributed a sizable check to the original business owner, and I received my share of the proceeds as per the agreement.

As you read this book, you will find that I have included policies, procedures, and forms that I used during the turnaround that may help any business owner manage or upgrade his or her own business. Please feel free to use anything and everything in this book to benefit you with your own business or business life.

Chapter 1

BEFORE ABC COMPUTER DISTRIBUTORS

*"The secret of my success is that we have gone to
exceptional lengths to hire the best people in the world."*

—Steve Jobs, Co-Founder of Apple

BEFORE I EVER DID A TURNAROUND, I WORKED FOR A PUBLIC
accounting firm and three other companies after I graduated from
college with a bachelor's degree in business administration in
accounting. At the graduation ceremony, my father asked me what
I wanted to do for the rest of my life with my accounting degree.
I told my dad that I wanted to be the president of a $100 million
company by the time I was forty years old. He just looked at me
and laughed.

These early jobs in my career provided me with the experience
and knowledge to later work with many distressed companies in
the following twenty years and successfully turn them around to be
profitable. My first job with the public accounting firm lasted for two
years. The only reason I worked there for that long— *precisely* twenty-four months—was that I wanted to take and pass the CPA exam.
Back then, you were required to have at least two years of public
accounting experience before you were eligible to sit for the exam.
I did not enjoy the business of public accounting, but I will always
appreciate the extensive accounting knowledge and business experience I gained during my college education and career experience.

I could not wait to get my two years' experience completed so I could quit and get a job "on the other side of the table." What I mean by "the other side of the table" is working for a company that is in business to make a profit. I knew that it was important for an accounting firm to be profitable, but it was not the same to me. Working on a client's financial records, doing an audit or a tax return for an hourly billing rate never got my juices flowing.

* * *

My second job was with a large wholesale grocery distributor that was a client of the accounting firm. I worked for the internal audit department for the company. My responsibilities were to go to all the company's divisions, review all the financial records, policies, and procedures, and write up my findings. Traveling around the country visiting all the company's different divisions was very interesting and professionally rewarding. The business knowledge I acquired while at this wholesales grocery distributor proved to be very valuable to me once I started doing turnarounds.

After six months, the CFO promoted me from the internal audit department to be the assistant controller at one of the divisions of the company. The divisional general manager had fired both the controller and assistant controller one Friday afternoon for reasons not disclosed to me. The company then sent the corporate accounting manager (his name was Ed) to the division to be the new controller, and I joined him as the assistant controller. This division operated two different businesses. The first was a distribution company that sold approximately $130 million of health and beauty aids to their franchised grocery stores. The second was a retail business, a chain of fifteen retail hardware stores. The hardware store chain did approximately $30 million in sales per year.

When Ed, the new controller, and I arrived at the division for our new job assignments, the financial records were a mess. We worked twelve-hour days, six days a week for the first two months to clean everything up. At that time, I was very young, only twenty-five years old. I was shocked that a $160 million division of a billion-dollar company could be in such an unreconciled financial mess. My "rookie" vision at that young age was that the executives managed all big businesses well, and the accounting records and financial statements were always timely and accurate. I was surprised and wrong.

Ed and I worked hard together to clean up the accounting disaster. During this cleanup, he was getting stressed and worn down. I did not think much about it at the time because I was feeling the same way. Ed was forty-five years old and married with no kids. When offered this divisional controller position, he did not want to take the job. Ed had enjoyed his comfortable corporate accounting manager position for the previous eight years. He had planned to turn down the promotion, but his wife had insisted that he take the job because of the increase in his compensation. The money was not that important to Ed. He did not want to change his current comfortable lifestyle, both at home and at work. Ed was a respectable professional and a complete introvert. He was the perfect definition of a "backroom accountant." Ed's personality was not a good fit to handle this controller position.

"Chasing the money" for a new position or promotion may or may not always be a good thing for your career.

In Ed's new position, there were thirty-five employees in the finance department. At Ed's old job as the corporate accounting manager, he had been responsible for managing six accountants, all of whom had similar personalities to his. They all would come to the office, grind out the accounting work all day, and go home in the evening. Ed's team required very little managing. They all knew their jobs, and Ed was more their friend than their manager. Ed's group of employees was responsible for consolidating the monthly financial statements for all the divisions and issuing the monthly financial package to the company's corporate management team. Ed's job as the accounting manager was not easy, but it was not stressful either.

The big difference was this controller position had many more responsibilities than Ed's old job. This type of professional situation was not in Ed's sweet spot, and he knew it. Also, unfortunately, when promoted, he and his wife were having tough times in their marriage.

One Saturday, after working six twelve-hour days in a row, Ed asked me if my wife and I would like to come over for dinner at their house. I accepted the invitation. After eating dinner, we planned to play the card game Hearts. The four of us had a very nice relaxing meal, which both Ed and I needed. After dinner, we all had coffee and dessert. My wife and I had brought an apple pie, vanilla ice cream, and a bottle of red wine. After dessert, our wives took the dishes into the kitchen while Ed and I cleared the table and got out the deck of cards.

Hearts is a fun game unless you get the queen of spades. Unfortunately, Ed's wife got the queen of spades three times in three consecutive games, and she was losing badly in points. The next time she received the queen, she immediately was outraged and threw the cards across the room. She started crying, went to her bedroom, and slammed the door. Ed froze. He did not know what to say or do. I saw the look on his face when she threw the temper tantrum. I felt so sorry for him because he was embarrassed that his wife had blown up over a card game. I told Ed that my wife and I were leaving because it had been a long week, and I needed to get some rest. We got up, both hugged Ed, and were out of there as quickly as possible.

The following Monday, Ed came to work looking like he had not slept the whole weekend. His eyes were glassy and seemed to be staring into space. I went to my office and started working on the month-end closing. About 11:45 a.m., I decided to check on Ed to see if he wanted to go to lunch together. When I arrived at his office, he was staring at the wall humming the tune for "Pop Goes the Weasel." I asked him if he wanted to grab a bite, and he did not answer me. I asked him again, and he did not acknowledge that I was even in the room. I tapped him on the shoulder and nothing.

I stepped out of his office and asked his administrative assistant to call 911 for an ambulance. I immediately called Ed's wife and told her what happened so that she could meet him at the hospital. Ed had had a mental breakdown due to all the stress in his personal and professional life.

> Ed's wife wanted him to "chase the money" for the controller promotion, but he was so unhappy and stressed that he had a mental breakdown.

I felt awful for Ed; he was such a good man. He was in a perfect position for his personality as the corporate accounting manager working with people who were just like him. When he moved to the new controller position, he was out of his element. The combination of the stress at home and work caused him to have the breakdown. If it had not been for his wife pushing him, Ed would have passed up the promotion. He would have been happy as the corporate accounting manager, and his stress level would not have been a problem.

> Stress is a terrible thing; it can control you and cause a mental breakdown or worse. I learned to watch for the signs of stress in my own life so that stress would not overtake me as it did Ed.

George, the general manager of the division, was Ed's boss at the time. After the EMTs took Ed out on a stretcher, George asked me what had happened. George was a nice person, but he did put significant stress on Ed to get everything cleaned up in his department quickly. I got the impression that George had an equal amount of pressure on him from his boss to get the accounting records cleaned up. George and I spent the afternoon together, talking about the whole situation with Ed and the finance department. I was lucky because Ed and I had had everything reconciled before Ed had the breakdown. After we analyzed the balance sheet, we reconciled the year-to-date income statement. Surprisingly, he asked me what I wanted to do if Ed was not able to return to the controller position.

I was shocked that he asked me such a question. I told him that I wanted the controller position and would hire an assistant controller to replace myself. George said he would sleep on the decision and let me know as soon as he learned more about the situation with Ed.

> This situation with Ed was a perfect example of promoting someone into the wrong position for his personality, and it ended in a real tragedy.

When I went home that evening, my wife and I went to the hospital to visit Ed. When we got there, he was in his hospital bed eating dinner. His wife, Dorothy, was sitting in the chair next to the bed. She jumped up when we got there and gave both of us a hug. Ed was happy to see us. After we had shaken hands, Ed asked me what had happened. He only remembered arriving at work that morning, and then the next thing he knew, he was waking up in the hospital bed.

I shared with him everything I knew. I asked him what he thought happened. Ed was never one to be talkative, but he was that night in the hospital. Our wives left the room to go to the hospital cafeteria to get more coffee so that Ed and I could discuss the issue privately. He told me that he hated being in the controller position. He did not want to relocate because he loved his old home and neighborhood. (The company had rented homes for each of us for a couple of months until we sold our houses and purchased new homes close to the division.) He said that the neighborhood where they currently owned their home was like one big family and he missed them all. Ed said he wished he had never left his old job. All the accountants he used to work with at the corporate accounting department were his friends.

Ed told me that he hated working the sixty-hour workweeks and that the division was considering purchasing another company soon, so the workload was not going to let up for several months. It was clear to me that this organization had pulled Ed out of his comfortable home, neighborhood, and job, putting his whole life in turmoil. His stress level just shut him down. The more I listened to Ed, the more I felt sorry for him. I had two cups of coffee as I listened to his story. I asked Ed what his plans were for the future. He said that he was going to try to get his old job back if he could. He asked me not to mention a word to anyone about what had happened. He planned to tell the HR department that he had recently started a new medication and the problem that sent him to the hospital in an ambulance was the result of the new meds. I told Ed I would support him however I could; his secret was safe with me. We had grown very close during our long work hours cleaning up the finance department. I wanted the best for Ed. Ed also told me that he was going to sit down with his wife and have a long talk with her. He was not going to let her push him around ever again.

> When hiring a new senior manager, like Ed, make sure to pay attention to his or her personality and temperament for the job. Ed had the experience and knowledge to be a reliable controller, but he did not have the character for the job. Ed was a "backroom" accountant type, or a "grinder," and the position called for someone who was outgoing and a leader with business knowledge. There is a difference between the two types of personalities: one can create success and the other can cause failure in the same position.

When our wives came back from the cafeteria, I was ready to leave. Ed got out of bed and hugged me. I knew that he felt less stressed now, having talked the whole thing through. He was pleased that he had just come up with some better decisions. We left and went home. My wife asked me a dozen questions about what Ed and I had talked about while she and Dorothy went for coffee. I told her the *Reader's Digest* version of Ed's story.

To make a long story short, Ed got his old job back. We stayed in touch for many years and had a great relationship. When Ed announced that he was going back to corporate, the controller position was mine. I hired my replacement for the assistant controller position. My work schedule was forty-hour workweeks except during the "monthly financial close week" when I came in an hour early each day and worked until 6:00 in the evening. I loved being home each night to enjoy dinner with my wife and family, so 6:00 was my deadline to leave the office.

After working there as the controller for two years, I received a phone call from an executive recruiter out of Baltimore. He said that he had a client looking to fill an assistant controller position with retail accounting experience. Initially, I told him that I had been the controller of this organization for two years, and I did not want to take a step backward with the "assistant" title. I had no idea how the recruiter had found me because I was not looking for a job. I enjoyed my position, my boss, and the people in the finance department. I was happy at home and pleased with how my career was going. Life was good.

I felt weird even talking to the recruiter because it was as if I was cheating on my company by speaking with him. He said that the job was in Philadelphia with a publicly traded company and told me the salary range they were offering for the job. At that time, I was making good money for my age, but the compensation for this position was almost double my current salary. I did not want to go backward to an assistant controller title, but the money was crazy good. I was loyal to my employer, but this type of increase was too much to pass up. At the time, my son was three years old, and my daughter was two. That kind of salary increase was "life-changing." I could provide a much better lifestyle for my family with that kind of increase in compensation. Still, I always had my friend Ed on my mind in a circumstance like this. Ed's wife had wanted him to chase the money for the promotion, but he was so unhappy and stressed that he'd had a mental breakdown.

My first job in public accounting was a "job," and I could not wait to get my two years in, so I could take the CPA exam and get out. Public accounting felt like a prison sentence to me. The controller position did not feel like work to me because I

> thoroughly enjoyed what I was doing in my management role
> with this organization. The job stressed Ed out and caused him to
> have a mental breakdown. With me, I enjoyed every day at work.

I flew to Philadelphia three times, twice for interviews and once to talk about the offer, the relocation package, the benefits, and a start date. Two weeks later, I was staying in a long-term-stay motel working at my new job. My wife and kids were back in Pittsburgh prepping our home for sale. The whole transaction went very quickly. We found a home in the new area. A week later, we had a contract on our house at the full asking price. Within two months, my family and I were in our new home, and I was comfortable in my new position.

I was with the health and beauty aids distributor/retail hardware store chain for two years in the controller position, and I learned a lot while working for that organization. When I left, I missed my team in the finance department.

* * *

At the young age of twenty-seven, I began working for a public company in the toy industry as the assistant controller. When I started, the company had fifty-five stores in thirteen states and did $105 million in sales. The company's headquarters was in Northeast Philadelphia. When I joined the organization, there were two hundred employees worked at the corporate headquarters and forty-five of the employees reported to me. I was responsible for managing the general accounting, accounts payable, cash management, payroll, and tax departments.

Six months after I joined the company, my boss, the controller, gave notice and left two weeks later. One week before he moved on to his new position, he called me into his office to tell me that it was management's decision not to replace him. He had recommended they promote me to take over his controller's position. Based on his recommendation, I was the controller the day after he left the company.

Three months after my promotion, the president of the company purchased another company that increased the number of stores from fifty-five to seventy-two. I received a thirty-day notification from the president about the acquisition. It was then my responsibility to hire seven new employees: two professionals, two junior accountants, and three accounts payable clerks. It was also my responsibility to manage the taking of all the physical inventories at the newly acquired stores. I was to oversee the addition of all the new employees onto our payroll system, open new bank and credit card accounts, and close the old ones, along with a list of thirty other financial and operational tasks. These acquisition responsibilities were in addition to managing all my current duties of our existing business, which was not easy.

> I knew that due to the rapid sales growth of the company,
> a small issue could quickly become a significant problem,
> and an undetected problem could cost me my job.

I worked for this company for eight years. During that period, the company tripled in size to over $300 million in sales. After the first couple of years of my young and naïve, "trial-and-error" management style, I knew that I needed to have excellent managers over the five departments reporting to me, or I would crash and burn personally and professionally. I knew that I was only as good as my management team. If I had a weak manager overseeing one of my departments, the other four managers and I would be at risk.

> I understood that I had to employ only quality employees,
> or everyone would get hurt and the company would
> suffer. Because I was so young and inexperienced, I
> knew that I needed mature and experienced people
> on my team to guarantee I would not fail.

Every three to six months, I reviewed each manager for the status of their department, their employees, the quality and accuracy of their work, and the timing of the completion of the monthly reporting. It was my job to be aware of any problems and any suggested solutions immediately.

I focused on open communications with the five managers who reported to me. Twice a month, we all went to dinner together at a local sports pub to relax and download any issues with each other. These meals enabled all of us to share our problems and to fix any inefficiencies as a team. These nights out as a group worked very well with the all the managers because, over time, we all learned to trust each other and protect each other's backs. Not only were the quarterly reviews good for keeping the managers professional, but the managers would not let the other managers fail. We all identified any weaknesses in any of the departments and discussed the resolutions of the problems. Each manager knew what their strengths and weaknesses were, and appropriately, we all dealt with them as a team.

After the six of us had been all together for a couple of years, the whole finance department functioned like a well-oiled machine. Each manager had checklists of their weekly and monthly responsibilities to accomplish. They also had the other managers' lists, so if the other departments got behind in their work, they could help each other. Because the company was a division of a publicly traded company, being late or inaccurate with the monthly and quarterly financial statements was not an option.

> I knew that systems, policies, procedures, communication, and reporting were critical to maintaining control of the company's financial records and its assets.

While I was the controller of the company, the president purchased five businesses, and the finance department handled each acquisition very efficiently. If we did not keep up with the workload, the whole company would fail, as well as its controller, which would be me! We consistently reviewed each functional area of all five departments quarterly with a goal of improving the productivity and efficiency of the work. I incented and rewarded employees when they found better and more efficient ways to enhance the production of their departments or other departments in the company. Not only did I compensate them, but I also did so publicly. I wanted to send a message to all employees that it is a good thing to improve everything in our work environment, and if you do, rewards will hit your wallet or purse, too!

In the eight years I was with the toy company, I learned a lot about the controller function for a large public corporation. However, more importantly, I learned how to be a good manager. I also learned how to treat the individuals who reported to me with respect.

My five department managers were my team, but they were also my friends. Those five managers all did an excellent job for the company. I am still proud when I think back to the difference between the status of the financial department when I joined the organization and the "well-oiled" efficient, productive team I left behind.

* * *

One Saturday afternoon, I was playing a round of golf with a good friend. The starter matched us up with another twosome. The two men, Hal and Nick, in the other golf cart owned a home-building and commercial construction company located right outside of Philadelphia. I knew about the company because they had several new home developments under construction in the local area. These two business owners and their organization had an excellent reputation as a quality home builder. During the golf match, I must have asked them dozens of questions about their business. That was normal for me because of my love for business. I enjoy learning about a new area of business in which I have had no experience.

After the match, the four of us had a beer together and talked for another hour. In the end, before we left the clubhouse, both Hal and Nick asked me for my business card. Later that week, I received a phone call at the office from Hal asking me if I would like to join them for another round of golf on Saturday. I gladly accepted because I had enjoyed our first round of golf together.

Saturday's golf match was different from the prior week's round of golf. We played for money this time. When gambling is part of the golf game, my game changes. My focus level on each shot is intense, and I think through every hole before I play it. Golf is a mental game with risk and reward on every shot decision, sort of like business. To make a long eighteen-hole story short, I was the overall winner in the foursome. I received several comments about being a "sandbagger." Life was beautiful on the golf course that day. In the clubhouse, my winnings were sitting at the bar ready to pay the tab for all the beer and food for the foursome.

After having one beer together, Nick asked me if I knew anything about the home-building business. I told him, other than what I had learned on the golf course over the past two weekends talking to him and Hal, I knew nothing about the construction industry. I told Nick that I had experience in the retail and distribution businesses, but not in construction. Nick asked me if I would be available to meet him and Hal for lunch on Monday. I told him that I could probably arrange that and asked where were we meeting. Nick said I should meet them at their offices at 11:00 in the morning, and we would eat lunch across the street at his favorite French restaurant. We shook hands. I paid the food and bar bill and headed home.

* * *

Monday, I arrived at the H&N Construction Company at 11:00 a.m. sharp. I was very impressed with the building and reception area of the company. The business was in a four-story red brick building in the heart of the quaint little town of Wayne, which was just outside of Philadelphia. The reception area was very modern and had beautiful fresh roses on the receptionist's desk. There was a sign next to the receptionist's desk: "Mr. Curry, welcome to H&N Construction Company." That personalized sign in the reception immediately gave me a warm "welcome" feeling. The receptionist's name was Angela as per her name sign next to the red roses. Angela was in her mid-forties and dressed professionally. She had a pleasant smile that did not change when she welcomed me. Immediately, Angela said, "Welcome, Mr. Curry. Nick is waiting for you in the conference room."

"Angela, how did you know my name?" I asked.

"Nick told me that you were coming at eleven o'clock, Mr. Curry. He also said that you were tall and a friendly guy. Plus, I looked up your profile on LinkedIn and saw your picture."

I gave her a big smile. "Well, Angela, when I grow up and own a company, I want to hire a receptionist who is just like you!"

"Thank you, Mr. Curry," Angela said with a chuckle. "Let me walk you to the conference room. Can I get you a bottle of water or a cup of coffee?"

"No, thank you, Angela."

When Angela led me into the conference room, Nick was there with a hot cup of coffee in front of him. The room was quite large with a big, beautiful mahogany table surrounded by a dozen high-back black leather chairs. The room had several windows on three sides, lighting up the whole conference room. Beautifully framed pictures of all home developments built by Hal and Nick's company covered the room's four walls.

When I entered, Nick jumped up, greeting me with a firm hand-shake and a big, hearty "Welcome to H&N Construction, Bob." There was a platter of bagels and fruit on the table with a pot of coffee, and H&N branded coffee cups. I felt a little like a celebrity with all this attention. Nick offered me coffee, a bagel, and asked me to have a seat. I poured a cup of coffee, added a little cream, and was about to sit down when Hal walked into the room. I stood back up to shake Hal's hand and then sat back down. I was not sure why I was there. I thought that I was meeting them for lunch, a nice meal with my two new friends from the golf course.

Hal sat down and thanked me for coming to the office. A moment later, he stood and asked me to walk with him around the room as he described the home developments they had built over the years depicted in the photos. I was impressed. When Hal finished, he asked me to follow him again. He and Nick walked me around the whole office to each department on all four floors of the building. The environment in this firm was fantastic. The employees all looked happy. Whenever the three of us walked into a room, every employee stopped what they were doing and stood up to welcome us. Nick and Hal introduced me to every employee, told me what each person did and how long they had worked for the organization. Most of the employees had been with the company for ten-plus years. I kept thinking about how the work environment created by these two business owners was incredible. I could see that this was a great place to work. We finished the company tour and ended up back in the conference room. The fruit and bagels were gone, replaced by a platter of sandwiches, chips, and cans of soda.

Nick said, "If it is okay with you, Bob, we decided to eat in, so we could talk and not be interrupted. It is quieter here than at the restaurant across the street."

Hal said, "It tends to be like a zoo over there at times."

I smiled and said, "It is okay with me." I was wondering what they wanted, maybe another round of golf this weekend?

When we all had a sandwich in front of us and a can of soda, Hal said, "We have invited you to the company because we would like to talk about business."

I knew something was up, but I had no idea what.

Hal continued, "Bob, we have been looking for a chief financial officer for our company for over six months, and to date, we have been unsuccessful in the search."

Nick added, "Bob, when we met you on the golf course, and you asked us all those questions, we started thinking about you as a candidate for the CFO position."

I kept the shock I felt off my face and continued to listen.

"We had checked you out," Hal explained, "and even though your experience has not been in the construction industry, we think you can do a great job here."

I looked at Nick and asked, "How do you know that? I could

understand you saying that you know how I hit a driver or an approach shot from a hundred and fifty yards to the green, but I have not told you anything about myself."

Hal picked up a stack of papers off the credenza behind him. He put them down on the table in front of him and then pulled out his reading glasses from his shirt pocket. Hal put the glasses on at the end of his nose. Hal was always very deliberate with anything he did, much like an engineer. He said that they had me checked out by a private security company.

This time my jaw dropped. Hal went on to tell me everything about myself from the time I was a child. They knew where I went to high school, including my grades and the sports I played. He told me about the college I graduated from, my studies, and how I did academically. He stated that my father owned three bowling alleys and that I had worked for him since I was at a very young age.

Next, he talked about my professional career. He read a paragraph from the report about my job with the public accounting firm and many of the facts at the wholesale grocery company where I had been the controller of the health and beauty aid and retail divisions. He then recapped my last eight years with the retail toy company. He said that the firm had grown by 300 percent since I had started working for them, and my department had been the foundation of the business supporting the company's aggressive growth. After describing the last fourteen years of my career for about fifteen minutes, he started with my family. He knew that I have four sisters and one brother. He told me where they all lived and what they all did for a living. He knew that I met my wife in college and we had gotten married a month after I graduated. He knew the names of my two children, Bobby and Jennifer. After about five more minutes of information about my family, including my credit rating, Hal took off his glasses and looked at me. I could only start laughing and shaking my head no! Hal asked me what was so funny.

I replied, "You researched all this information about me just because I won forty dollars off you and Nick on the golf course Saturday?"

Nick started laughing and then said, "Bob, since the first time we met you, we were very impressed." He explained that they had talked about hiring me for the CFO position for their company and decided to invite me to play golf again that past weekend to get a better understanding of my personality.

> Hal and Nick hired employees based on the individual's personality. Education, work experience, and skills are essential, but not nearly as important as personality. They want to match the personality with the job description, the company's corporate culture, and the personality types of the rest of the employees in the organization.

Nick went on, "Bob, you can learn a lot about a person riding in a golf cart together for eighteen holes." Nick said that after I had accepted their invitation to play another round of golf, they decided to do a background check on me before the second meeting. That way, if everything proved to be okay with my personal history, they could start talking to me about joining their company. All they would have to do is have me undergo a drug test before they wrote me an offer letter. I could hardly believe they would do such a comprehensive background check on me before they even talked to me about the position.

> Hal and Nick never offered a person a job with their company before they did a complete and comprehensive background, criminal, drug, and credit check on the candidate.

Nick said, "Bob, we have never offered a person a job with our company before we did a complete and comprehensive background, criminal, drug, and credit check on the candidate. I guess it is evident that we are interested in you joining our organization here. We have a minimal amount of turnover with our firm because we treat people with the respect that they deserve. We pay every employee a fair salary for his or her position. We bonus everyone in the company from the company's profits. Fifty cents of every dollar of profit goes back to the employees as bonuses. Hal and I believe that the way we make money with our business is to hire the best people in the area, treat them with respect, give them the tools to do their job, provide them an excellent environment to work in and compensate them fairly. We do a performance review with all employees in the company every January and July. We share with them what they are doing right and what they may be doing wrong. The review times in this firm are easy to deal with because we employ the best people. Everyone loves working here and respects their job. We have not had an employee leave the company in two and a half years. We had a great CFO six months ago, but he was in a horrible car accident and did not make it. The position has been open since then because we have not been able to find the right person. We are hoping that you are the right person for the job. This hiring system we use has worked for us very successfully for the thirty years that Hal and I have been in business together, and Bob, we are not going to change it now."

> Hal and Nick believed that the way to make money in their business was to hire the best people in the area, treat them with respect, give them the tools to do their job, provide them an excellent environment to work in, and compensate them fairly.

To say the very least, I was stunned. I had no idea that this was why they invited me to lunch. Hal and Nick were straightforward and deliberate about their hiring practices. They did not advertise to fill the CFO position; they went out and found a senior manager for their company on the golf course.

Hal asked, "Bob, what do you think about this? Did you expect that we were going to offer you a job today?"

"No, Hal. I expected a cheeseburger, French fries, and a diet coke."

Hal laughed goodheartedly at my expectation. "So, Bob, is it okay if we start talking business now?"

"Sure, Hal, you have already knocked my socks off in the first forty-five minutes, why stop now?"

H&N Construction did a performance review of all employees in the company every January and July. They shared with each employee what they are doing right and what they may be doing wrong. The review times in their firm were easy to deal with because they employed the best people. Everyone loved working there and respected their job. At the time of my hire, H&N had not had one employee leave the company in the previous two and a half years.

"We have no idea what your company is paying you, but we will increase your compensation by twenty percent in the first year. You will be part of a management bonus program in which fifty percent of the company profits go to bonuses to the employees. The managers' shares are twenty-five percent of the earnings. The managers distribute the balance to the employees based on their productivity and seniority with the company. Then twenty-five percent of annual profits are bonuses for Nick and me. The company retains the remaining twenty-five percent to generate future profits. Bob, we have a solid balance sheet. The money that we reinvested back into the company has kept the business with a minimal amount of bank debt, which is where we want it, in the small loan balance category.

"If you accept the job, we will give you an employment contract that will state everything that I am telling you right now. We will also give you a one-time bonus of twenty-five percent of your starting salary if you are still with the company in three years. That is our investment in you to put some 'golden handcuffs' on you to stay with the organization to make it successful long-term. We want you to move into one of our current home developments under construction. We will defer your mortgage payments for five years and forgive the debt if you are still with the company at that time. So, Bob, how does this all sound to you?"

"Well, gentlemen, you successfully have taken the decision entirely out of my hands. I would be an absolute crazy man if I did not accept such an offer for this CFO position. I have two things that I must do before I can talk to you about formally accepting your offer."

"What is that?" asked Nick.

"I must speak to my wife, and then I should do a background check on the two of you gentlemen."

Nick laughed and said, "That is okay with me; just make sure that you get the right Nick. I have a son with the same name as mine, and he is a wild man! I am not sure what his background check would say."

"Bob, I am assuming that you would not object to taking a drug test, would you?" Hal asked.

"Hal, I have never smoked a cigarette or taken any illegal drug in my life, so that would not be a problem."

"Bob, I didn't think so."

> The employees in the company were one big team supporting each other to make the business very profitable. This group of employees was like a "Dream Team" case study of a successful business. I believe the reason the company was so successful was that the two owners made the hiring process the most important function they were responsible for accomplishing.

Naturally, I accepted Hal and Nick's lucrative job offer to be the CFO of H&N Construction Co. This position was the best job I ever had in my life. Hal and Nick were good people and great bosses for every employee who worked for the organization. They did not delegate the hiring responsibility to anyone else, especially when hiring senior members of the management team. They were very meticulous in offering candidates a job. They treated every employee with respect. They gave each employee the opportunity to be successful within their organization. These business owners were "first-class" managers.

After working for H&N Construction Company for four years, all the CFO functional areas of my departments were running efficiently and required very little of my "hands-on" time. Hal and Nick promoted me to be the CFO/COO for the organization in which every vice president in the company reported to me, and I was the only executive who answered to Hal and Nick. This promotion gave me incredible experience managing the non-financial departments of the organization, including the sales and construction departments. The new areas that I was responsible for were a significant challenge and helped me grow professionally to be ready for a CEO position.

A national developer purchased the company after I was with the organization for eight years. The developer was only interested in buying the land contracts that H&N Construction owned. They acquired the corporation, so then they possessed the land contracts. The new organization did not hire one employee from H&N, which was, in my opinion, a mistake on their part. Hal and Nick made a huge profit from the sale of the company and shared 50 percent of the profits with the employees, just as they had done for many years. Some employees received a settlement check larger than any amount of money they had ever made in their whole career.

Hal and Nick were fantastic owners. It seemed that I had a job for life back then. The sale of the company made me very sad. Nick and Hal were my bosses, but more importantly, they were my best friends. I trusted them 100 percent of the time. They both were honest and very loyal to their employees. They treated their employees like family, and in return, the employees treated them the same. Turnover was nonexistent in the company during the eight years I worked there. If not for the sale of the company, I would still be working there today because I loved going to work.

Employee turnover is a costly business expense, but not for H&N Construction Co. because they invested the time and money in the hiring process to materially reduce any hiring mistakes.

The day of the settlement of the sale of the company was both a sad and happy day. Everyone had to pack up his or her possessions at the office, which was very tough. However, when all the employees received the envelope with their share of the settlement, suddenly the day got better! I decided that I was going to deposit my settlement check in the bank and take the next year off to travel the world and play golf. I planned to play as many of the "America's 100 Greatest Public Golf Courses," as listed by the *Golf Digest* magazine, as I could.

The settlement was on a Thursday, and by the following Monday (four days later), my life changed again. My travel and golf dreams did not even last for a week.

For the rest of my career, I will always remember the lessons I learned from Hal and Nick at H&N Construction Co.

Chapter 2

AMERICA'S 100 GREATEST PUBLIC GOLF COURSES

"As a business owner or manager, you know that hiring the wrong person is the most costly mistake you can make."

—BRIAN TRACY, MOTIVATIONAL PUBLIC SPEAKER
AND SELF-DEVELOPMENT AUTHOR

FRIDAY, DECEMBER 1

THE DAY AFTER THE SETTLEMENT WITH H&N CONSTRUCTION Company, I was on the golf course early in the morning. It was a warm day for December, in the low sixties. The starter on the first tee matched me up with a good friend of mine, Kevin. I love golfing in the fall because usually there are not a lot of people on the course. If the weather was right, I could play eighteen holes in three hours or less.

My friend Kevin worked for a computer floor-planning company. If you do not know what a "floor planner" is, their business is to finance computer distributorships, much like a bank that uses their customer's inventory and accounts receivables as collateral for the company's line of credit. Kevin was two or three years my junior and had red hair with a military-style cut. He worked out, pumping iron seven days a week. It was easy to tell, especially when he was wearing a golf shirt; his arms and chest were huge. Kevin was a

25

decent golfer. I think he would have been much better if his muscles didn't get in the way, and he had no patience for putting.

Kevin was a good person and fun to be with on the golf course. We always had a good time together, and there was even a little "trash talking" on the golf course at times by both parties. The fun part of my golf matches with Kevin was "getting in Kevin's head" during a round of golf when we had a little wager on the outcome of the eighteen-hole contest. When I could get Kevin thinking about the possibility of missing a short putt, he could not make a three-footer to save his life. It was fun for me to find an opponent's Achilles heel on the golf course and then start taking advantage of it. Kevin and I have played golf many times together, and we always enjoy a very healthy competition.

Kevin asked me on the first tee, "How did you get out of work to be golfing on a Friday morning, Bob?"

I told him I had become officially unemployed as of Thursday at five p.m., so I had decided to start my life as an unemployed executive with a round of golf. "But, Kevin, do not feel sorry for me. I have more money in my bank account now than I have ever had in my life."

He looked at me with a puzzled expression. "How is that, Bob?"

Rather than continue to play with his mind, I told him, "My employer sold the company, and the acquiring company did not hire any of the existing employees. Therefore, I am unemployed. The acquiring company bought our business just to own the land contracts to build homes on the property. The two owners of the business shared one-half of the proceeds of the sale with the employees. Every employee received a big check yesterday, making them happy for a long time."

Kevin knew Hal and Nick and said that he had heard great things about their construction company. He understood that it was the best company to work for in the Philadelphia area.

I said, "Kevin, whoever told you that was *not* lying."

"So, now that you are a free man with some money in the bank, what are you going to do about finding a job?" Kevin asked.

"I am not looking for a job. I am taking the next year off. I plan to play a round of golf on every golf course on *Golf Digest's* 'America's 100 Greatest Public Golf Courses' list. I plan to schedule the geographical location of all the courses on a map and then put together a plan to travel around the most efficient route to play all those courses within twelve months. My wife and I are planning to fly into a city on a Thursday night, play three rounds of golf on three different courses on the list and fly home on Sunday night. My wife's parents are going to watch our kids while we are gone.

The plan works out well because my in-laws love Bobby and Jennifer. Kevin, now you know the number-one item on my bucket list. Enough talk about my employment status. You are up first. While you are hitting your first drive, please don't think about that lake on the left side because, if your ball goes in the water, you probably are going to lose the first hole."

Kevin gave me a smirk. "Bob, after I take you for everything you currently have in your wallet, we need to talk more after we finish the round."

"Okay, knock it in the water—oops! I mean, keep your drive away from the lake."

* * *

After playing eighteen holes, Kevin and I walked back to the clubhouse.

"Well, Bob, are you going to buy me lunch since you have all my money?" Kevin asked.

I patted my friend on the shoulder. "If you would have taken my advice and not hit your drive in the lake on the first hole, you probably would not have been in such a bad mood for all eighteen holes today. You probably would have played much better."

Kevin gave me a sour but playful expression. "Okay, okay, but can we talk a little business now before you go jumping on an airplane with your golf clubs and a suitcase? I have a favor to ask you."

"What is that, Kevin?" I asked.

"Well, I have a client, a local company that is struggling to make a profit, and they need some help. Are you interested?"

"Interested in what?"

"Interested in doing a consulting engagement to turn this company around to be profitable again? Bob, I know how you ran Hal and Nick's company. I believe you can do the same for this company and make it profitable again in no time."

"I have never done any consulting work in my life," I responded incredulously. "I would not even know how to start."

"Well then, Bob, how about you become the president and CEO and manage the company back to profitability from that position?"

"Kev, this situation sounds like this job would get in the way of my bucket list golf journey. Moreover, what makes you think that the owner of this company is going to hire me as the president and CEO?"

"Bob, I agree that it would delay your and your wife's travels, but if you accomplished this, you would be able to start a golfing trip to play America's *two* hundred greatest public golf courses. This owner is in real financial trouble and needs help. My company is going to hire a turnaround consultant to fix this business, or we are going to foreclose on the loan and liquidate all the assets of the corporation. I am getting a real 'black eye' with my company because of this client. We stand to lose somewhere between four and seven million dollars unless I figure out how to fix this problem. Bob, seriously, if this owner gets an attorney and files for bankruptcy protection, it could cost me my job."

I could see in Kevin's eyes that he was serious.

"What kind of business is it, what are the annual sales, how many employees, where is it located, and who owns the company?" I asked.

Kevin explained, "It is a computer distributor that sold fifty million dollars last year in computer hardware, software, and service. It is a good business; it just has an owner who is a total jackass. The company is located less than two miles from here, and I believe they have about fifty employees. Let's meet tomorrow morning, and I will have a copy of my complete file on the company for you to review."

I weighed the idea in my mind for a moment and said, "I will review the information, but I am not going to make you any promises. I have never done a turnaround, and I do not know even how or where to start. However, I will commit to reviewing the information and at least give you my opinion on how to fix the business to be profitable. Kevin, who owns the business?"

"How about I invite the owner to meet us here tomorrow at the golf course an hour after you have reviewed the file, and we can all play eighteen holes together?"

"Okay, but who is the owner?"

"Bob, you will meet him tomorrow."

Obviously, Kevin didn't want to give me his name, so I turned to other matters. "Okay, Kevin, what do you want for lunch?" (I always buy Kevin lunch with the money he has just pulled out of his wallet to settle the bets from our golf matches.)

After I got home from the golf course and took a shower, I turned on my computer. There was already an email from Kevin. I guess he was so excited when I told him I agreed to review the information that he could not wait to get the financial statements to me right away. He sent me three years of financial statements (income statements and balance sheets) from his client. I opened the file, and Kevin had deleted the name of the company. I had no idea why he was so secretive about the company and its business owner.

I reviewed all the financial information and made several pages of notes and comments about what I saw as the issues and problems with this company. I printed the financial statements. I made some schedules and graphs of the top issues that I saw from the economic data that would paint the picture for Kevin of the problems with this company.

- I made a schedule of the sales payroll dollars and sales payroll expense as a percentage of sales. The sales payroll dollars had been going up each year, while the sales had gone down slightly each of the three years, which made no good business sense to me.

- The service department payroll went up each year while service revenue dropped by 10 percent each of the previous three years. The service department payroll as a percentage of sales, when graphed, showed a terrible trend.

- The gross profit dollars and percentage had gone down each of the three years.

- The accounts receivable balance had increased each year, even though the sales were down. That information told me that whoever was responsible for collecting the receivables was not doing a good job.

- The inventory balance for a computer distributor was excessively high for this type of business. The problem with computer inventory, because the technology was changing all the time, is that a laptop sitting in the warehouse inventory could be obsolete in six months because the manufacturer had released a new machine that was quicker with more features and benefits. When the computer manufacturers release a new computer model, the old models lose 40 to 50 percent of their retail value. If I owned or managed a computer distributor, I would try to keep the inventory as close to zero as possible to reduce the chance of the laptops becoming obsolete before they are sold to a customer.

Several other issues on the income statement and balance sheet were negative trends. None of them was as important as the ones listed above. Well, I take that last statement back. The issues listed above were problems caused by the main problem with this company: its ownership and management team. Kevin had said that the owner was a "jackass." Usually, if the owner is a jerk, the management team falls into the same category.

I spent forty-five minutes reviewing the file and making notes, and I started to put all the information in a folder to give to Kevin in the morning at our meeting. I sat there thinking for a minute that I could spend another hour or two to develop a complete analysis of the information so that Kevin could hand it over to a turnaround consultant, and he could hit the ground running when he started the engagement. I knew that I was not going to earn fees for my time, but I thought that I could spend a few hours to help my buddy, Kevin. He had looked so stressed when he told me that he was in fear of losing his job over this client. Besides, I wanted to keep him as a friend because he usually lost twenty dollars to me after every time we played a round of golf together.

I worked all afternoon and put together a comprehensive analysis of this business even though I did not have all the necessary information, such as employee headcount by the department, the chart of organization, and the number of active service contracts. I scheduled and graphed every issue that I identified as a problem. Documenting information in a table supported by graphs are great tools when explaining the information to a "non-accountant" type of person. I organized the papers, developed a table of contents, and made three copies of all the information.

The first item listed in the table of contents was a summary listing of the problems that I identified, sorted by the most financially significant first to the least important. I developed a disclaimer agreement noting that I was not issuing an opinion about the company or the management team. Since I did not even know the name of the business or the owner, I felt that I should cover myself legally just in case someone challenged my comments. I made up three binders and put them in a big envelope for Kevin's review in the morning. I planned to have a short meeting with Kevin, showing him what I had done with all the information that he had sent me. I expected to hand him the envelope, have a fifteen-minute discussion, and then get out on the putting green to practice before our round of golf.

Chapter 3

YOUR TITLE WILL BE "PRESIDENT/CEO"

*"Don't be a time manager, be a priority manager. Cut your major
goals into bite-sized pieces. Each small priority or requirement
on the way to ultimate goal become a mini goal in itself."*

—DENIS E. WAITLEY, AMERICAN MOTIVATIONAL
SPEAKER, WRITER, AND CONSULTANT

SATURDAY, DECEMBER 2

SATURDAY MORNING, I ARRIVED AT THE GOLF COURSE AN
hour early for my scheduled meeting with Kevin. My goal was to get
some practice in before meeting Kevin. I knew that if Kevin started
digging into the information that I put together and our meeting
dragged on, I would still have time to hit some balls and practice my
putting. When I got to the golf course, Kevin was already there on
the putting green. He said he wanted to practice his putting before
our meeting because he was not going have his butt kicked on the
golf course by me two days in a row.

We decided to sit in the clubhouse first, review the information
together, and then later hit some balls. When I handed Kevin the
binder that I created the night before, based on the look on his face
as he opened the cover, he could not believe that I had done this

much work to put together an analysis in one day. First, he stood up and held out his hand to shake hands. He said, "Bob, you have no idea how important turning this company around is to me."

"Kevin, please sit down so we can go over this so that I can get out on the golf course."

"Bob, I am serious!"

"Kevin, I know you are serious. That is why I did all this work and put this together as I did."

We started to go over every detail that I had documented that was a problem. When we finished, the owner of the company walked up and tapped Kevin on the back to get his attention. I could not believe we had been sitting there for two hours going over the information. It honestly seemed like we were there for maybe a half an hour. Kevin and I stood up, and Kevin said, "Bob, you know Craig, don't you?"

I shook Craig's hand and sat back down. I had known Craig for about three years. I had met him first here at the country club.

Craig said, "Bob, Kevin tells me that you are going to come to work for me and help our company out." As Craig was talking, I saw Kevin cringe.

I replied, "No, Craig, I am not, there must have been some confusion on Kevin's part."

Kevin, with complete frustration in his voice, told Craig, "What I told you was that I was in the process of talking to Bob about the opportunity to join the company to turn it around. I did not say that Bob agreed to anything."

Craig saw the papers on the table and asked if those were from his company's financial statements. Kevin told Craig that last night he had emailed me three years of the company's financial statements. Kevin said that I had been kind enough to develop a complete analysis of his business. Craig pulled up a chair to the table and grabbed one of the binders I had made for this meeting. Craig said, "I would love to hear your comments about my company, Bob."

I glanced at Kevin, and he knew from the look on my face that I did not like Craig. Craig had a bad reputation at the club to the point that he had a tough time finding other members to play a round of golf with him. He was loud, cocky, and offensive. When I encounter people like Craig, I stay away from them. I let them be their obnoxious selves around others, just not me. I showed Craig, in an abbreviated way, my notes and graphs. I explained to Craig that his company's sales were down slightly over the previous three years, but his payroll costs were up. His gross profit dollars and percentage were both on a downward trend. The receivables and inventory balances were up.

Craig asked, "What's wrong with the receivables and inventory?"

"Craig, if your sales are down and your receivables are up, that means that your average day's sales outstanding—DSO—is up, which means your employee responsible for collecting the receivables in your company is not doing a good job. If your inventory is up, that means that the firm is at risk for obsolete inventory since the technology changes all the time."

Craig asked, "Well, Bob, what do you recommend we do to fix these problems?"

"Craig, I recommend that you get a turnaround guy to take over the company and fix these issues quickly," I suggested.

"Bob, why don't you join us to fix the problems?"

"Because, Craig, I have a date with America's one hundred greatest public golf courses over the next year."

Kevin said, "Craig, Bob just received a nice settlement from the sale of the company that he worked for, and he is planning on a long-extended golf trip playing the top courses in the nation."

Craig said, "Bob, that trip can wait, help us become profitable again."

I just remained quiet. I did not like Craig, and my attitude was not changing about him from this conversation.

Kevin saw my temperature rising, and he interrupted Craig. He said, "How about we play eighteen holes and talk about this later?"

I quickly responded, "Kevin, great idea! Let's go." We all got up, and Kevin collected all the folders and started to put them back in the envelope I had given him.

Craig said, "Can I have one of the binders?" Kevin told Craig he would give him one later.

Kevin and I rode in the same cart for the round of golf. Kevin knew not to say anything about Craig because he was aware I was on the edge of walking away and never talking about this computer company again.

When we finished the eighteen holes, we went and had a beer. Craig left right away because he had to pick up his kids, or "his brats," as he put it. When Craig was gone, Kevin started.

"Bob, I have an employment contract for you from my company. Your title will be president and CEO. Your salary will be more money than you have ever earned. Craig will be chairman of the board with no daily responsibilities or decision-making authority. He has an office in the building but will not have authority to sign checks, hire, or fire anyone. You will have the ultimate authority to manage the business."

Kevin continued, "Bob, Craig recently fraudulently signed collateral reports overstating his company's assets. If he gives you any problems, we can prosecute him for fraud and put him in jail. I am pretty sure that he is going to behave while you are managing the company back to profitability."

I sat at the bar and read the contract while Kevin sat there. I redlined four issues in the language of the agreement. "Kevin, my first change to the document is that I receive 15 percent of the sale price if the company is profitable when sold. The second issue is that if Craig interferes with any of my decisions, you and Rick will remove him from the company's offices for good. The third issue is, if I am fired for any reason, I will receive one year's salary as a severance payment. The fourth item is that your company will purchase a director and officer insurance policy in my name covering me for at least five million dollars from any risk of managing this distressed company. I am going to forward this document to my attorney to review. Kevin, if you can get those issues approved, I will do the deal."

Kevin had a huge smile when I told him that I would take on the challenge. He said that he would call his boss immediately, talk to him about these items, and call me back as soon as he got a positive response. I said okay and went home.

The whole night, I was wondering if I had made a good or bad decision. If I did an excellent job, that jerk, Craig, would receive most of the benefit from my turnaround efforts. Then I switched my thoughts to Kevin; I would hate to see him lose his job because of Craig. I decided that I needed to stay focused on the company and Kevin, and not Craig if I was going to accomplish this turnaround.

I received a phone call later that evening from Kevin, confirming the approval of my deal. Kevin said that he wanted to meet me at eight a.m. Monday morning, at Panera Bread. He wanted me to meet his boss, Rick, for breakfast so we could all sign the employment agreement. Kevin said that Rick wanted to meet me before he signed the contract. Kevin told me that after the three of us met; Rick said we were all going to meet with Craig and tell him his plan. Craig was going to stay out of my way, or they would move him out of the office. I stated to Kevin that I would prefer Craig to be gone immediately, but if I had his and Rick's commitment that if Craig started acting up, their team would remove him, I was okay with that. I had scanned and emailed the employment agreement to my attorney as soon as I'd gotten home from the golf course. Later that evening, he'd called and said that the contract was okay to sign; there was nothing in the language that was a problem.

I sat at my desk at home and prepared for the meetings with Rick, Kevin, and Craig's management team on Monday morning. I planned to meet with the company's management team after the meeting with Craig to introduce myself and review my goals for the organization. Initially, my goals were:

- The company would be cash flow breakeven within forty-five days of my start date.

- I would schedule "one-on-one meetings" with each employee on the management team within the first seven days to evaluate each manager.

- Then I would evaluate the management team to determine who would be staying and who would not within thirty days. If there was turnover on the management team, I would recruit and hire the replacements within forty-five days.

- Within the first month, all managers would evaluate their staff to determine who would be staying and who would not.

- There would be sales, financial, and operational reporting implemented measuring all the key performance indicators (KPIs) within thirty days.

- There would be an approved operating budget for the company for next year completed before the end of December.

- I would review the operating expenses of the business to identify where there is profit leakage within the first thirty days and resolve the problems within forty-five days.

- Sales of hardware and software would grow by at least 50 percent in the first ninety days compared to the same period in the prior year.

- Sales of the service department would increase by at least 25 percent in the first ninety days compared to the same period in the previous year.

Chapter 4

MY GOLF TRIP IS OFFICIALLY POSTPONED

"Get the right people on the bus and the wrong people off the bus."
—JIM COLLINS, AMERICAN BUSINESS
CONSULTANT, AUTHOR, AND LECTURER

MONDAY, DECEMBER 4—DAY 1 OF WEEK 1 OF THE TURNAROUND

I ARRIVED AT PANERA BREAD AT SEVEN THIRTY A.M. FOR MY meeting with Kevin and his boss, Rick. Rick, much like Kevin, was a big man and looked like he just retired from the military after being a navy seal for twenty years. He was wearing a suit, but I could tell that he worked out in the gym his whole life. He was big and thick! I remember meeting Tony Robbins, the motivational speaker, in person a few years ago. Rick reminded me of Tony. He had his hair cut very short in the classic military style, and he stood very erect. Rick was a nice person, but I would not want to be on his wrong side.

Over the weekend, I had reviewed all the financial information from Craig's company again and updated the reports and my comments. I was concerned that I was walking into a hornet's nest with this endeavor, so I wanted to be exceptionally prepared. The meeting with Kevin and Rick went well. Rick was very blunt with me about this turnaround. He stated that he was tired of Craig's lies and the fraudulently filed collateral reports. He told me that if I did not think that I could fix all the problems with this business, he would enjoy shutting this company down and prosecuting its owner for the balance of the unpaid loan. All I could think about was that this was my first experience at working in the turnaround industry and it appeared that this line of work was not going to be easy. Rick told me that Kevin has fully endorsed me to handle this assignment. He also said that if everything went well, their floor-planning firm would have more turnaround opportunities for me in the future. I was not sure yet that I wanted to be involved with doing turnarounds as my next career move. I could see that Rick was a "no-nonsense guy," and that I did have his support. Rick and I signed two copies of my employment agreement, one for his files and one for mine. We all shook hands and went to our cars to drive to Craig's company, which was now my new job opportunity. The signing of the employment agreement firmly canceled or at least postponed, my journey to America's one hundred greatest public golf courses for probably at least a year.

The three of us arrived at ABC Computer Distributors at the same time. I parked my car in the parking lot and waited for Kevin and Rick to do the same. The three of us walked up the sidewalk to the front door of the company. There were three parking lot spaces right next to the front of the business's entrance with reserved signs for the parking spots. The first sign was "Reserved for the President." Within that space was a brand new $100,000 Mercedes-Benz. I stopped and looked at the car and asked Kevin if this was Craig's car.

Kevin lowered his head and said, "Yes."

I asked Kevin if he knew if the company was paying for the vehicle. He stated that he did not know if the Mercedes was a company car or Craig's personally. I took out a notebook from my briefcase and wrote a reminder to myself to check on Craig's car to determine if this distressed company was paying for the vehicle.

The three of us walked into the reception area. I went up to the receptionist's desk and asked for Craig. I told the receptionist that my name was Bob Curry and I was here with Kevin and Rick. I said that Craig was expecting us. She smiled, and I asked her name. She stated that her name was Tina.

Tina was very young, maybe nineteen years old. She had long blond hair and a pleasant smile. She picked up the phone, called Craig, and told him that we were waiting for him in the lobby. Craig came to the reception area, shook hands with each of us, and invited us to follow him to the conference room. As Craig led us to where we were going to meet, I thought to myself that the woman in the receptionist position was excellent. Tina had greeted us with a friendly smile and had had a "happy" voice on the phone when she called Craig.

> I believe that the receptionist position of a company, the person who is the first contact with the customers either on the phone or in person, is a vital position in an organization.

When we arrived at the conference room, there was a tray of doughnuts, bagels, and pastry and a pot of coffee in the middle of the conference room table. We all sat down, and Craig asked Kevin about the agenda for the day. Rick immediately spoke up and said, "Kevin and I have just hired Bob to join the organization as the new president/CEO of ABC Computer Distributors."

As Rick was talking, I poured myself a hot cup of coffee and added a little cream.

"Craig, Bob will have the ultimate authority to lead the company in the immediate future. He will be responsible for hiring and firing, signing all checks, and growing the business profitably. You, Craig, will have no day-to-day operating responsibility or authority as of today. I do not want you to interfere with Bob managing this business. You are welcome to maintain your office here if you choose, but we do wish that you would gather your belongings and move out."

I looked at Rick and Kevin; they wore stern expressions as Rick talked to Craig. Craig said nothing to Rick when he finished speaking. I believe that Rick had had this conversation with Craig before; he was just repeating himself in front of me to confirm what Rick told me earlier.

Craig looked at me and asked with a very sarcastic tone, "Do you want my keys to the front door?"

I answered him, "Craig, I believe that it would be best for the employees and the company if you would leave and find a new business venture. We need everyone here to be confident and energized. I know that it is going to be difficult for you not to lead the organization when you are here since you have been the president for such a long time. However, concerning your keys, is that your Mercedes outside in the president's parking space?"

He said, "Yes, why?"

"Craig, is it a company car or your vehicle?"

He said, "The company is paying for the lease."

"Craig, please do not take offense at this, but I am going to cancel the lease and return the car to the dealership."

"Bob, is that necessary?"

"Craig, yes, it is. I plan to turn over every rock in this company to eliminate any wasteful spending, regardless of what it is or whom I offend. My sole mission here is to make this company profitable and cash flow positive. This company spending money on a hundred-thousand-dollar car does not improve the opportunity for the success of this turnaround. Please arrange to provide yourself with another vehicle to drive, because that car is going back to the dealer as soon as possible."

Rick looked at me with a smile on his face. He knew my move was bold and aggressive to take the owner's car away from him in the first hour of my employment. He was aware of the need for this type of management style to turn this company around financially. Craig reached into his pocket, pulled out his car keys, and put them on the conference room table. I did not make a move to pick up Craig's keys off the table; that was going to be someone else's job, probably the company's controller. Craig got up and left the room without saying a word.

Rick and Kevin looked at me. Kevin told Rick, "I told you that we had the right guy to turn this company around quickly."

Rick then told me that I had his full support, and he was just a phone call away if I need his help. Kevin left the conference room and said he was going to find Craig and bring him back. Kevin wanted to get Craig to walk me around the company and introduce me as the new president/CEO of the organization. A minute later, Craig and Kevin reentered the room.

Craig suggested that he bring his management team to the conference room to introduce me. Then they could all individually introduce themselves to Kevin, Rick, and me. I nodded and told Craig that would be great. "However, Craig, before you go gather them up to meet us, could you please sit down, and give us a little information about each member of your management team?"

Craig sat back down. "Which manager do you want me to talk about first?" he asked.

"You can start with anyone," I told him. "Please just give us a little background information about each person."

Craig first ran down the members of the management team:

- Craig, the owner/president

- Darren, the controller

- Tom, the sales manager

- Roger, the service manager

- Alan, the purchasing manager

- Donna, the human resources manager

- Trish, the training manager

- Tim, the warehouse and shipping manager

"Tom, the sales manager, has been with me the longest, ten years," he started. "I recruited Tom's wife, Nancy, from a competitor. Tom and Nancy came as a package since they were married. Unfortunately, Tom is useless to the rest of the salespeople, but he works hard to promote Nancy's sales. He has every potential customer phone call that comes through the receptionist forwarded to him, and then he passes all the possible sales calls to Nancy. The funny thing is, Nancy does not need his help. She is very talented and can certainly be very successful without him. As of the end of November, Nancy is responsible for fifty-five percent of the total sales for the company. I do not understand their relationship. She works hard at looking good and keeping herself fit. Tom, well, Tom is the total opposite. He is overweight, looks ten years older than his age, and wears a bad toupee. Tom and Nancy got married for fifteen years ago. I do not understand that relationship."

I then asked, "Does Tom have regular sales meetings?" Craig just looked at me and did not answer the question. Then I asked, "Does Tom have weekly, monthly, or quarterly sales reporting by a salesperson? Are there sales training classes for the sales team? Does Tom go on sales calls with the other sixteen salespeople? Does he have hardware vendors come in and do product training for some of the high-end products?"

"Bob, let me quickly answer all your questions—no, no, no, no, and no."

"Boy, I can now see a consistency in his sales management style! I do have a clear picture of Tom's good qualities now, which would be his wife, Nancy. He sounds more like Nancy's sales assistant rather than the sales department manager."

Craig said, "Yes, Bob, you are right."

"Craig, as we were walking through the office to this conference room, I noticed that all the employees were women. Are there any males that work here?"

"Bob, there are nineteen women—sixteen salespeople and three sales support—and only one male in the sales department. Once you are around the office more, you will better understand the answer to your question. I like having beautiful women around the office. I do all the hiring of the sales department and the rest of the company. I believe that it is just as easy to hire an attractive female employee as it is to hire an ugly one. I like being around beautiful women, so I hire mostly females rather than males. Coming to this office and seeing a bunch of beautiful women is a good thing!"

I asked, "I understand, but can they sell?"

"Some can. Others, probably not," Craig said with a sickening smile on his face.

"I have one last question about Tom before we move on to the next manager. Are you kidding about all of this?"

"No, Bob, I am not kidding."

"Okay, I just had to confirm that this was a true story about your sales manager, the sales team, and soon-to-be my sales manager and sales staff."

Craig shrugged and continued, "Next is Darren. Darren is the controller. He has worked for the company for seven years. Darren is very intelligent and does a great job. He probably is much better at his job as the controller than I need to run this company. No, I take that back. I do not know if you have realized it yet, but I am a salesperson. I believe that I am an outstanding salesman. I could sell snowballs to an Eskimo. The problem with the company is that I am not good at managing people. I am too much of a 'smartass' to be a good manager, and that is why the company is in financial trouble."

Craig continued, "Getting back to Darren, he could probably be much more efficient for this company. The problem is that I do not know what to ask him. My management solution to every problem is just getting more sales to take care of yesterday's mistakes. I believe that we are now in financial trouble because of my problem resolution strategy. 'Getting more sales' is not working anymore. Bob, I understand that you have been a controller and CFO for the past companies that you worked for recently. You would be able to use Darren's talents better for you and the company just because you will know what to ask him to do.

"Next is Roger, the service manager. Roger has been with the company for seven years. Recently, I promoted him from senior technician to service manager. Unfortunately, Roger is an excellent computer technician, but a terrible manager of people. I put him in charge of the department because I caught my old service manager stealing laptops from the warehouse and selling them to his friends for cash."

Kevin asked, "How did you catch him?"

"One of the stolen laptops came in for service," he explained. "The technician checked the serial number for warranty purposes and found that the laptop was a stolen computer from our company. When we threatened the laptop owner that we were going to report him to the police for the possession of stolen property, he ratted on my service manager."

Rick asked Craig, "What did you do with the guy, the old service manager? Did you prosecute the thief?"

"No, Rick, I just fired him. He is now working for one of our local competitors. He is probably stealing from them now. That is how I compete with my competitors. I send them my employees who are thieves."

"Craig, that reminds me, I wanted to ask you if you do background checks on candidates to be hired by this company."

"No, why? Do you think that I have a bunch of pedophiles working for me?"

I bristled at his question. "No, I have no idea who is working for you—and now working for me."

Craig gave me a weird look and continued, "Back to Roger. He is an outstanding technician, but he hates the manager's job. He wants his old job back, and I promised him I would do that as soon as I hired a new service manager. I have recently interviewed a couple of candidates but have not found anyone who will take the job. I am not sure why, but I think that this company may have a bad reputation in the Philadelphia market area. I have had a hard time finding good people to work for me. This problem is growing into a real issue for us. Right now, I have a problem with the sales people because they refuse to sell service contracts. Our service department has a terrible reputation with our customers. The salespeople believe that if they sell a service contract, the service technicians are going to screw up the service call and then the customer will never purchase hardware or software from that salesperson in the future. They do not want to lose their customers, so they stopped selling service."

"Craig, as of today, do you have a solution to the problem?" asked Kevin.

"No, and now I do not have to worry about it anymore since Bob is here. It is his problem now."

I took notes as Craig was talking. I knew that one of the first things that I was going to have to do was to fix this service department. In reviewing the financial statements of the company over the past three days, I knew that the gross profit margin for selling hardware averaged 10 percent, the software was 15 to 20 percent, and service was 66 percent. It does not take a Rhodes scholar to figure out where to focus my efforts when starting this turnaround.

Craig continued, "Next, we have Alan, our purchasing manager. Alan has been with the company for less than a year. He is excellent. Alan knows the product, has all the contacts with the vendors, is a respectable negotiator, and gets along with everyone in the company. Right now, he is the heartbeat of this operation. Nancy will give him an order to purchase twenty-five laptops, a server, and several different kinds of software. He has the order all bought out within a few minutes and never screws up the details, which could be a disaster. If Alan messed up one of Nancy's customer orders, she would kick his butt. Nancy would rip him a new one if he shipped the wrong product to one of her clients. What I do not like about Alan is that he is an excellent golfer, and he kicks my butt every time we play a round of golf together."

"I am so surprised that you would admit that anyone could beat you on the golf course, especially someone working for you!" I kidded.

"You are a smartass, Curry, huh?"

"You know I am kidding, Craig!" I said with a smile.

"So, does that mean you were also kidding about getting rid of my Mercedes?"

The smile quickly faded from my face. "No, unfortunately, I was not kidding about that."

Craig sighed and went on, "Then we have Donna, our human resources manager. Donna is good at what she does, but she is a pain in my butt. She wants to do everything by the rules, and that just is not who I am. I am the type of person who likes to live in the gray area. She is very strict when it comes to following the rules, following the rules, and following the rules! For example, when we fired the old service manager for stealing laptops, I had to document the transaction six different ways for his personnel file because of Donna. Rather than immediately booting the guy out of here for stealing and forgetting about him forever, she made a big deal about the proper documentation for his personnel file. She also said that she wanted to prosecute him because we are setting the wrong precedent by letting him off and not making him pay for what he stole. It sends the wrong message to the rest of the employees of this company. She has been with the company for two years. I hired her because I was getting too many lawsuits from employees. Since she joined the firm, we have not had a lawsuit filed against us."

"What have been the topics of the employee complaints?" I asked.

"I don't remember," he said, "but I know that we have not had any employees sue us since she has been here." (I later learned from Donna that, when she joined the organization, Craig had two new sexual harassment complaints filed against him by women on the sales staff.)

"Wow, she must have one of those 'fixer' types of personalities," I said.

Craig shrugged again and went on, "Tim is the warehouse and shipping manager. Tim is my cousin and has been with the company for about eighteen months. He works hard, but he is not the brightest light bulb in the company."

It must run in the family, I thought.

"Tim makes mistakes," Craig continued, "but Alan catches most of his screwups before the product was shipped to the customer, so Nancy does not castrate him, too."

"Do you have any other relatives working for the company?" I asked. I wanted to know how much nepotism that I was going to have to deal with in the near future.

"Yes. Frank, one of the sales staff, is also my cousin. I hired him to sell service. Most of the women here do not know how to sell service properly. I hired Frank to go along with them on the sales calls to sell service contracts. And then, of course, there is Trish."

"How are you and Trish related?"

"She is not related to me, but we have been living together for the past six months."

That got my attention. "Okay, please tell us more about Trish."

"Well, I met Trish at an industry trade show in Philadelphia. She owned a training company and was doing computer training for several large corporations in the area. I thought it would be a good fit if I purchased her company, and she could come here and work for me. I thought it was a real 'win-win' deal. She could sell her training services to our whole customer base, and we would pick up her existing customers to sell hardware, software, and service. After she had joined the company and I paid her the purchase price for her business, we started dating after a month. She moved in with me during the second month after our first date. That was six months ago, and since then, she has not sold a training contract, and neither has the sales team. Buying her training company is a deal that I wish I could reverse."

"Are you two still involved, Craig?" I asked.

He said, "Yes, we are, but it is not going well. I have three kids that I have custody of every other week, and Trish has three children. Her kids are a pain in my butt and are spoiled brats. My kids are also spoiled, but they are *my* kids. When the six kids are at the house every other week, my home is crazy. The kids fight with each other all the time. I have given up trying to separate them. I just let them fight."

I said, "Thank you, Craig, for your comments. I appreciate all the information. How about you go find all your managers and bring them in here now?"

We all sat back and waited for Craig to return with his team. Rick and Kevin sat there shaking their heads as if they could not believe what they had just heard for the past half hour.

Rick spoke up and said, "This business is a mess. What were we thinking when we decided to loan this guy money? We must have had a fragile moment when we made that decision." Rick turned to Kevin. "Were either of us sober when we signed those loan papers? Bob, good luck, you are going to need it."

"I do not think so, Rick," I said. "It is not about luck. It is about getting rid of the weak players and managing the top-tier employees to success. Craig's philosophy is different. He gets rid of the managers that steal from him and hires a bunch of attractive women for the office."

Okay, I thought, *now I know more about the battle in my future.* According to what Craig had just told us, I had a management team consisting of:

- Tom, the sales manager, was useless to sixteen out of the seventeen salespeople, other than his wife. His wife was responsible for 55 percent of the total sales of the company while the other sixteen salespeople sold 45 percent, which made Tom almost untouchable. Of the other sixteen employees on the sales staff, fifteen were female, and one was male, the male being Craig's cousin, Frank. Tom had the receptionist forward every potential customer who called into the company to his wife. The other fifteen women were attractive, but about half of them could not sell the products or services.

- Nancy was a keeper. I wrote a note to myself in capital letters in my notebook to meet with Nancy as soon as possible. I need to make sure that the change in management would not upset her to the point where she wanted to leave the company. With her history of sales volume, she could have quit and gone to work for any computer reseller in the area. If she were to leave the company, we would have to shut the doors of the business within a week.

- Darren sounded like he could be an asset for this turnaround. I knew he was going to be very busy developing financial and operational (sales and service) reports measuring the productivity in those two departments. He would also be preparing the following year's operating budget for the business immediately and dealing with the year-end closing.

- Roger was not going to be the service manager anymore, as soon as I could replace him. I knew that the secret to the profitability of this company was to have an experienced service team. We needed the sales staff to have the confidence to sell service contracts to all our customers, and the service department needed to do an excellent job for their service customers. The service revenue gross margin was a much higher percentage than any hardware or software products. Recruiting and hiring a new service manager was probably my number-one priority to begin this engagement.

- Alan also sounded like a definite asset to the management team, thank goodness. This business was a reseller of products manufactured by other companies, except for the service department. Without an experienced buyer for the company, I would have another significant exposure in that functional area. I hoped Craig's information about Alan was accurate.

- Donna, the HR manager, sounded like she was worth keeping also. She must have had a dominant personality if she could keep Craig under control. With all the females in the sales department walking around and Craig's appetite for attractive women, this place was like a lit firecracker for sexual harassment lawsuits. Donna might have been another person like Darren, who sounded like a breath of fresh air in this crazy place!

- Tim, the "dim light bulb" warehouse manager, who was Craig's cousin, would probably be gone as soon as I could reduce the inventory in the warehouse to make him obsolete.

- And then there was Trish, Craig's training manager, who had forgotten how to sell or train as soon as Craig purchased her business and paid her in full for her company. It was apparent that she was not a real "money-maker" here.

After a few minutes, Craig returned to the conference room with his management team. The first thing I noticed was that this was not a group of happy people. There was not a smile on any of their faces as they entered the room. I saw a big difference between this management team and the team I had worked with at H&N Construction Company. In the first thirty seconds, I could tell they did not like working here. After Craig finished introducing the management team, he stated to everyone that Kevin was the account manager for the company that was financing this business. Craig referred to Kevin as "the Banker."

Then it was Kevin's turn to make the introductions. He first introduced his boss, Rick. Rick immediately stood up and spoke for a few minutes to the management group. He talked about how the business had been losing money for the past year and a half and how he was looking forward to an increased effort from this management team to turn this business around. Rick told the group that Kevin would explain why we were there that day. Kevin stood up and stated that he also looked forward to positive results from this management team, starting immediately. Kevin then introduced me and told the group that I was the new president and CEO, starting that day. Before I said anything, I pulled out my notebook with the bullet points I wanted to talk about with this group.

I first shared a little about my background and professional experiences. I told them that my primary mission in joining the company was to make the business profitable again. I then explained to the managers that I would be meeting with each of them, one on one, during the following two days. The goal of our meetings would be for me to learn and understand from each of them their job challenges. I asked everyone to prepare for the meeting by creating a list of problem topics for us to discuss. At the end of the two days, I wanted to be able to understand all the problems and issues that were holding any of them back from doing a great job and this company from being profitable.

Next, I told the group I had a list of questions for each of them that I wanted them to be ready to discuss at our upcoming one-on-one meetings. "I hope you all have something to record notes on right now, so we will not have to go over this information twice," I said.

All seven managers, including Craig, got up and left the room to get a tablet on which to take notes. I wasn't surprised that they had come unprepared.

Kevin looked at Rick. "These people are in for the shock of their lives under Bob's leadership."

"GOOD!" Rick responded.

When everyone returned and was ready to write, I told Darren he was first on my list. Darren was a big man, around six-foot-five, and not your typical-looking accountant. Darren was forty years old and married with three kids. He was not the shy type; he could talk to anyone about anything. He had passed the CPA exam and was attending Villa Nova University at the time to graduate with an MBA degree sometime soon. Darren was easy to like, and the rest of the management team thought of him as the leader of the group. Most of these people did not care for Craig, but they did appreciate Darren. He was a very hard worker, and when I met him, I knew he was going to be an asset to me for this turnaround.

"Darren, I would like you to have the following ready to review when we meet: I would like to see the current month's income statement and balance sheet. I am assuming, the books will be closed soon for November," I said.

Darren replied that he had finished most of the financial closing and soon the statements would be ready for my review. I was already impressed; it was early December, and he had a lot of the work done for the monthly close.

"This year's operating budget by month, if possible," I continued.

Darren said, "Not possible, sir; there currently is not a budget for this company."

"Well, get ready, we are going to have one soon!" I said. "Bank account reconciliations. How many operating cash accounts are there?"

"There are two bank accounts, the business operating account and the impressed payroll account, Mr. Curry."

"Are they both reconciled as of the current month? And please call me Bob."

"Yes, by the time we meet, I will have a formal reconciliation ready for you for each account, Bob."

"Good, please call the bank and get new signatory cards for

the two accounts. I want to add my signature to the accounts and remove Craig."

Darren hesitated, looked at Craig for approval, and then said, "Okay."

I knew that I had just shocked these people, but that was okay in my mind. This management team had been on a perpetual holiday under Craig's leadership. Now they were all going to have to work for a living from this day forward. I continued giving Darren the rest of my list.

"I would like to see a copy of the company's loan statement for the past three months. I want to review the current detailed aged accounts receivables and accounts payable listings. And the last physical inventory reconciliation—Darren, when was the most recent inventory taken and what were the results?"

"At the year-end last year, eleven months ago....There was a large loss recorded for the prior year."

"Please print a current inventory also for us to review," I requested.

"Okay, sure thing!"

"Then I would like to review a copy of the company's most recent borrowing base calculation report. Do you do them weekly or monthly?" I added.

"I do one every time we borrow money from the line of credit," Darren explained.

I nodded. "Okay, next, I would like to see a copy of the latest payroll run. And, finally, I want to see a copy of the car lease for the Mercedes that the company is currently paying."

Darren looked surprised about the request for the car lease, but he did not comment. He just added it to his list. I pushed Craig's keys to the Mercedes over to Darren and told him I would talk to him later about the keys.

Craig interrupted, "Why are you reviewing all this information, Bob?"

I wanted to give Craig an incredibly sarcastic answer, but I maintained my control. I said, "I only know how to manage a company by one method, and that is by the numbers. To accomplish that, I need to review all the information that is currently available, so I can make good business decisions in the future on how to stop this company from bleeding cash and move it on its way to profitability. Currently, I have no idea what information is available until I review all of it in the one-on-one meetings with the people in this room. After I finish meeting with each manager, I will develop a plan on how we are going to move forward as a management team with this company. I am going to ask everyone here to focus on their job more than they ever have before in the history of this company because this turnaround is not going to be easy."

Craig cleared his throat and asked, "When do you think that you will have this plan prepared for my review?"

"Well, Craig, with all due respect, the plan is not for your review. As of today, as Rick stated earlier, you no longer have any operating or decision-making authority for this company. I am the new president and CEO of this organization, and I have the sole responsibility to make this company profitable again. Right now, this business is losing almost ninety thousand dollars per month. You have made many decisions that have put this company in this distressed position. I do not need your opinions or advice on how to operate this business in the future. Today, the management of this corporation is going to change materially. Today is a new day at ABC Computer Distributors. Craig, I want you to know that, right now, in front of this group of managers, I need you stop interfering with the future success of this company. I am going to be leading this team, and they are going to need to follow my directions. I refuse to be unsuccessful with this company's turnaround. If you do interfere in the future, I am going to have to ask you to move out of your office and leave the company."

"Bob," Craig protested, "maybe you forgot that I am the sole shareholder of this corporation."

"No, I am not forgetting, Craig. I suggest that Rick, Kevin, you, and I meet immediately after this meeting to discuss this issue in private."

"Fine!" Craig replied with a huff and remained quiet for the balance of the meeting.

The expressions on the faces of all the managers got very serious.

"Darren, where did I leave off on my list?" I asked, wanting to get back to the business at hand.

"You wanted to see a copy of the car lease, sir," Darren replied.

As I thanked him, I noted that Darren had called me "sir" again. He and the rest of the group must have been a little intimidated by my responses to Craig's questions.

"Thank you," I replied. I then asked Darren to create a spreadsheet of the payroll broken down by the department containing the following information (see page 366):

- Department title
- Employee's name
- Date of hire
- Annual salary

- Commission (if applicable)
- Total compensation
- Date of last salary review
- The dollar amount of the previous salary review

I also requested another spreadsheet for each salesperson on the sales staff, as follows (see page 367):

- Employee's name
- Date of hire
- Year-to-date sales (hardware and software)
- Year-to-date gross profit (hardware and software)

- Year-to-date sales (service)
- Year-to-date gross profit (service)
- Year-to-date sales (total) and year-to-date gross profit (total)

Then I asked for a spreadsheet for each of the technicians on the service staff, as follows (see page 368):

- Employee's name
- Date of hire
- Employee's hourly billing rate

- Year-to-date hours billed
- Year-to-date billings dollars

"Darren, is there any monthly sales reporting that you maintain right now?" I asked.

Holding up a finger for each of the reports he did have, he replied, "We have sales by invoice, sales by customer, and sales by salesperson reports."

"Great! How about we schedule our meeting for this Tuesday at three o'clock, so you have time to prepare all this information?"

"That sounds fine. I can be ready by then and thank you for giving me the extra time to gather all this information."

Tom was next on my list. Tom was a huge man, but not in the way Darren was huge. Tom looked like he was fifteen months pregnant. Unfortunately, he was probably seventy or eighty pounds overweight. Tom was somewhere around fifty years old but looked older. He wore an ill-fitting toupee that looked like he had it on backward. The moment I met him, I had a hard time seeing past his "rug." Tom was a big friendly person, but, according to Craig, he was not the strength of the management team.

"Tom," I began, "do you have any current sales reporting for your sales team?"

"What do you mean?" he asked.

That question, coming from the sales manager, scared me. "Well," I explained, "do you have sales pipeline reporting, such as a list from each salesperson of which customers they had sales calls with and the results of each call?" (See page 363.)

"No, sir, I don't."

"Do you have any targeted customers assigned to each salesperson?"

"I have not assigned any targets for the sales team."

"Do you have any sales status reports, by client, available from the sales staff?"

"No, unfortunately, we do not have or use any operational sales reporting."

I was determined to keep asking Tom questions until I got at least one "yes" from him. "Well, then, do you have monthly commission reports by salesperson by month?"

"Yes, I have that information."

Jackpot! "Good, we can start there. Do you have the current commission plan for your sales staff, Tom?"

"I have the commission plan in my head," he said. "Do you want me to write it down for you and email it to you?"

"Yes, that would be great. How often do you have your sales meeting? Weekly?"

"Monthly, usually the first Monday of each month," he replied.

"Okay, do you have notes or minutes of these sales meetings?"

"No, I do not, sorry." He cast his eyes downward.

It seemed like there would be no more yesses to come from Tom, but I kept trying. "Do you ever have any sales contests for the salespeople to compete and win prizes?"

"No, we have not had any sales contests yet."

"Do you have any sales training for your team?"

"Unfortunately, no."

Right then, I wrote a bunch of *no's* on my list of questions for the sales manager. I had a lot of work to accomplish in the sales area. "Since you have very little to prepare for our one-on-one meeting, are you available to meet today at one o'clock?"

"Yes, Bob, I am available. Maybe we could go to lunch together. Would that be okay?"

"Sure, Tom, then let's make it at twelve thirty rather than one o'clock."

"Sounds good," he agreed.

So far, my first impressions were that Darren was a "keeper" and that Tom had better wake up and get to work soon. I was sure that I did not want to lose Nancy's sales volume, so I was going to have to turn Tom into a sales manager, which was probably going to be quite a task. Tom, at first glance, seemed like a very lazy manager!

"Donna, you are next," I said, and she perked up. "I have a written list for you, and I made a copy of it for your review." I handed her the sheet of paper. Since Donna was the HR manager, much of what she did was confidential. I did not want to ask her my questions in public. She could prepare her responses to my list of questions, and we could talk later about each topic. For example, one of the issues I wanted to discuss with her, but not in public in front of the management team, was whether there were any open, unresolved sexual harassment complaints in the company.

"Are you available tomorrow morning at eight to meet?" I asked.

Donna agreed to the time, and I moved on to the next manager.

"Roger, how are your service technicians doing recently?"

"Good, sir!"

"Do you have any monthly operating reports for your service techs?"

"No, sir!"

"Do you know the hours billed or revenue by month by service tech?"

"No, unfortunately, I do not."

"Are there any customer complaints about your service team?"

"There are, sir, on a regular basis."

"Do you have any training classes available for the service department?"

"No, sir, we do not."

After a few questions with Roger, I knew there was no hope for a positive exchange, so I stopped asking. Roger was not going to have much to prepare for our one-on-one meeting, so I scheduled him immediately after my lunch with Tom, at 2:00 p.m. I looked away from Roger to the next new face.

"Alan, how are you, sir?"

"Great!" he replied enthusiastically.

"I do not have a list for you, but are you available to meet today at three thirty?"

"Yes, I am. That time is okay with me," Alan readily agreed.

I turned to the next person at the table.

"Tim, how are you, sir?"

"I am doing fine, Bob!"

"How about I come see you in the warehouse at nine thirty tomorrow morning after my meeting with Donna?"

"That is okay with me."

"Okay, great, I will see you then."

Tim wrote down the time of the appointment in his little notebook.

I turned to the last face at the table. "So, you must be Trish since I have everyone else on my list is checked off."

"Yes, I am Trish."

"Good, Trish, do you have time to meet tomorrow morning at eleven, here in this conference room?"

"Yes, I will be sure to add the meeting to my jam-packed calendar."

I could not tell if Trish was being sarcastic or not, but it did not matter right now. I knew that her attitude, effort, and results here at the company were going to have to change quickly or she would soon join the large group of the population in the whole world who did not work for ABC Computer Distributors.

"Just to confirm the day and time with everyone, the list of the one-on-one meetings are Tom at twelve-thirty today, Roger at two o'clock today, Alan at three thirty today. Donna, we will meet at eight a.m. tomorrow, Tim at nine thirty a.m. tomorrow, Trish at eleven o'clock tomorrow morning, and finally Darren at three p.m. tomorrow. I will meet with everyone in either the conference room or my office, and Tim, you and I can talk in the warehouse."

Everyone nodded.

I further explained the purpose of our meetings: "Each of you should plan on the meeting lasting no longer than one hour. I maximize the time for all meetings to one hour. Please come prepared with your list of questions and issues that you believe are problems with your department or anywhere in the company. Please bring a notepad and take notes during the meeting. Chances are, when we finish our meeting, there will be some assignments for each of you. Feel free, when we meet, to be very open and honest. My goal is to eliminate every problem or roadblock that is causing this company to lose money. I want this to be the most profitable computer distributor in the United States next year. For that to happen, we all must work together as a strong management team with totally open communication."

They all nodded, and I turned to Tom, "Before the end of this week, Tom, I would like to schedule a meeting with your sales group to introduce myself and share with them what I am going to expect from each salesperson in the immediate future."

"When would you like to have that meeting?" Tom asked.

"How about Friday afternoon at two o'clock?"

"I will make that happen."

"Also, Tom, please make sure that everyone knows that attendance is mandatory."

"I will make sure everyone on the sales team will be there!"

> I schedule all sales meetings on Friday afternoons because some salespeople have a bad habit of taking Friday afternoons off for personal reasons. I like to have my sales reps work a forty-hour workweek. When I have my sales meetings after lunch on Friday, I know that the sales department is not going to quit for the day after a Friday morning sales call.

I thanked him and turned to Roger. "I would like to schedule a meeting with your whole technician group on Friday at three o'clock p.m."

"Okay, I will have every technician here for the meeting on Friday."

I thanked him too, and then I covered the next-to-last item on my list. "This management team is going to have a weekly management meeting every Wednesday. So please add to your calendars a management meeting every Wednesday at one o'clock p.m. for the next three months. Attendance at the meeting for this group is mandatory. There will be an agenda distributed to all attendees twenty-four hours before the meeting listing the topics to discuss. Please do not ever be late for the meetings because there are cash penalties for anyone who shows up after one o'clock. I will explain the cash penalties further at the meeting this Wednesday. Is everyone here okay with that time and day for the meeting?"

No one objected.

"Finally, the last bullet point on my list: Does anyone have any questions to ask Kevin, Rick or me?"

"What do you expect Craig to do in the future?" Trish asked.

I thought it was an odd question for her to ask me. "I will let Craig answer that question."

His face was a shade of red, Craig replied, "This all happened so fast, I haven't thought it through yet."

Trish asked a second question: "Are any of us going to get fired?"

"That's a question I *will* answer," I replied. "Trish, every employee in this company must work hard for this company to be profitable. I am going to expect everyone to give an extra effort during the next three to six months, or this company is going to be shut down by these two men, Kevin and Rick. The more money this company loses, the more risk for their company. I firmly believe that the level of risk this company is right now is as much as they can handle. I am sure that no one here wants to start collecting unemployment compensation as everyone looks for a new job. ABC Computer Distributors is a good company and can be very profitable if everyone works together and pulls the rope all in the same direction. So, Trish, the simple answer is no one who currently works for this company will have a job if we do not quickly turn this company around to be profitable. I hope that my message was clear for everyone here. Are there any other questions?"

The room was silent.

"This meeting is over," I concluded. "Okay, team, GO WITH CONFIDENCE!"

Everyone but Craig, Kevin, Rick, and I got up and left the room. Rick stood and closed the conference room door. He sat back down again, looked at Craig, and said, "I want you to know that our company is engaging Bob to turn this company around. We do not want you to interfere with his efforts. If you want to stay here, you cannot interrupt his leadership and direction for the management team. If you do, you must leave the company. We currently have a legal issue with you right now regarding your signature on a fraudulently reported collateral report with the overstated borrowing base calculations. My company does not want to have to press charges against you and foreclose on the loan. You have an opportunity to get out of this mess if you let Bob do his thing and make this company profitable again. If you can be a productive and positive asset to this company, we would appreciate it."

"Okay, how can I help?" he asked.

"Craig, you said before that you could sell snowballs to Eskimos," I said, "How about you go out and start selling computers and service contracts rather than snowballs to your old customers?"

"Are you asking me to take over the sales manager position?" Craig asked.

"No, just go out and sell and turn over your customer orders to Alan in purchasing to fulfill."

"So, you want me to be a salesman?"

"Yes, that would work fine for me, but I want to caution you, you are no longer managing any of the employees in this building."

"Okay, but if I start selling, can I have my Mercedes back?"

"No. I will give you a five-hundred-dollar monthly car allowance. You can keep the Mercedes if you pay the monthly lease payments, then you can use the monthly car allowance to offset the lease payment."

"No, turn the vehicle back to the dealer, that lease is twelve hundred fifty dollars per month."

"Okay, Craig," Rick chimed in. "Are we in agreement now, and do you understand your future role with this company?"

"I will sleep on it this week and get back to you later with my decision," Craig replied.

"Okay," Rick said, "but please remember not to interfere with Bob's leadership with this company."

"I understand, you have hammered that issue enough today for me to understand your message."

The four of us stood up, shook hands, and Rick and Kevin left. Craig said that he was going to have Trish drive him home since he no longer had a vehicle.

"Before you go, is there an office that I can use?" I asked.

"There is an open office next to mine. I suggest you use that one. I think that it is clean with a phone and computer."

"Okay, thank you."

I went to the empty office, sat down, and began to write down everything I had learned during the meeting. I posted all the scheduled meeting dates and times for the one-on-ones and the management meetings for three months on my calendar. I also entered a message in Outlook to remind me to create the agenda for the management meeting and distribute it before noon on Tuesdays. I posted the meeting with the sales team for that Friday at 2:00 p.m. and the service department at 3:00 p.m.

*   *   *

My first one-on-one was with Tom, the sales manager. I wondered, after hearing Craig's description of Tom, if, rather than calling him a sales manager, I should refer to him as Nancy's assistant. However, I knew I needed to keep a positive attitude about Tom because I did not want to lose Nancy and her sales volume. Tom and I went to lunch at his favorite Italian restaurant, which was only a few blocks away from the office. I rode with Tom in his car, a big Cadillac, to the restaurant. He needed the extra room of a big vehicle so he would be able to fit behind the steering wheel, due to the size of his midsection. When we arrived at the restaurant, Tom went in the front door and walked over to the corner table without saying a word to the host. I followed him because he looked like he knew where he was going. After we sat down, the server came over with two cups of coffee, put one in front of Tom, and she asked me how I liked my coffee. I said, "No sugar, just a little cream would be good."

She looked at Tom and said, "The special?"

He said, "Of course!"

I asked Tom about the special of the day. Tom said with great passion, "Meatball lasagna, with a side salad, dessert, and coffee, all for one low price. Bob, the lasagna here is amazing!"

Wow, I thought, *that is a lot of food for lunch!* I told the server that

I would have a Caesar salad with chicken. The server scribbled down our orders and walked away.

"Bob, I should apologize. I left my list of issues to talk about back at the office on my desk, but I have it committed to memory."

"Tom, to get this company profitable again, I am going to need your help. Can I depend on you?" I asked.

"Bob, yes, of course. I do not know what Craig has told you about me, but I am a company man. Nancy and I love it here. I have been with ABC Computer Distributors for a long time, and I do not want to see this company fail, and neither does Nancy. I do not have to tell you that Nancy is responsible for over fifty-five percent of the sales for this company."

"Craig has said very little about anyone on the management team, and what he did say I had a tough time believing. However, Tom, I do have a question to ask you. I am a numbers guy, but for the life of me, I do not understand this."

"What is that, Bob?"

"If Nancy is doing over twenty-seven million dollars in sales this year, why are all the rest of the sixteen people on the sales team only doing a total of twenty-three million? That means that we have sixteen people each averaging one million four hundred thousand annually. Nancy is doing more in a month—two million three hundred thousand—than any of the rest of the salespeople are doing in a year. I would be embarrassed if I was one of the other salespeople in the department."

"I understand what you are saying. Bob. There are several reasons why Nancy is so successful, and there are many reasons why the others are not."

"Well, I would like you and me to figure out what those reasons are and correct them. Then I also want to understand the reasons that make Nancy so successful. I would like to start training the salespeople Nancy's secrets that makes her such an extremely successful salesperson. Let's develop a plan to make that happen, and soon."

"Bob, I believe that one of the key issues with the sixteen salespeople is lack of sufficient effort."

"What you're telling me is that they are lazy and not motivated. We need to turn up the heat on these people. They need to feel the pressure to either produce or find a new career."

Tom agreed, "We need to light some fires and get the rest of the salespeople productive."

"As the sales manager, you are going to have to push them hard. If Nancy can do over two million three hundred thousand dollars a month with her customers, why cannot the other salespeople do the same numbers? We need to kick the salespeople's butts out of the office and get them meeting with our customers. Every company out there needs computer hardware, software, and service."

"You tell me what you want me to do, and I will get it done."

"Great! I appreciate your attitude, Tom. I sincerely appreciate it. I will develop a list of large local target companies. I would like you to assign those companies to all the salespeople, including Nancy. I will also develop a new sales incentive system, and then we need to start measuring and tracking the sales team's successes. Tom, I want our salespeople in large companies. I want to see big orders, not these one-, two-, or five-laptop orders. I want to see one hundred, two hundred, or five hundred computers on the customer orders."

"I agree. That is one of Nancy's secrets to her success. Most of her customers have at least a thousand or more employees. She schedules visits with all her customers every month, and she does not miss an order if there is one out there."

"Okay," I said. "I will develop my plan in writing and forward it to you for your review. If you agree with everything, then together, we will implement it, and start materially growing the sales with the balance of the sales team. If you do not agree with any issues of the new plan, just let me know. We can talk about it and get coordinated. Is there anything that I could do to help Nancy increase her sales volume?"

Tom leaned forward. "I am glad that you asked me. Right now, we have three sales assistant people that support the sales department by writing up the orders when received from the customers. They process the orders and then forward them over to Alan in purchasing to buy out the products. There are times when these three girls cannot stay current with processing the orders. It may take those three employees ten days to two weeks to process all the open customer orders at times. There are many times when customers get angry because we are not getting them their products quick enough."

"What do you suggest we do to resolve the problem?" I asked.

"I think if we add one more sales assistant to the department, we will be able to stay current in the future," he suggested.

"I have an idea. How about if we hire an additional support person and have that new person report directly to Nancy? That way, her orders are a priority for the new person and up to date. The new employee could also download some of the processing of Nancy's sales orders to the other three girls if she gets backed up."

"That is a fantastic idea," he said. "Nancy would love you if you did that. The reason Nancy is so successful is that she fights hard to take care of her customers."

Since Tom was Nancy's manager, I asked when the best time would be for me to schedule a meeting with her so that I could introduce myself.

"I will check her schedule, find out when she is going to be in the office, and find some time for her to meet with you," he said.

"Okay, great, but please don't forget! It is important."

"I will not forget," he promised.

The server came over and poured some hot coffee in our cups. Tom asked if the food was on its way. When she assured him that it was, I asked him, "How often do you get a chance to go out on sales calls with the other salespeople on the sales team?"

"Unfortunately, not very often," he admitted.

I took a thoughtful sip of my coffee. "Can I ask you to start scheduling at least one sales call with each of the salespeople over the next two weeks? Let me tell you why. I would like to know how many seasoned salespeople we have, and which ones are the rookies."

"I think that it is about half and half. About half of the sales force are pretty good salespeople, and the rest are okay, nothing special."

"In your opinion, what is the problem? Why are they not selling more?" I asked.

"Part of the problem, Bob, is most of the girls were hired by Craig because he met them out at a bar one night and offered them a job to try to get them to go to bed with him. There was a two-month period six months ago when a new girl was starting every week in the sales department. When the first couple of the girls were hired, I started doing some sales training with them. However, when I learned that they had no computer knowledge, sales experience, or motivation to learn how to sell our products, I quit trying. What they did have was cleavage. I just got fed up with the whole situation and told Craig that he was responsible for getting these—or his—girls selling, I was not going to waste my time."

I raised my eyebrows. "What did Craig say?"

"He said okay and then did nothing. Some of the girls figured out quickly that they were not going to make enough money to live unless they got out and started selling."

"I understand your situation," I assured him. "I probably would have done the same thing. However, now we need to support and manage them so they can be productive, or we need to weed them out."

"How do you suggest we do that?"

"I will develop my sales incentive plan over the next couple days. You review it, and if you have any comments, let me know immediately. Then we will introduce it at the next sales meeting this Friday. Please start scheduling yourself to ride with a different salesperson on sales calls, one in the morning and one in the afternoon, every day. I would like you to take notes on each person—what they did right and what they did wrong. I would like to keep the productive people on the sales staff and get rid of the ones that don't sell enough product and services to cover their base salary."

When Tom acknowledged that plan with a nod, I switched topics. "I would also like to talk to you about the service department. Craig said that the service department is delivering poor service, so the sales team stopped selling service contracts. Is that accurate?"

"The service department at this company has never been good," he explained. "First, there is poor management, as well as poor hiring practices. No one tested the candidates who interviewed for a service job. We hired a bunch of service technicians who were terrible and knew very little about servers and software. Craig recently fired the service department manager because the guy was hitting on Trish. Trish was flirting with him, and Craig did not like it."

"But Craig told me that the old service manager was stealing laptops from the warehouse and selling them to his friends for cash," I said, perplexed.

"That is not true, Bob. Craig is a very jealous person. If someone looks at Trish the wrong way, Craig is ready to fire him."

"Hmm . . . Craig did not tell me the truth, hard to believe," I said dryly. "You know, Tom, when someone lies to you like that, it is hard to believe a word that comes out of their mouth in the future. Because you brought it up, tell me more about Trish."

Tom was happy to oblige. "Nine months ago, Craig bought Trish's training company. He overpaid for it and paid her cash for the deal. As soon as she got some money in the bank, she stopped working, but of course, she still comes to work every day and collects her big salary. What a bad deal that was. Craig should have never purchased her company."

The server brought us our food. The piece of lasagna on Tom's plate was huge. Then there were two giant meatballs smothered in meat sauce. I had not eaten that much food at one sitting in my life. On her next trip, the server brought me my salad and freshened up our coffees again. She asked if she could get us anything else. Tom told her he would love some bread. I did not say a word, but I knew that I would have had to take a nap all afternoon before I went back to work if I ate all that food on Tom's plate, plus bread.

Tom was quiet while we ate. Before I was able to finish my salad, he ate all his lasagna, meatballs, almost a loaf of bread, and a side salad. The server returned, took Tom's plates away, and put a piece of cherry pie with vanilla ice cream in front of him, and then warmed up his coffee again. The server asked if she could get me a piece of cherry pie, but I declined. I finished my salad just as Tom was finishing the last bite of his dessert. It was hard to believe how much he had just eaten for lunch.

"Is Nancy a good cook?" I asked, breaking the silence.

"Nancy has never cooked a meal in her life," Tom replied with a smile. "I married her fifteen years ago, and I remember once she made me a ham sandwich while I was watching a football game on a Sunday afternoon. I almost fell off the couch when I saw her there holding the sandwich. Other than that one time, Nancy has not prepared any of our meals."

I laughed as he continued, "We go out and eat at different restaurants in the area every night. We eat here about four nights a week. They save this table for us each evening."

I looked around. "Beautiful table, Tom!"

Tom just laughed.

"Before we go back to work," I said, "let's recap what we have agreed to during this lunch, okay?"

Tom agreed enthusiastically.

"I will develop a target list of big corporations in our geographic area for the salespeople to go after to develop new business sales. I am going to write up a new incentive plan for the sales team and send it to you for your review. Once we both agree on the strategy, we will present the plan to the sales staff at the next sales meeting scheduled for this Friday at two o'clock. You are going to announce the sales meeting to everyone on the sales team and let everyone know that attendance at the meeting is mandatory. I think we should include the sales assistants and probably Alan from purchasing. What do you think?"

"I agree."

"So, you will make sure everyone knows about the meeting?"

"Yes, I will," Tom said, pulling a pen from his front shirt pocket. He began jotting down notes on his napkin.

Even on a napkin, taking notes was a good idea. We had covered a lot during our lunch despite the silence while Tom ate.

> It is always a good business practice to bring something to
> take notes with when you are in a business setting, whether
> it be a lunch or a formal business meeting. If you write down
> important issues to remember, you will never forget them.

I went on, "You are going to check Nancy's schedule and let me know when she will be available to meet with me this week. I am going to speak to her about hiring a new sales assistant to report to her directly to process her orders. You are going to start attending sales calls with each of the salespeople over the next two weeks. You will go on a sales call in the morning and one in the afternoon so that you can visit at least one customer with every salesperson on staff. You are going to write an assessment of the salesperson for each sales call. After, you will sit down with the salesperson to discuss what they did right and what you think that they need to do to improve their sales skills. You will also give me a copy of the assessments for my review."

Afterward, Tom and I shook hands, and he said, "Bob, together, along with Nancy, we are going to grow this company and make it profitable again."

I thanked Tom for his time. The server brought the check for our lunch. I gave her enough cash to pay the total for our meals, plus a big tip. We then went back to the office together.

My first meeting with Tom had been such a pleasant surprise. If I had just listened to Craig's description of Tom, I would have materially misjudged him. I walked away from my first meeting with Tom thinking that he was going to be a valuable member of this turnaround management team. The other things I learned from our lunch meeting were: first, boy can Tom eat; and second, I could not believe a word that came out of Craig's mouth!

*   *   *

When Tom and I arrived back at the office, Roger was in the reception area waiting for me. It was 1:50 p.m. and our one-on-one meeting was at 2:00 p.m. I shook Tom's hand again, thanked him for his time, and asked Roger to follow me to the conference room.

When I first met Roger, it took me approximately ten minutes to figure out that the service manager's position was way over Roger's professional skill level. He was trying to keep his head above water but was losing the battle. As I was interviewing him, he told me that Craig had put him in this position against his will. The last service manager was terminated one day at 5:00 p.m. According to Roger, that was normal for employees who worked for Craig.

Roger was in his mid-thirties, about five-foot-six inches tall and always wore a gray sports coat over a white shirt, with no tie. Immediately after I met Roger, I knew that he had a "follower's" personality. Roger did not want to manage the service group; he was most comfortable repairing customer's servers and network systems.

Roger was supposed to be one of the most qualified technicians for the company, so Craig had promoted him because of his abilities with a computer, rather than his management skills. Roger was the type of person who got along with everyone but could manage no one, including himself. The whole department was feeling the problems of Roger's weak management skills, and the customers were experiencing the same pain. Roger had no idea how to dispatch the techs to customers' locations for installations and repairs. Because of this problem, the sales team had stopped selling maintenance contracts. Not selling service was a major problem for the company's profitability because service contracts were the most profitable sales category.

I first asked Roger, "How long have you been the manager of this department?"

"About three months, Mr. Curry, the longest three months of my life."

"Roger, please call me Bob."

"May I speak freely to you, Bob?"

"Of course, Roger!"

"I hate this job. I do not want to be the manager of this department.

It stresses me out and takes me away from what I am good at, repairing customers' computer systems."

"Why did Craig promote you if you did not want the job?"

"Because he fired the old service manager and had no one to replace him. Therefore, he promoted me. I have no idea why."

"Why did Craig fire the old service manager, do you know?"

"Yes, Craig walked into the old service manager's office one afternoon, and Trish was sitting on his lap. That evening, Craig fired him, and asked me to help the old service manager clean out his office."

"Wow! Roger that is not the story that I heard."

"I know. Craig is very good at lying. I believe he does it without even thinking about it. I have caught him in several—no, I take that back, many lies. Anyhow, I think Craig promoted me just because I was in the office on the day he caught Trish and the old service manager. If I had not been in the office that afternoon picking up parts for a customer's network, I probably would have never been promoted."

"Roger, I am guessing that the company's customers are missing you right now while you are in here hating your manager's job," I said.

Roger shook his head. "I have been working four evenings a week at our customer's locations because no one else in the service department can technically handle network and service problems as well as I can."

I knew what I needed to do. "Okay, Roger, I hear you loud and clear. I will commit to you that I will recruit and hire a new service manager as a priority and get you back into the field as quickly as I can."

"Bless you, sir!" Roger said with a happy sigh.

"In the meantime, how can I help you right now?" I asked.

Roger did not hesitate with his reply: "You can go to your office immediately and start the recruiting process. The quicker you hire a new department manager, the better."

"Okay, my friend, I can do that," I agreed with a laugh. "I sincerely appreciate your absolute honesty."

I pulled out my notebook and wrote down some notes:

- *Number-one priority: recruit and hire a new service department manager.*

- *Roger is an asset to this company with his high-end technical server and network skills.*

- *DO NOT BELIEVE ONE WORD THAT CRAIG TELLS YOU! So far, Craig is zero for two on what he told Rick, Kevin, and me about his management team.*

* * *

My next one-on-one meeting was with Alan at 3:30 p.m., which was an hour away. I decided to walk over to Alan's office to see if he was available right then rather than wait another sixty minutes. His door was open, so I gently knocked on the wall next to the door to get his attention. As soon as he saw me, he stood up from his chair and came to greet me with a handshake.

Alan was the purchasing manager. He was about five-foot-ten and skinny. Alan did not have an athletic build, but according to Craig, he was an outstanding golfer. Alan was a single guy and approximately forty years old. He had graduated from the University of Florida on a golf scholarship. That was a little surprising because Alan weighed no more than 140 pounds. I later witnessed his skills on the golf course. He hits his drives off the tee like a bullet, and his irons were like lasers hitting the golf ball right at the pins. He was a great partner in a scramble golf tournament because he was long off the tee and hit most of the fairways.

The purchasing manager is a critical position for a computer distributor. He needs to know about all the different computer products and the most current technology releases. The purchasing manager needs to understand which vendors have the best prices for each product and parts of which there are thousands and thousands. Alan was very good at negotiating and maintaining the company's on-hand inventory.

Every salesperson depended heavily on Alan. The salespeople would receive a customer purchase order (PO), then the sales support department would write it up and turn the PO over to Alan. Alan would take care of everything else. Everyone loved Alan. He was always getting gift cards for dinners from the salespeople as a thank-you for doing a great job with their customer's large orders. It was evident to me that Alan was a backroom "money-making machine." I do not know what his capacity was with the current level of sales volume, but I knew that I was going to test it. It was my current plan to double the sales volume very quickly. If he continued to perform at his current level, he was going to receive a handful of gift cards wrapped up in $100 bills from me. Alan was what I call a "hidden asset."

Alan looked at his watch and said he thought our meeting was scheduled for 3:30, but he had time to meet now since I was free. I closed his office door, sat down, and pulled out my notebook to record any notes from our conversation.

> Years ago, I learned to show respect to fellow employees by not just barging into their office unannounced. I always gently knock on the door to get their attention, and then stand at the door until the employee invites me into the room. Showing respect for fellow employees builds camaraderie!

"So, Mr. Curry, how can I help you?" Alan asked.

"Please share with me anything about your department or within the company that you believe is getting in the way of this business being profitable."

Alan reached into the top drawer of his desk and pulled out a notebook. He opened it to the first page, and there was a list of bullet points. *Hmm, that's a good sign,* I thought, *Alan listened to me at that morning's meeting.*

Alan said, "Nancy gives me more orders to purchase products for her customers than the rest of the total sales team. That makes no sense to me. If there are several of the salespeople employed here who are not selling anything, why is the management team letting them be here and eat up the cash and profits?"

"You are right, and I am developing a plan to deal with that problem this week."

He went on, "The three sales assistants are swamped with work, more work than three people can handle. They work very hard and are under enormous pressure to get the customer orders processed. When they are rushing to get the orders done, they make a lot of mistakes."

"In your opinion, Alan," I asked, "what is the solution to this problem?"

"We need to add a sales assistant to the department to get caught up. We need to hire an additional person immediately. The backlog of work at times is creating canceled orders because the customers are tired of waiting for delivery."

I wrote myself a note to talk to Donna about recruiting and hiring an additional sales support person.

"The company's credit rating with some of our vendors is bad. Craig runs out of money after paying the payroll at times and stops paying our suppliers. There are many times when I have customer's orders on hold until Craig sends the vendor some money to pay off some of the older invoices."

"I would ask for your suggested solution to the problem," I said without a hint of humor, "but I think we both know how to solve that issue."

"Bob, the employees all come to work every day and walk up the sidewalk from the parking lot to come into the building in the front door. As the workers are walking to the building, they walk past a hundred-thousand-dollar Mercedes. We are not paying our vendors on time to get our customer's orders shipped on time, but the company can afford a big expensive Mercedes? Bob, that makes no business sense at all."

"Alan, that car is going back to the dealer within the next couple of days."

"You are kidding, right?"

"No, I am not!"

"Good!" he said with great enthusiasm. "Bob, I see some

employees here work long and hard hours, but then other employees draw a big salary and never do anything positive around here."

I gave Alan a knowing look. "Even though I have been here less
than a day, I know who you mean. I will have the problem fixed
within a week or two."

The look of relief that crossed Alan's features was short-lived,
and he continued, "Craig wants me to maintain four million dollars
of inventory on hand here in the warehouse. He wants me to have
the highest moving products on hand, so the salespeople can receive
an order, and have it delivered the next day. This business decision
makes no sense to me at all. I can have product drop-shipped to
our customers for orders within forty-eight hours. If the customers
want the product quicker, they can pay a slight premium to have
it overnighted and receive the products within twenty-four hours.

"Many times, we have the situation where we are shipping products out of the warehouse and filling the balance of the order by
drop-shipping it from one of the master distributors. Those double shipments—shipments from two locations to fill the customer's
order—confuses the customers and delays payments of our invoices.
Many times, we will get a partial payment for the shipment from the
warehouse. Then we must send the customer a 'proof of delivery'
for the drop-shipped product to get the balance of the invoice paid.
If I had it my way, we would have no inventory in our warehouse.
I would have all the shipments drop-shipped from our suppliers.
When there are situations where we are being paid to load software
on the computers from here, we could bring in the whole order to
our warehouse, load the software, and ship the entire order from
this location."

I smiled. "Well, Alan, your wish has just come true. Effective
immediately, do not bring in another order to this warehouse that is
not for a customer's purchase order. I am planning on running the
inventory down to zero as quickly as possible by offering spiffs—
bonuses—for the sales team." (A "spiff" is an immediate bonus for
a product sale. Typically, spiffs are paid by an employer directly to
a salesperson for selling *specific* products.)

"Well, Bob, those were all the issues I had on my list." He looked satisfied and hopeful.

"Okay, now I have one issue for you, Alan."

"What's that?"

"I want to get rid of the inventory as soon as possible."

"Do you want us to return the inventory to where we purchased it?"

"Is there a restocking charge for returns?"

"Yes, there is, fifteen percent."

"Okay, then no, I do not want it returned. I want to spiff the salespeople to sell the inventory as quickly as possible. I agree with you, it makes no sense to me either to have inventory on hand when our suppliers can ship our customers the product in two days."

"I agree with you, Bob. It was Craig's idea to have inventory. He used to say, 'How can I sell the product if I don't have it?'"

"Well, Alan, I have a different concept. I would rather have money in the bank than inventory in the warehouse. As you know, the big problem with computer inventory is that it becomes obsolete very quickly. I read an article this past weekend that said that computer inventory loses one percent of its value every month. One percent of $4 million is forty thousand dollars. I rather have our vendors deal with that risk rather than ABC Computer Distributors."

"The other benefit of getting rid of the inventory is that it will save me a lot of time not having to worry about if we have the product in the warehouse. I can buy out the orders quicker and not have to worry if there is inventory on hand."

"Would you be able to keep track of which salesperson is selling product out of the inventory? I am going to offer a spiff program and reward the sales team for selling the inventory in our warehouse to get rid of it."

"Yes, Bob, that would not be a problem. I could do two things to help you out with moving our warehouse inventory quickly. I could provide each salesperson with a listing of all the computers that we have and the prices. Then I could provide you a monthly report showing the number of computers each salesperson sold out of the inventory."

"That would be great. Please print a computer inventory for each salesperson and give them to Tom so he can distribute them. Please let him know about my plan that the salespeople will get a twenty-five-dollar bonus for every computer that they sell out of our inventory."

"I will meet with Tom before the end of the day. It will not take any time at all to print those inventories for the sales department."

I was very pleased with how this meeting was going; our conversation was fast paced and productive, but I still had two more requests to make of him.

"This next idea is confidential until I formally announce the program," I told him. "I would like to offer a four-year college scholarship to a senior in high school who comes from an underprivileged family and cannot afford to go to college. I want our management team to form a committee to find a student in high school who has the grades, intelligence, and maturity to excel in college, but who does not have the money to pay for the tuition, books, room, and board. What I would like you to do, Alan is to talk to some of your vendors that you deal with daily to participate in the program. They can either donate money, laptops, iPads, etcetera, for the future college student. I plan for ABC Computer Distributors to donate at least a hundred and twenty thousand dollars next year to this program from our profits. I would love to have our vendors match our contribution. Alan, if you are uncomfortable asking our vendors for the money, come and get me when any of the sales reps are here, and I will ask. You can tell them that they can participate in the selection of the student."

"Bob, are you kidding? I can handle our vendors. I will be happy to request some of the big vendors open their wallets for such a great program and chip in for your idea. A scholarship program is such an easy idea to get them to contribute. I do have one question. This company has lost money for the past two years. How are we going to afford to contribute that kind of money?"

I waved my hand as if the problem were already solved. "Alan, I plan on lighting some fires under some of the sales and service people to increase their productivity. Some of the nonperformers are going to disappear soon. We are not going to spend the company's money on people who refuse to work hard and make this company profitable. I am planning on this company doing at least a hundred and twenty million next year."

"Wow! If we do those kinds of sales next year, we will be very profitable."

"I know, and when we are, I would like to help some students get a college degree."

"Bob, I love the idea!"

His enthusiasm encouraged me, and I made another request. "Please ask some of our vendors to teach our sales team about their new products. At my past employers, we called it a *Lunch and Learn*. For the privilege to have the attention of our sales force for one hour to teach and promote their products, they must donate one of their products—a desktop computer, laptop, iPads, etcetera—as a door prize for those attending, plus they must buy lunch for the group. I would like them to donate to our scholarship fund also."

"That one is easy. Bob. I have vendors begging me to have a meeting with our salespeople. They are always asking me if they could attend our weekly sales meetings. We used to do this a while ago, but Craig used to take all the door prizes himself. He never shared them with the sales team. Eventually, they all stopped coming to the vendor's meetings since they seemed to be only for Craig's benefit."

"I am so surprised when I hear greedy stories like that about Craig," I said, closing my notebook.

"Really?" asked Alan.

"No, I have heard bad stories about Craig many times. Over at the country club, everyone dislikes him."

Alan chuckled at my dry humor, then said, "You have given me some exciting projects, Bob. I will make these happen, the scholarship funding and the *Lunch and Learns*."

"I appreciate your hard work and honesty," I told Alan sincerely. "I am going to ask you in the future to bring to my attention any other problems you see so I can deal with them also. You do not have to be formal about how you communicate your suggestions—send me an email, text me, or let's go get a cold one after work some evening."

"Will do! It is a breath of fresh air to have someone leading this company who is easy to talk to and will listen to constructive suggestions."

"I am going to clean up this business, Alan, and then we are all going to have some fun and make a bunch of money."

I stood up, and so did Alan.

"Well, Bob, I want you to know that you have my absolute support for your mission." He reached out his hand for a shake.

"Alan, it has been a pleasure," I said shaking his hand.

We exchanged a few more acknowledgments of how productive our meeting was before I went back to my office to get myself organized. I had a lot of information from my conversations with Tom, Roger, and Alan that I needed to write down so I could organize everything, develop a plan of attack, and solve these problems. In my notebook, I recorded the following items regarding my top priorities to improve the company's cash flow quickly:

- The service department is bleeding right now and needs help. The techs need a new leader.

- The service department needs direct supervision, systems, reporting, incentives, and a customer survey program to self-govern the quality of the technician's fieldwork.

- There are people on this payroll that should not be here because they are unproductive and a negative influence on all the employees who want to see this company successful.

- We need to add an employee to the sales support department, and that person will report to Nancy based on the backlog of orders plus the anticipated increase in sales in the future.

- I need to get rid of that big Mercedes as soon as possible, which would make progress with employee morale and improve cash flow by getting rid of those monthly lease payments.

- We need to reduce the inventory in the warehouse. There is no need for this company to have this much stock on hand.

- Alan is going to stop buying computers for our inventory, print an on-hand inventory for every salesperson and give it to Tom to distribute to his sales team.

- Alan is going to keep an accounting of which salesperson sells computers out of the on-hand inventory so I can pay a $25 spiff to the sales staff based on the number of computers sold.

- Alan is now responsible for getting donations from our vendors for the scholarship program and scheduling lunch and learns for our employees.

* * *

During the time of this turnaround, on Monday nights, I played in a men's basketball league at the local YMCA. Playing basketball had always been a great stress release for me. I played for the same team for several years, a group of former college "ballers" who love to run and gun the whole evening. We blew most teams off the court in this men's league. Because we ran so much, we all alternated in and out of the game on a regular basis.

Our team had a bunch of players who used to be young and aggressive on the court. Now, fifteen or twenty years after graduating from college, the players had slowed down their speed, but not their passion. After the games, we all needed to recover from the fatigue and "rehydrate." There was only one proper way to rehydrate after our basketball games, which was having a beer or two at Duffy's Sports Bar. We watched *Monday Night Football*, but only until the end of the first half because all of us needed to get home to our wives and get to work the next morning.

One of the guys on my team, Chris, and I were the only two rehydrating that evening. I had known Chris for many years. We met on the basketball court at the "Y" when I first started at H&N Construction and were friends almost immediately. Chris and I sat and talked for three hours about basketball, football, family life, and our jobs. Chris worked for a competitor of ABC Computer Distributors. He was their service manager and had been employed by the same company for over nine years. He started as a service technician and earned a promotion to manage the group after three years. Chris was six-foot-six and weighed 230 pounds. He was a handsome guy with a very natural smile on his face almost all the time. Because Chris was such a tall man with a strong but friendly personality, he was a natural leader. I liked Chris; I liked him a lot. When Chris told me something, whether it be good or bad news, I could depend on its being the truth. I asked Chris what he believed was his next move for his career.

"Bob, I am not sure. Someday I would like to do the same thing that you are doing, take over a company and clean it up in a leadership role."

"Hmm . . . Chris, why don't you join my management team and help me clean up this company? We can kick butt and make this company very successful together!"

"Bob, are you serious?"

"Yes, Chris, I am very serious. There are two significant problems with this company, sales, and service. I will take charge of the sales department, and you can take over the service department. Roger is the service manager right now and is a fish out of water in the manager role."

"Bob, I know Roger. I have met him several times at some technical training classes over the years. He is not service manager material."

"Chris, I know. He would be the first one to agree. He needs to be replaced soon if I am going to make any quick progress with cleaning up the service department."

"I have got to be honest with you. Craig tried to recruit me recently. I checked that guy out, and he is not someone that I would ever work for in my life."

"Yes, I know and agree with you. However, Chris, I have an employment contract with the company's bank to be the new president and CEO of the organization. Craig has no responsibility or decision-making authority with ABC Computer Distributors anymore, as of this morning. I can make him move out of the office if he starts interfering in any way."

Chris took a sip of his drink. "Bob, you know that he is going to interfere. That is just who he is, a cocky jackass!"

"Yes, I know. Today was my first day at the company. Craig had a hundred-thousand-dollar Mercedes sitting in his parking space in the front of the office. I had a meeting with the bankers and Craig first thing this morning. I told Craig that his car was not going to be the company's liability after today, and he handed me the keys. My first step toward expense reduction was Craig's company car."

Chris laughed. "I bet he enjoyed that. Did he cuss you out?"

"No, just put the keys on the table, gave me a sarcastic comment, and walked out of the conference room."

"Are you serious about this, Bob? You want me to come to work with you?"

"Yes, Chris, I am—I am very serious. I need your help."

"I earn big money, Bob. You probably cannot afford my salary."

"Let's talk again in the morning, and we will work out a deal."

"I have to work in the morning, Bob. I am not the president of the company like you. I have to get up every morning and go to work for a living."

"Okay, then let's meet for lunch tomorrow right here at noon, but we cannot drink any beer tomorrow."

"I never drink on the job," he assured me, although he knew I didn't think that would be an issue. "I will be here, especially since I know that you are going to pay for the lunch. I know that it is going to be a business lunch for you recruiting a new superstar service manager."

"Chris, I will buy you lunch anytime. I will even pick up the tab tonight."

"You should, Bob! I rebounded those bricks that you threw up at the basket the whole night. I knew when you took a shot that I better get under the basket because there was going to be a rebound for another one of your missed shots."

"Chris, I know, it was a bad night for me. I only scored twenty-two points. You had a great night shooting! You scored—was it three or five points, right? Enjoy your evening, Chris, and I will see you at lunch tomorrow."

After I paid the bar bill for Chris's and my rehydration that evening, I sat in my car for a few minutes and jotted down notes while everything was fresh in my mind. I hate forgetting anything, so I am regularly writing stuff down. This way, I can relax knowing that I will not overlook the issue in the future. That evening, my notes were:

- *I need to schedule a meeting with Tom's wife, Nancy. Nancy is the number-one salesperson for the company. I need to win her over, so she trusts that ABC Computer Distributors is going to turn around and be very profitable in the future. Nancy is a very valuable employee.*

> It is always important to identify the top 10 percent of the employees in the company to ensure that they are happy and have the tools to do their jobs. They need to know that you are supporting them because they are helping you and the company.

- *I need to prepare for the meeting with the sales team. I also need to create templates for reports that I am going to ask the salespeople to maintain in the future.*

- *At all our meetings (sales, service, and management), we will take minutes, so everyone knows what they will need to accomplish. The minutes are for follow-up with those given assignments at the meeting. The meeting minutes should keep everyone accountable for any assignments made to the managers.*

> As the leader of the company, I always prepare in advance for meetings. Meetings are costly when you add up all the salaries of the participants. Meetings should be efficient with a good exchange of information.

- I need to review the current sales commission schedule to determine if it needs to be updated to incentivize the sales team. I want to motivate the sales team to grow the sales volume of this company. (There are occasions where the commission plans have issues, which open the door for salespeople to cheat. When that happens, the salesperson earns compensation, but the company does not benefit from the transaction.)

- I need to recruit and hire a new service manager. The service department should be the "money-making" department in the company. The service department's gross margin on sales should average at least 66%. Properly managing this staff will make this tech group very successful. I plan to find a reliable leader with service department experience and then build this unit with qualified and experienced technicians. (My evening with Chris was very favorable toward accomplishing this critical goal.)

> A good commission plan for a sales department is essential. It should pay commissions to those salespeople who work hard and produce profitable sales. I believe it is best to pay a sales commission when there is a "win-win" situation, meaning both the salesperson and the company benefit from the transaction.

Chapter 5

I HAVE ONE SUGGESTION— GET RID OF YOU!

"A key to achieving success is to assemble a strong and stable management team."

—VIVEK WADHWA, AMERICAN TECHNOLOGY
ENTREPRENEUR AND ACADEMIC

TUESDAY, DECEMBER 5—DAY 2 OF WEEK 1

I ARRIVED AT THE OFFICE AT 7:30 IN THE MORNING, AND Donna was sitting in her office as I walked past her door to go to the break room to get a cup of coffee.

When Donna saw me, she called out, "Are you ready for me?"

I turned around, poked my head into her office, and asked, "Is there any good coffee in this place?"

"I have my private stash of good stuff here," she said. "Not like the crap that tastes like mud that is in the break room. How do you like your coffee, Bob?"

"Oh, thank you very much!" I said, surprised and delighted. "Just a little cream, please!"

"Got it," she said. "Where are we meeting? In your office?"

"Yes, my office."

"I will come over and bring my notes when your coffee is ready."

"Okay, thank you! See you in a few!"

Donna arrived at my office door five minutes later, carrying a handful of papers and my coffee. "Here is your coffee, Bob, and a copy of my notes listing the things I would like to discuss with you."

"Thank you," I said taking the coffee. "Okay, it is your meeting! Talk to me." I got up and closed my office door.

"These are significant issues. I hope you are awake."

I took a sip of my coffee. "I am, I promise," I replied, enjoying Donna's her humor despite her serious demeanor.

"Bob, I have had three women come to me this past week complaining that Craig was sexually harassing them."

"Are you serious?" I asked incredulously.

Donna looked taken aback. "Bob, I take these sexual harassment issues very seriously, as do the people making the complaints."

"No, I did not mean it that way. My comment is that Craig harassed not *one*, but *three* different women to the point that they came to you to file complaints. I will deal with this issue this week. Getting Craig out of here makes all the sense in the world right now. What do you have documented about these complaints?"

"I asked each woman to write up exactly what happened. I have two grievances filed in their personnel files and one more coming."

"Okay, please give me a copy of each. Consider this problem solved as soon as I have the third written complaint. I am going to deal with this problem, maybe as soon as this week. What's next?"

"This company's employee manual, performance review policy, or hiring procedures are all probably twenty years old, outdated, and plagiarized from other businesses. The human resources infrastructure of this company is terrible. I feel embarrassed every day that I come to work as the HR manager because I am working for a company that does not have all current standard forms and HR policies."

"Let's put together a list of everything we need and then we will start working on it. I know that there are websites on the internet or HR consulting firms where we can purchase everything you are listing. Let's do some research to see what buying everything that we need costs and make a good business decision very soon."

"Bob, there is a lot that we need," she said without hesitation.

"I know, I understand, but do you know how you eat an elephant?"

She looked at me quizzically.

"One bite at a time."

She chuckled and said, "Okay, I will put together a list, prioritize it, and do some research then get back to you with my recommendations and the cost to update everything."

"You go ahead, make the decision, and get your department updated. I don't need to make this decision. It is your baby!" I assured her.

"Thank you, Bob, I appreciate that! Resolving these problems is important to me." Donna went on, "No employees in this company have been given a performance review in the past two years."

That did not surprise me. "Okay, Donna, at the management meeting on Wednesday, we will talk about this. Do we have a performance review policy and forms to be used?"

Donna answered, "No, sir, we do not."

That did not surprise me either. "Well, Donna, as I see it, we have two options then. I have old forms from my prior company. I will review them, make changes where needed, and forward them to you. That is the first option. The second option is for you to get online and purchase the forms we need today, so you are ready for the management meeting on Wednesday."

"If you don't mind, Bob, I would like to pick option two. I would rather purchase what we need than have you spend your valuable time working on forms I can buy in ten minutes."

I couldn't argue with her suggestion. "I do have better things to do with my time than make up some HR forms. You do the research and make the acquisition. At the management meeting Wednesday, we will announce the company-wide performance review. That is going to force you to get our procedures and forms done quickly."

She smiled confidently. "I will get it done and be ready for the meeting, I promise. That is everything on my list. Oh, and here is the existing chart of organization for your review. Do you have anything for me?"

"Yes, we need to recruit and hire an additional sales support employee. I am considering having the new employee working directly with Nancy."

"I think that may be a good idea, but I also believe that Nancy would be a tough person to work for if we want to retain any sanity for that employee."

I quickly scanned the chart Donna had handed me (see page 90). "Okay, let's get some candidates for the position, and we can deal with the chart of organization issues after we find the person."

"Okay, I will get on that immediately and start looking for a candidate. Bob, I want you to know that I am here for you. I want this company to grow and be successful. I want to be here long term."

"Donna, I appreciate your attitude and support. I had already determined that you would be a definite long-term asset for this company the first time I met you. You are valuable as an employee, a manager, and probably even better as a friend. My door is always open to you also. I have one last question for you."

She motioned for me to ask.

"Craig shared with me that he fired the old service manager for stealing computers. Is that true?"

"No, it's is not," she said flatly and offered no further information.

So I asked, "Did Craig terminate the service manager on the spot because he and Trish were flirting?"

"Yes, Bob, that's true. I had a hard time documenting that transaction in the employee's file."

I thanked Donna for her time and the coffee, and I sat down at my desk to write down my notes from our meeting. It seemed I had walked into a hornet's nest here with all this crap going on. Turning the company around was hard enough of a challenge without having to deal with the owner hitting on virtually every woman in the office. My notes read:

- *The sexual harassment complaints against Craig are a real problem. I have decided to terminate him this week, or there could be significant lawsuits against the company soon. Three sexual harassment complaints are three more than I can or want to handle.*

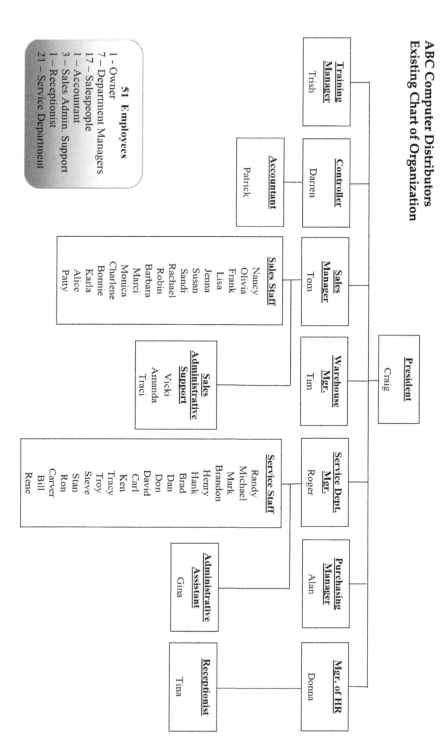

ABC Computer Distributors
Existing Chart of Organization

President
Craig

Training Manager
Trish

Controller
Darren

Accountant
Patrick

Sales Manager
Tom

Sales Staff
Nancy
Olivia
Frank
Lisa
Jenna
Susan
Sandi
Rachael
Robin
Barbara
Marci
Monica
Charlene
Bonnie
Karla
Alice
Patty

Warehouse Mgr.
Tim

Sales Administrative Support
Vicki
Amanda
Traci

Service Dept. Mgr.
Roger

Service Staff
Randy
Michael
Mark
Brandon
Henry
Hank
Brad
Dan
Don
David
Carl
Ken
Tracy
Troy
Steve
Stan
Ron
Carver
Bill
Rene

Purchasing Manager
Alan

Administrative Assistant
Gina

Mgr. of HR
Donna

Receptionist
Tina

51 Employees

1 – Owner
7 – Department Managers
17 – Salespeople
1 – Accountant
3 – Sales Admin. Support
1 – Receptionist
21 – Service Department

• *Not having current policies, procedures, an employee manual and HR forms represent significant exposure to the company. It is Donna's priority task to get this accomplished as quickly as possible.*

* * *

At 9:30 a.m., I walked out to the warehouse to find Tim. He was sitting at a small desk, doing some paperwork. "Tim, how are you doing?"

"I am doing well, Bob," he said, standing up and coming around the desk.

We exchanged a quick handshake. "How about you give me a tour of your warehouse and then we can talk?" I suggested.

When we began our tour, I immediately noticed that the big warehouse garage door was wide open. I looked around, and there were no security cameras or any security system at all. There was a lot of inventory on the racks. "Tim, are all these computers open stock or are they here for a customer order?"

"They are all open stock inventory," he answered.

An alarm went off in my head. "Is there any security in the warehouse?"

"No, none, sir."

"Okay, then, do me a favor and keep that garage door closed and locked?"

Tim agreed and shut the big garage door. After a few more minutes of surveying the warehouse, we went to the conference room to sit and talk.

"Did you create a list as we talked about in our meeting Monday morning?" I asked.

"Yes, I did." Tim pulled a piece of paper out of his pocket and unfolded it. I could see that this meeting was very important to Tim. The first thing he said was that he wanted to help make the company profitable again and that he had some ideas on how to help make that happen. I urged him to share his ideas with me.

"There should be a security system monitoring our inventory in the warehouse," he began. "Right now, employees can walk into the warehouse anytime and take anything they want with no supporting paperwork. That should stop immediately."

"I agree. What do you suggest?"

"Well, I think we should lock the door to the warehouse. I realize it was wide open this morning, but some of the techs hanging around in the warehouse wanted to bring in some fresh air. Anyway, there is a split door entering the warehouse from the office. I can open the top half and lock the bottom of the door. If anyone wants anything from the inventory, they need to come to the door and request it from me. We should have an inventory adjustment form approved by the person's supervisor before I give them anything out of the warehouse. Then, once I provide them the computer, software, computer part, or whatever they requested, we both sign the form confirming that they received the inventory. I would then give the form to Darren to record the transactions at the end of each day. He would adjust the computerized inventory and the accounting records, reducing the value and the unit count of the product. Last year when we had that huge inventory loss, I was offended. I am accountable for the inventory in the warehouse. Now that you are here, I am happy because I can see that things are going to change around here."

I nodded enthusiastically. "I think that is an excellent idea. I believe we should implement this procedure immediately. I suggest that you design the inventory request form and let me see it once completed. Then we need to write procedure, so everyone knows the rules around here. On Wednesday, we will present the process and form to the management team and get everyone's buy-in on the change."

"Does everyone on the management team need to approve this, or just you?" Tim asked.

"Well, good question. Ultimately, I am responsible for everything that happens here. However, I like to have the management team present ideas and changes to procedures, and then I endorse them. If I constantly tell everyone what they should do, the whole management team would be a bunch of puppets. I don't want puppets working for me. I want highly qualified, intelligent, hardworking, creative people on my management team, with strong leadership skills. Just like you are bringing this issue to me, you are now responsible for improving the procedures with inventory movement in this company. That is a great thing, and I appreciate you for doing this."

> I like to have the management team come up with the ideas and changes to procedures, and then I endorse them. If I constantly tell everyone what they should do, the whole management team would be a bunch of puppets.

Tim got a big smile on his face. He looked at me with that smile and said, "I like you, Bob!"

"Tim, I like you, too! What else do you have on your list?"

"You asked about a security system earlier. We need to have one installed in the warehouse monitoring the inventory."

I couldn't have agreed more. "I have a friend in the security system business. I will give him a call to come here and give us an estimate on installing a monitoring system in our warehouse. Does that make sense to you?"

"Yes, sir, it does."

I wrote myself a note to give my friend Charlie a call.

"Bob, right now, when we need to stage computers for sale to a customer, the service guys come into the warehouse and do all the staging. If you don't know what staging is, it is starting up the new computers, loading software, and then running diagnostic programs to make sure that everything is working before we repack them back in the box and then ship the computers to the customer. It is a straightforward process, but it does take time."

"So, what is the problem?" I asked.

Tim explained, "I believe that those service guys should be out at our customers' offices billing for their service work, rather than in the office staging machines. A high school or college kid with very little knowledge of computers could do the staging as well as our technicians and just as quick, but at one-third of the cost. I suggest that I be responsible for all equipment staging in the future. That way, our service team can bill more and get this company profitable again."

I liked where this was going. "I suggest you talk to Roger and work out the issue with him. Tim, this is great, do you have any more ideas?"

"Yes, I do. Recently, Nancy came to talk to me about preparing for her multimillion-dollar customer order of ThinkPads. She said the laptops would need several software programs loaded on the machines before we ship them all to her big pharma customer."

I wanted to ask Tim about the big order, but I did not want to interrupt him. I was sure that I would find out about this transaction later when I met one-on-one with Nancy.

"Bob, Nancy is very friendly, but at times, she is a little intimidating."

"I am sure she means well. It is her hard work and large orders that pay for your and my salaries," I explained to Tim.

Tim gave me a look that told me he understood, and then said, "I am setting up a system so that we can stage fifty computers at a time. If we are going to have to set up and download software for as many as three and a half thousand computers, we must prepare for the project, so we can get the machines staged and shipped quickly. If I could hire two high school or college kids on a temporary basis to come in to help stage the order, we could get it done a lot quicker at a minimal cost."

"Well, Tim, you are four for four. I agree with your idea. Please talk to Donna about finding some young people. She will help you. Since it is so close to the holidays, we should check to see if any of our employees have kids home from college who would like to earn some money before they must go back to school. If you get those machines staged and shipped quickly, Nancy will love you."

"We will stage all the machines, repackage them, and deliver them to the customer's offices faster and at a lower cost than this company has done in the past," Tim said happily.

Potential space constraints concerned me, and I asked, "Are you going to have enough room in the warehouse to store those laptops while you are staging them?"

"According to Alan in the purchasing department, we have the option of having a thousand machines delivered at a time, so space will not be a problem. But even if we get the whole shipment on one delivery, we will be able to handle warehousing the whole order. I have a plan."

I gave him a big smile. "Tim, there is nothing better than a man with a plan!"

"I like that, Bob. I think that I am going to use that in the future, is that okay with you?"

"Sure, it is yours to use, buddy! I am very pleased you have thought this all out."

"Bob, I love my job. Craig is my cousin, he gave me the job, and I appreciated it. Nevertheless, I do not like the things that he does around here, so I stay away from him as much as I can. I want to work here for a long time. I love my job!"

Tim had indeed made it abundantly clear that he loved his job! "Okay, please send me an email about everything we discussed today so I can help you accomplish each strategy."

"Will do, Bob, and thank you for your time!"

"Tim, I should be the one thanking you. This was a great meeting!"

* * *

At 10:55, I grabbed a notebook and went to the conference room for my meeting with Trish. At 11:15, Trish walked into the room and sat down. She was only fifteen minutes late, which surprised me. I estimated that she would show up for the meeting at least twenty to thirty minutes late. I knew how busy her schedule was doing virtually nothing for this company.

She said, "Bob, what do you want to talk about with me?"

"Well, Trish, you were at the meeting Monday morning when I asked everyone to develop a list of issues to discuss what changes we need to make to the company to become profitable again. Did you take the time to create a list?"

"Bob, I don't need a list. I only have one suggestion."

"What is that? What's your suggestion?"

"My suggestion is to get rid of you and make Craig the president of the company again. I don't get it. He owns the company," she said petulantly.

I did not let her attitude get to me. "Thank you for the suggestion, Trish. It is appreciated," I said kindly.

"Bob, are we done for now?" she said as she got ready to stand up.

"Yes, unless you have something more constructive to say," I said directly.

"Don't I have a right to speak my mind?" she asked, gunning for a fight.

"Yes, Trish, of course, you do. I have not stopped you from saying anything, have I?"

"Bob, I think you have a bad attitude."

I just sat there and looked at her without saying another word. After about fifteen seconds of silence, which seemed like fifteen minutes, she got up from her chair and left the conference room. I was glad that transaction was over. I knew from everything that I had heard about Trish that I needed to avoid her like the plague. She was trouble, and trouble was not what I need now.

> From the first time that I met Trish, I knew that she was going to be trouble because she had a chip on her shoulder about me. She wanted to start a fight with me so she had a reason possibly cause legal action against me. I learned a long time ago before meeting Trish, nothing good comes out of an argument with an employee, especially one like Trish.

Since my meeting with Trish had lasted only five minutes, I had some free time. I went back to my office, sat down at my desk, and called a good friend of mine, Charlie.

Charlie was the manager of a loss prevention and security department for a large manufacturer in the area. He had recently retired and started a security consulting firm to provide advice to companies like ABC Computer Distributors. I had a feeling I needed to have a security system installed in the warehouse quickly, so computers did not start disappearing with Nancy's possible big order coming in soon. I called Charlie and asked him to inspect our office and warehouse. I wanted him to recommend what we needed to protect this company's assets.

"I'm free tomorrow late afternoon," Charlie told me. "When would you like to meet? However, Bob, before you answer, I must warn you, my consulting services are going to be *very* expensive. It is going to cost you the price of a big steak and a glass or two of red wine."

"I can handle that," I responded.

We agreed that Charlie would come over and walk the building late in the afternoon on Wednesday. "We can do our security work and then go to dinner after," he suggested. "I am not going to eat all day tomorrow so that I can order the biggest steak on the menu!"

I laughed, but I knew that he was serious. "It will be my pleasure to buy you the biggest steak on the menu tomorrow night and get caught up. It has been a long time."

After finishing my call with Charlie, I developed the management meeting agenda and then walked around the office to give each member of the management team a copy (see page 357).

(see page 357)

*　*　*

I arrived at Duffy's Sports Pub at 11:45 a.m. to meet Chris at noon. He was already sitting at a table in the corner with a cup of coffee in front of him. I walked over to the table. He stood up, and we shook hands. The coffee cup was half empty, so I figured Chris must have been there for a while. He was wearing blue jeans and a golf shirt.

"Chris, is this how you usually dress for work?" I asked as I slid into my seat.

"No, Bob, I took the day off. My wife and I had a long conversation about your job offer, and we talked until about two a.m. I forgot to set my alarm, and we both woke up at nine this morning. I called the office to tell them I was taking a personal day."

"So, Chris, was your wife in favor of your coming to work for me to turn this company around?" I asked hopefully.

"She was! She took the positive point of view. She said that it was time for me to take on some risk with an opportunity that has a big reward. She also said that my talents and leadership skills would help me to excel and grow to into a 'C' level position."

"It is awesome that you have a wife who will support you with your career challenges and trusts your skills." I knew how that felt because my wife was the same way.

"She does not like the owner of my company and thinks that it is an excellent time to make a move if you and I can come to terms."

"Well, Chris, I have not yet met your wife, but I like her already!"

"She is an exceptional lady. I respect her. She has always supported me during our whole married life. She is also smart, funny, sexy, beautiful, and a great mother."

I could tell that Chris loved and respected his wife. "You are a lucky man, and I am very happy for you. You know what they say, 'Happy wife, happy life!' So, are you interested in the service manager position?"

Chris stated again that he did not want to work for Craig because of his abysmal reputation. I assured Chris that I was now the president and CEO and the owner has no daily decision-making responsibility for the firm. Chris and I talked for two hours about the company. He wanted to know more about what I had planned for the long-term future of the organization. I told Chris that I had a 3:00 p.m. meeting scheduled with Darren, the controller. I suggested that Chris follow me back to the office so we could continue talking until that 3:00 p.m. meeting.

Chris said, "My time is yours. I have the whole day off."

We arrived back at the office at 2:30, and I walked Chris to the conference room. I asked him if he would like another cup of coffee.

He said, "If I have one more cup, I will float away!"

"Okay, please sit here a minute. I am going to ask our HR

manager, Donna, to come to the conference room to meet you for a few moments. While you are here, I want you to fill out an employment application and a release to do a background check."

He looked surprised about the background check, so I explained, "Doing background checks on all employees is a firm rule of mine at any company where I am responsible for hiring management and staff. Am I going to find problems when we do a background check on you?"

> Never, never, never make exceptions for something like a background check or drug test for a friend. First, it could put you at risk with a discrimination law suit with other new hires or employees. Also, I neglected to do a background check with a business associate that I was doing a large business deal with and it turned out that the gentleman was a convicted felon for SEC fraud. Unfortunately, the client found out about the SEC problem before I did and it cost me over a half a million dollars in consulting fees. Never make exceptions with the types of hiring practices, it will cost you every time.

"No, Bob! Of course not."

"Well then, you have nothing to worry about, right?"

"I know, it just shocked me a little. I did not expect it since we are friends."

I did not make an exception, of course. I went to find Donna and she was in her office. I asked her to take an employment application and a release to do a background check to Chris in the conference room. I also asked her to stay with him to answer any questions until he completed the documents.

"Okay, no problem!" she agreed. Then a look of confusion crossed her features. "Bob, may I ask, who is Chris?"

I smiled. "Chris is going to be the new service department manager for this company as soon as possible. Do we have a relationship with a clinic in the area that does drug testing?"

"We do not right now, but I will check into it," she said.

"Okay, please check right now so we can send Chris there immediately after he leaves here to get a drug test." I had no doubt Chris would pass such a test, but it was still mandatory.

"Okay, I will handle it. I hope Chris does not bite me when I tell him to report to a clinic to get a drug test."

"He is a big guy! I bet that his bite hurts, so be careful!" I laughed and then said more seriously, "Chris is a big teddy bear. You are going to love working with him! He is the best!"

After Chris completed the HR documents, I went back to the conference room to talk more about the details of his coming to work for me. We discussed his salary, bonus, and employee benefits, including reimbursement for technical training classes. When we finished our meeting, we shook hands, and Chris said that would get back to me once he discussed the situation with his wife. He also added that he was sure that she was going to agree with the move.

After Chris left, I asked Donna to do Chris's background check immediately. I told her that if Chris's discussions went well with his wife and there were no problems with the background check and drug test, I wanted to be in the position to offer him the job. She told me she would get it done for me immediately.

I looked at my watch; it was two minutes to 3:00. I had a meeting scheduled with Darren at 3:00, so I had to hustle to get there on time. I grabbed a notebook from my office and immediately went to the conference room. I got there at 2:59 p.m., in time for our one-on-one meeting. I hate being late for anything.

Sure enough, Darren was sitting at the conference room table with a stack of binders and a tablet in front of him, ready to take notes. I had such a good feeling about Darren; this manager had great potential. I was shocked that a quality person like Darren would work for a business owner like Craig with Craig's poor reputation. I sat down at the table and told Darren that this was his meeting. He handed me a sheet of paper with a long list of bullet points.

Darren first wanted to download some bothersome issues concerning Craig. "Bob, I have never liked how Craig acts around several of the women on the sales team. I have submitted my written resignation several times, and Craig talked me into staying with a little 'stay' bonus and a promise that he would change his ways around the women." Darren wanted me to know about the written resignations because he did not want me to get the wrong impression if I heard rumors. Darren continued, "I respect the women in this company, and when Craig treats the female employees like hookers, it bothers me."

I assured Darren that I was dealing with the "Craig problem" and would have it resolved soon.

Darren also told me that Craig had filed "fraudulent" expense reports to be reimbursed by the company. Craig had been stealing money from the company for at least a year and a half. With a look of distaste, Darren said, "Craig has charged lots of his personal expenses to the business." Darren thought that Craig believed no one could save the business from going under, so he had been stealing as much as he could because the money was coming from the bank's loan balance and not his equity in the company.

This information about Craig did not surprise me at all. "Darren, please develop a schedule of the expense reports that you know are non-business–related reimbursed expenses. We will deduct the total of any personal expenses that the company reimbursed him for from his next paycheck. However, I must warn you to get the schedule done soon because Craig is not going to be around very long."

Sounding pleased, Darren asked, "Bob, are we talking months, weeks, or days before you get him out of here?"

"I think it is more like minutes, hours, or days, but no longer than a week," I told him.

"Okay, it will be a top priority on my list to get it done quickly." Darren opened his notebook and wrote down a reminder to recap Craig's expense reports.

"Does the company have any corporate credit cards?" I asked next.

"Yes, Bob, there are corporate American Express cards."

"Who all has a card?"

"Craig and Trish are the only ones in the company who have the AMEX cards."

"Are there personal charges on the company's card statements?"

"Are you kidding? Craig uses that card for everything, including his vacations and gifts for his children."

"Okay, then, please schedule those personal items also and add it to the expense report list. By the way, the same will be true for Craig's best buddy, Trish."

Darren impressed upon me that he cared about ABC Computer Distributors and did not like to see the owner stealing from the company. He felt that if the company did file for bankruptcy protection, it would reflect very poorly on him since he was the corporate controller.

I understood how he felt and assured him of that. Now I needed to get those cards back. "Please collect the cards and cancel them with American Express. You can tell Craig and Trish that we only pay business expenses that they have in the future from an approved expense report. Once I have approved the expenses, we reimburse the employees for all business-related expense reports within seven days. If Craig or Trish hassle you at all about this issue, tell them to see me."

Darren nodded and then introduced the next item on his bulleted list: the current month's income statement and balance sheet. Darren handed me both statements. I glanced at the income statement for November, which showed the company had lost $104,000 for the month and almost $1.15 million year-to-date. (See the financial statements on pages 358 and 359.)

"Bob, as I told you Monday, we do not have an operating budget for this company. However, yesterday, Patrick and I developed several worksheets in Excel to facilitate the creation of this company's first operating budget with support schedules for revenue. There will be one for the sales of hardware and software and a second for service, the cost of goods, payroll broken down by department, and all the operating expenses. I also developed a spread schedule for the balance sheet accounts."

No company should ever be in business without a well thought out operating budget. A budget can best be defined as the company's plan on how the business is going to be managed during the next year. A good budget forces the management team to think through the following year on how they are going to manage the business for the next 12 months. Many well-managed businesses also develop a long-term budget for 3 to 5 years in the future.

A good budget should include a balance sheet, income statement (month by month for at least one year), a bullet point list of assumptions used to create the plan. The budget should also include a cash flow forecast for the same period.

If your business does not have an operating budget, it is like trying to steer a boat in a wind storm without a rudder. Without a plan, you can never know where you are going.

"Great, Darren, good job! Please make sure that you break down the cost of goods sold for hardware and software combined, then a separate schedule for service. Also, please create a spreadsheet of all monthly expenses for the past twelve months, sorted by the largest expense category to the smallest. This type of schedule helps me to review the new budget totals compared to the prior year. If you would send those schedules to me, I will review them, give you my comments, and then forward them back to you immediately."

Darren wrote another note on his tablet to remind him to send the budget schedules to me.

"Let's schedule a budget meeting for early next week," I suggested. "Are you available next Monday morning at nine a.m.? I want to start working on the budgets as soon as I make some decisions about the changes I am anticipating. It is important to me to determine the breakeven point for the company."

"Okay, Bob. If I am not available, I will cancel whatever I have scheduled to make sure that I will be at the meeting. Do you mind if I bring Patrick to that meeting? Patrick is going to be my budget expert for this company."

> For any company that I have worked with to improve the financial results of the business, one of the first things that I always do is create a breakeven analysis.
>
> The benefits of the analysis are: it reveals the amount of sales and gross profit the business needs monthly to cover the fixed and variable expenses. It also shows the amount of cash required to be on hand to operate the business. There are many more benefits, but these two listed are some of the most important outcomes.

I told him to feel free to bring Patrick to any meeting, and then he continued down his list. "Bank account reconciliations. Here are the reconciliations of the two accounts for your review. Behind the reconciliations are new signature cards for each account. If you sign them right now, I can have them delivered to the bank this afternoon to make the changes to the accounts."

I signed both cards and handed them back to Darren, and Darren called Patrick to come pick up the cards and take them to the bank immediately. While we waited, I scanned the bank accounts, and there were weeks that the bank balance was hundreds of thousands of dollars, sometimes as much as $1.2 million sitting idle in the bank. I asked, "How often do you pay down the loan balance with available funds from the checking account?"

"When we see that there are available funds in the checking account, Patrick calls the bank on Friday afternoons and has our bank wire the available balance to Kevin's bank to pay down the loan balance."

Less than a minute after Darren's call to him, Patrick entered the room, holding his car keys in his hand. I stood up, shook his hand, and introduced myself.

Patrick said, "Mr. Curry, I am thrilled you joined the organization. I look forward to working with you, sir."

"Patrick, it is a pleasure to meet you, too. And thank you for helping with these signature cards."

"No problem, sir," Patrick said, then quickly left for the bank.

I had a good feeling about Patrick and asked Darren to tell me what kind of employee he was. I was pleased to hear Darren describe him as "the best." He told me that Patrick works hard, churns out the work, is always accurate and gets along with everyone.

"I would like to place an order for ten more just like Patrick, if that is okay with you," I joked.

Darren laughed, and we continued discussing all the items on his list. "Here is a copy of the aged accounts receivables and accounts payable."

"Darren, are there any problems with customer receivables?" I looked at the report, and it was not bad—not as bad as I expected. There were some very old uncollectable receivables in the report. I told Darren that I wanted to see the paperwork for every one of the delinquent receivables within the next few days. I asked him to print a detailed AR schedule for each company with a copy of the paperwork attached so I could visit the company and hand deliver the invoices to the client. "Please make sure that all the invoices on the schedule are valid receivables with backup documentation, so I do not get embarrassed when I visit the client. Starting next week, I would like to meet weekly to review the receivables and talk about any problem accounts. And, Darren, I plan to schedule customer visits with current problem accounts to introduce myself and ask them to stay current with paying our invoices for our company."

"Yes, sir. When would you like to have the AR meetings?"

"When do you get the daily mail and have the checks posted on the customer's accounts?"

"The checks are posted by no later than one o'clock p.m. daily."

"Okay, then let's schedule a meeting every week on Wednesday at two o'clock p.m., immediately after the management meetings."

"Okay, that sounds good to me, Bob." Darren handed me a sheet of paper. "Here is the copy of last year's physical inventory reconciliation. As you can see, we had a substantial inventory write-off—a hundred and fifty-five thousand dollars."

"I heard that the old service manager here was stealing laptops from the warehouse and selling them for cash to his friends. Is there any truth to that rumor?"

> It is important for the controller and the sales manager to review the status of the delinquent accounts receivable (AR) weekly. Both managers should be accountable for the current condition of this asset. If accounting does not manage the AR, it can become out of control very quickly and turn the asset into an expense.

"Not that I am aware of, Bob. I knew that he got fired, but I am pretty sure that it was not for stealing computers."

"I had a meeting with Tim, the warehouse manager, and he had some great ideas about inventory control in the future. Please meet with him so the two of you can talk about controls and paperwork procedures."

"Okay, Bob will do." Darren wrote down another note in his notebook as a reminder to meet with Tim. "Here is the copy of the company's most recent borrowing base calculation. You will note, Bob, that currently, the company's loan balance is larger than the borrowing base calculation by two hundred thousand dollars."

My eyes widened. "How did that happen? I have never seen a bank advance funds to a company for more than their collateral in my career."

Darren explained, "The last borrowing base report was calculated and given to Craig. He asked me to change the numbers when the company was at its borrowing limit. When he told me to change some of the figures, I refused. Craig took the report from me, redid the numbers himself, and sent it directly to the bank."

"Who signed the revised report?" I asked.

"Craig did, but I refused to add my signature to the report. I am not interested in going to jail for fraud for anyone, especially Craig."

Craig almost put Darren in a terrible position by filing a fraudulent collateral report with the bank.

"Darren, the guys from the bank said that Craig fraudulently filed a collateral report. How did they know? Did they do an audit?"

"Yes, there were two reasons they knew about the false report. First, the bank noticed that Craig had signed the report, which was the first time they had seen his signature on the report. I had signed all the rest of the reports. The second reason was that they asked me why I did not sign it. I told them I didn't sign it because it was wrong. Then they did an audit of the records. The bank guys were grumpy at Craig after the audit."

"I know those guys get a little perturbed about fraud," I said dryly.

"They were angry, and then suddenly in a few days, Bob Curry shows up, with the bank officers announcing that you are the new president and CEO. Seeing you did not surprise me even a little bit."

"Well, Darren, I am glad to be here. I have never done a turnaround before, but I think that I am going to enjoy this one."

"So am I! I am excited about the changes you are going to implement," he said, and I thanked him. He handed me a few printouts. "Here is a copy of the last three loan statements that you requested. As you can see, the loan balance is averaging approximately six million three hundred thousand dollars for the last three months. The interest rate on the loan balance is four and a half percent, and the monthly interest expense was twenty-three thousand." He handed me a binder. "As you requested, this binder contains the most recent payroll reports. We have two more payrolls before the end of the year."

"I am going to review this report and give it back to you as soon as possible," I told him. "I need to check the year-to-date payroll costs for a couple of individuals who are not going to be on the payroll after this week."

"This is the copy of the Mercedes car lease that the company is currently paying."

"Please review the contract for the Mercedes and determine if

there are any penalties for returning the car to the dealer and terminating the lease."

"I did that already after you gave me Craig's car keys at the
meeting Monday. We can return the car without penalty. My brother-
in-law works in the leasing department at the dealership. It is always
nice to know people in the right places!"

I agreed with a nod. "Let's get that car back to the dealership as
soon as possible."

"Yes, sir. Patrick and I will make that happen."

I told Darren that if he needed to hire a temporary accountant to
get all this work done in a week, he had my permission. Darren said,
"Bob, my wife is out of town for a week visiting her mother, so I am
happy to stay late each evening to get these schedules completed."

Darren was saying and doing all the right things to become a long-
term, valued member of the management team for this turnaround.

"Bob, I have a list of several other issues that I would like to talk
to you about, things like the year-end audit, the property and causality insurance, health insurance, and taxes. I would like to schedule
a meeting with you later this week. I have some preparation to do
before I will be ready to talk to you about these other issues."

"I am available to you anytime, twenty-four hours a day," I told
him.

"Thank you, Bob. How about we meet Thursday morning early?"

"Thursday morning is fine with me."

"I am an early riser; I could be here at seven a.m. The place will
be empty and quiet. Are you good to meet that early?"

I told Darren that the early morning hour worked for me too.
Then I had a thought: "Darren, please call Patrick and see if he is
still at the bank. If so, please ask him to ask the bank officer when
he would be available to come here to meet as soon as possible. I
want to meet him and explain my role here. And I think rather than
add my name to the account; I want to close the old accounts and
transfer the balances into new accounts. I want the old accounts
frozen and no new checks written on the existing accounts right now
until completing this transaction."

Darren called Patrick, who was, indeed, still at the bank. Patrick was able to schedule the bank officer to visit the company Thursday morning at 9:00 a.m. Darren asked Patrick to tell the bank people that the company was going to open two new bank accounts and to freeze all activity in the old accounts.

"Darren, do we need to order checks immediately for the payroll account?"

"Bob, all the employees' payroll checks are paid via direct deposit, so we do not hand out any paychecks. We only need to tell the payroll processing company about the new bank account."

"Can you take care of that, please?" I requested.

"Sure, Bob, no problem." Darren wrote down another note, so he did not forget to follow-up on the issue.

I finished the meeting with Darren and carried all the reports and information back to my office. I set it down on my desk and started to organize everything when Kevin and Rick appeared at my door. I stopped what I was doing, stood up, and shook their hands.

Kevin said, "We were driving past the building, coming back from a visit of another one of our customers, and decided to stop in to see how you are doing. I am sorry that we showed up unannounced. You have not changed your mind, have you?"

"No, but let's go talk in the conference room. People here have mentioned that the walls in these offices are paper thin. Everyone has told me that conversations can be heard in the rooms next to us like there are no walls at all."

Once we were in the conference room, I shut the door and sat down at the table opposite to Kevin and Rick.

Rick said, "Bob, I am happy that we hired you, and we trust you to recover our investment here. Whatever your concern is today, we will support you."

"Gentlemen, thank you for your comments. I appreciate your support. I have a fiduciary responsibility to this company and your bank. I want to let you know that I am terminating Craig and Trish. Craig has had several sexual harassment complaints against him recently. Trish has not sold a training program in the past six months, nor has she taught one training class. She has a terrible relationship with all the sales staff, so they will not promote or sell the company's training classes. I plan to make this Friday their last day at work. There are other problems with Craig and Trish, but those issues are not as important since I have made my decision already. I thought that you should be aware of this."

Rick said, "Bob, this is now Kevin's account. You do not need me to participate in the management of this account any further. I put this company into your and Kevin's control."

"Good, Rick, I will not let you down!"

Kevin said, "Bob, call me anytime you want to chat about anything. I appreciate your updates, but they are not necessary. ABC Computer Distributors is now your company to fix. You are qualified, and I am not going to get in your way. If you need me, I will be here for you."

"Great, gentlemen! Thank you for coming in and have a great evening."

Rick said, "Same to you, Bob, and please get rid of Craig before I lose my temper on that guy."

I saw the look on Rick's face and quickly said, "Yes, sir!"

* * *

Tuesday evening, I received a phone call from Chris. He wanted to know whether I would consider hiring some of his service techs, should they be interested in coming with him to ABC Computer Distributors. I told him that I was open to the idea, but probably not all on the same day that he was going to start. I also told Chris to tell his technicians that maybe after the first of the year would probably be the best timing.

"But, Bob," Chris explained, "you need to understand something about these technicians. They are all stationed full time at clients' locations. The cool thing is that you never see them. All you do is write them paychecks every two weeks and invoice the client monthly for two and a half to three times the amount of the technicians' salaries. These guys are money-making machines!"

"Chris, that is a different story. How many guys want to join you here?"

"Bob, pretty much every one of them, but I would only ask maybe five at a time. So, maybe three groups of five technicians."

"Chris, I don't think that we should ask any of your old techs to join our company. We need to place an advertisement in the Philadelphia Inquirer stating that ABC Computer Distributors is looking to recruit and hire more computer technicians. If we don't handle it this way, your old owner is going to sue us for raiding his organization and his customers. I do not want to start having to spend company funds for legal fees so, here is the plan. Tomorrow, we will have Donna place an advertisement in the Inquirer. Any of your technicians who are interested in a job with our organization will have to send us a letter and resume as per the advertisement. We will then have documentation that any technicians that we hire in the future all responded to the ad rather than us raiding his company. In order to protect our ABC Computer Distributors from a big messy lawsuit, we need to be very professional and go through this hiring process in a 'business-like' manner. So, you can tell your people that they should watch for our advertisement in the Philadelphia Inquirer and respond to it immediately. I will speak to Donna to place the ad tomorrow when I get to the office. By doing the recruiting and hiring process this way, we also may find some other qualified technicians in addition to your group."

Chris stated enthusiastically, "Bob, I like your idea and agree that is the right way to handle this. Now I understand why you are the president of the company."

"Thanks, Chris."

"But, Chris, I must warn you—and them—they are all going to have to pass a background check and a drug test before they go on our payroll."

"Bob, is there any way that we could waive all that stuff?"

"No, Chris. Everyone gets treated the same in the organization that I am managing. I had to take a pre-hiring drug test and background check, just like the one you took."

"I will make some phone calls this evening, but, yes, that will probably work fine for these guys."

"So, Chris, do you and I have a deal? And when is your start date?"

Chris said he was going to sleep on everything tonight and call me by noon tomorrow. I hung up the phone and got my notebook out of my briefcase to make some notes about this call with Chris:

- It appears that the deal with Chris will be finalized tomorrow by lunchtime, which is a significant accomplishment in the first week of this turnaround. He would not have called me about bringing his techs with him if he was undecided about accepting the position.

> Background, credit, and drug tests should always be required when hiring a management position or an employee whose job includes visiting clients. It would be a very bad situation if you unknowingly hired a convicted felon or someone with a drug problem to manage one of the departments in the company.

- Hiring technicians from Chris's company is going to be a positive cash flow transaction for our business. These future additions to our service department show how important relationships are in business. If these technicians come to work for our company, it could mean a $1 million annual profit to our organization (and the loss of the same amount by one of our competitors).

- Talk to Donna in the morning about placing an ad in the Philadelphia Inquirer to recruit and hire highly qualified computer technicians.

Chapter 6

YOU FIX IT, OR I AM OUT OF HERE!

"Your past does not equal your future."

—TONY ROBBINS, AMERICAN AUTHOR, ENTREPRENEUR,
PHILANTHROPIST, AND LIFE COACH

WEDNESDAY, DECEMBER 6—DAY 3 OF WEEK 1

ON MY THIRD DAY AS PRESIDENT AND CEO OF ABC COMPUTER Distributors, I started work very early. I arrived at the office at 7:00 a.m. I planned to prepare the agenda for the sales and service department meetings scheduled for Friday afternoon. I had been thinking about different ways to motivate the technicians to improve the quality of their service calls and reward them for positive results. I opened my laptop and saw that Darren had sent me all the budget schedules that he had promised to email me at our one-on-one meeting the previous day. I opened each file, reviewed each report, and emailed the reports back to Darren. I did not have a comment on any of the schedules other than, "Good job, Darren!" Next, I started writing down my ideas for the sales and service department meetings, and my cell phone rang. I saw that it was Chris on my caller ID. "Good morning, Chris, what's up?"

"Bob, I'll accept your offer, but I want the salary to be five thousand dollars more than you offered."

"I will give you a twenty-five hundred dollar signing bonus, but the salary stays the same if you start in two weeks," I told him. "I will send you an offer letter documenting everything that we agreed upon in regard your employment (see page 360). If you agree to the terms and conditions as noted in the offer letter, I want you to sign and date it, scan it, and email the offer back to me."

Chris said, "Wait, you agreed to the signing bonus too easy! How about increasing the signing bonus to five thousand? And, Bob, by the way, I went and took your stupid drug test yesterday afternoon."

"Well, did you pass, Chris?"

"Yes, of course, I passed it. I don't put any of that crap in my body. And, besides, if I did, my wife would kick my butt out of the house, and I would not be able to be there to be a good father as my kids grow up."

I laughed and said, "Welcome aboard! See you in two weeks."

At 7:30 a.m., Tom walked into my office. I was surprised; Tom did not seem like an early morning type of person. Tom told me that Nancy wanted to meet with me that day at 1:00 p.m. "She has a sales call this morning and will return to the office after lunch."

"Thank you, Tom. I will add the meeting to my calendar."

"Bob, can I help you with anything else?"

"Yes, my friend! Please start attending sales calls with each salesperson."

"I have already started. I have my first sales call this afternoon with Olivia, and two tomorrow with Patty and Rachel. Friday morning at eight thirty, I am going out with Jenna to meet a new customer, and Barbara was trying to get an appointment on Friday at eleven thirty. I should hear back from Barbara later today if she was able to book the appointment with the customer."

"Wow, Tom! Super! That is great! Please make sure that the two of you are back here by two o'clock on Friday for the sales meeting."

"I will!" he assured me. "I know how important the first sales meeting is going to be with these people, so I will not be late."

I shook Tom's hand and thanked him. I believed that Tom's riding with the salespeople and evaluating their skills would also motivate them to get into the field and close more deals.

No sooner had Tom walked out of my office, then Frank, one of the sales staff, arrived. He knocked on my office door asked me if I had some time to talk. I introduced myself to him and asked, "What can I do for you, Frank?"

Frank was short, probably five-foot-three. He was approximately thirty years old and dressed as if he were a model for *GQ Magazine*. His hair was blond and curly as if he had it dyed and permed once a month. Personally, I thought his hairstyle looked silly, but that wasn't how I would be evaluating his abilities.

He had come to meet me because he wanted me to know that Craig had hired him to sell service. He said he was the "service sales expert" for the company. He told me that he attended sales calls with all the other salespeople except for Nancy to help them sell service contracts.

"Why doesn't Nancy invite you to join her on her sales calls? She sells more service than anyone in the company!" I asked, my curiosity piqued.

"Because we were on a sales call together about a year ago, and I dozed off a little during the meeting. Nancy never asked me to go on another sales call."

"Can you blame her? I am sure that you embarrassed her in front of her customer."

"I make one mistake, so she never invites me to another sales call? Do you agree with that, Bob?" he asked, and I was surprised that he had even admitted falling asleep on a sales call.

"Frank, you didn't make a mistake. You were sleeping! You can't make a mistake while you are sleeping, can you?"

Frank just shrugged. "Well, anyhow, Craig did not have confidence that all these women in the sales department could sell service contracts, so he hired me to be the expert. All the salespeople schedule an appointment with their customer, and I tag along on the sales call. The salesperson would sell computer hardware and software. Then she would introduce me as the service expert, and I would attempt to sell a service contract."

"Frank, what did you do before you joined ABC Computer Distributors?"

"I sold cellphones at Best Buy."

"Frank, how many service contracts have you sold, year-to-date, this year?"

"I have no idea," he admitted. "Do you expect me to remember every sale for eleven months?"

"No, Frank, of course, I don't." I picked up my phone and called Darren.

Darren answered, "Yes, Bob, can I help you?"

"Yes, Darren, how long would it take you to tell me what Frank's year-to-date sales are, through today?

"Bob, hold on, I have the sales report right here. Frank has sold fifty-five thousand dollars in service contracts for the year through the end of November. Do you want me to check if he has sold any contracts in December?"

"No, Darren, that will not be necessary, but thank you!" I hung up the phone and turned to Frank. "I am wondering how you pay your bills."

"Why would you ask me that?"

"Well, Frank, Darren just told me that you have only sold fifty-five thousand year-to-date of service contracts. The commission on fifty-five thousand is eight thousand two hundred dollars. I believe that your living costs, based on how you dress, are more than eight thousand two hundred dollars for the year."

"You are confused. I am salaried. I don't get paid any commissions for sales."

"Frank, you are telling me that you are a salesman for this company, paid a salary, and your annual sales are fifty-five thousand? What is your salary?"

"My salary is seventy-five thousand."

"It is hard for this company to be profitable when you have only sold thirty thousand dollars less than the total cost of your salary and benefits."

"Bob, you do not understand."

"What don't I understand?"

"I don't know if you are aware, but Craig is my cousin," he said as if that explained everything.

"Yes, I believe I have heard that before, but what does that have to do with anything? Frank, you are working for a company that is losing money every day. You would be sadly mistaken if you believe that a family relationship would waive your responsibility to work hard to be a positive impact toward profitability for this organization. Frank, could you please share with me why you came to talk to me this morning?"

"We had not met each other yet since you joined the company, and I just wanted you to know that I was the only service salesman in the company."

"How come you have not been selling service contacts?"

"Because our service department sucks."

"Okay, Frank, you have helped me out today. I would like to thank you for your time and for sharing everything with me. I am now full of information to start this turnaround. Have a great day, and please go sell some service today."

"Okay, Bob, I will do that."

> My father once told me a long time ago, "Every time you use your emotions in a business situation you lose, and every time you use your intelligence, you win." Whenever I feel myself getting emotional or angry in a business transaction or any situation, I immediately recall what my father told me, and I start using my brains and put my feelings aside.

I stood up to shake his hand to get him out of my office as quickly as possible. I wanted to fire him in the next five seconds, but I restrained my emotions.

I translated what Frank had come to say to me. He was Craig's cousin. Therefore, he was not required to work hard or do his job, which was to sell service contracts. I have no time for people like Frank. I was trying to turn this company around *because* of people like Frank. As Frank walked out of my office, I felt good about myself for using my father's advice again. I opened the notebook that was on the corner of my desk and wrote myself a note to deal with Frank soon. He was now on my list with Craig and Trish. Dealing with those three would get this company a little closer to cash flow breakeven.

I could now finally start preparing for Friday's sales and service department meetings. I knew that I had considerable work to accomplish, so my goal was to begin immediately so if something interrupted me—like Chris, Tom, or Frank this morning—I would still have plenty of time to be ready for both meetings. I started listing the bullet points that I wanted to talk about at the sales meeting (see page 361).

My cell phone rang again, and I saw that it was Chris. "Chris, buddy, what's up, my friend?"

"I went to work this morning and handed my letter of resignation to the owner of the company. The letter stated that I was giving a two-week notice. He read the letter and immediately got very mad at me. He asked me who hired me. I told him that I was not going to talk about that right now. Then he got madder. He said that if that was how it was going to be, I should pack up my stuff and leave immediately. Bob, I could not believe how bad he treated me after working for him for over nine years. He was extremely rude. He had one of the technicians follow me to my office to pack up my stuff, so I did not steal anything from the company. I could not believe it. I made that guy all kinds of money, and he treats me like dirt. I am mad and hurt."

"Chris, where are you?"

"I am at home. Bob, you are the first person that I called, other than my wife."

"Okay, Chris, you have a couple of different options, all of which are good by me. First, you can come to work immediately. That way you can get started with your new position right away. That will distract you from getting any angrier than you already are, and you can do something constructive with your time. On the other hand, you can start on Friday. Friday afternoon, I am having two meetings, one with the sales department at two p.m. and one with all service department employees at three p.m. I can introduce you then to both the sales and service teams. The third option would be for you to start your new job on Monday. Which do you prefer?"

"How about I come in for only the two meetings on Friday afternoon?"

"That would be good, too, Chris."

"That way, I can relax, settle down, and enjoy some quality time with my wife. I can also get stuff done around the house that I have been ignoring too long."

I suggested that Chris be at the office at 1:00 p.m. on Friday. First, we would talk, and then he would meet with Donna to complete all the rest of the new hire paperwork. At 2:00, I would introduce him to all the salespeople at the meeting. Then after the sales meeting, at 3:00, he and I would meet with all the service people for the first time. This plan sounded good to Chris. Does that work for you, Chris?"

"Bob, I will see you Friday at one o'clock."

"Good, I will send Donna an email to make her aware that you are going to be here on Friday at one o'clock. She will have the hiring and benefits paperwork all ready for you to sign."

Always document the hiring terms and conditions in a well-written job offer letter to a candidate, so the business relationship does not begin with any confusion between the two parties. The job offer letter should include at least the following information: the start date, the starting salary, any signing bonus, any sales commission plan, any management bonus plan, employee benefits, any relocation cost reimbursement, and the name of the candidate's supervisor.

"Sounds good. I feel better already, Bob!"

"Good, spend some quality time with your beautiful wife and give her my best!"

"Thanks, I will! See you Friday."

"Chris, did you receive and sign the offer letter?"

"Yes, Bob, I did. How about I bring the letter with me on Friday?"

"Okay, Chris, I will see you Friday afternoon."

I was thrilled to have heard from Chris because I was afraid he was going to get a counteroffer from his company to keep him from leaving. There was little or no chance that was going to happen now. That was the main reason why I'd offered Chris a signing bonus. It was an insurance policy so he would not accept a counteroffer from his boss to keep him from leaving the company. Finding and hiring an exceptionally talented service manager like Chris was a significant win for me. I had known Chris for several years, and I was very excited to have him as part of my turnaround management team. Life was good!

> Whenever hiring a new employee, you should always notify the employee in writing in the job offer letter that they are on a **ninety-day probationary period** with the company. The ninety days gives you and the company the opportunity to carefully evaluate the employee and determine if the individual is a good fit for the position. The probation period gives you the chance to terminate the employee with minimal exposure for a wrongful termination lawsuit initiated by the employee. This policy has two benefits: it helps the company get rid of a "bad hire" and you can do it with minimal risk of paying legal fees.

I had set the reminder alarm on Outlook to go off at 12:50 because I had a scheduled meeting with Nancy at 1:00. I picked up the notebook and pen off my desk to make notes and looked up; Nancy was standing there at the door to my office. I stood up, walked over, and shook her hand. I said, "Nancy, I am Bob Curry, and I am pleased to meet you."

She shook my hand and sat down in the chair. I closed my office door and sat down in the chair next to her.

Nancy was between thirty-seven and forty years old but looked younger. She had long, thick, curly jet-black hair that shined. She had on a dark navy suit and a white silk blouse and wore a multi-colored scarf around her neck that went perfectly with her outfit. It was easy to see that Nancy worked out in a gym on a regular basis. She was about five-foot-eight (six feet tall with heels) and walked with confidence. When she entered a room, people surely noticed.

"Nancy, it is very nice to meet you. I have heard nothing but wonderful things about you."

Nancy said, "Mr. Curry, I have a problem, and either you fix it, or we will never be able to get to know each other."

I understood that Nancy had quite a strong personality, but I did not expect to have that opening statement from her in the first minute that we met. "What is your problem and how can I help?"

"Mr. Curry, I have a purchase order in my hand for over seventeen million dollars for laptops and software from one of my largest customers. Large orders this size require special handling with purchasing for pricing and approved by our bank. There probably will be an issue with sourcing the product, but that is another story."

"Okay, I agree with that, so what is the problem?"

"Since you are brand new here, I took the order to Craig for help. I just came from his office, and he told me that there was no way that we could accept and process this purchase order because our line of credit with our bank is at its limit. Therefore, we could not finance the receivables and inventory for my customer's purchase order. I am going to tell you what I just told Craig. If this company cannot handle processing this order, I will be working with a new computer distributor within twenty-four hours. I am sure that if I walk into another computer distributor with this order in my back pocket, they will hire me within five seconds."

"Nancy, I am sure you are right. Please give me five minutes, because I need to make a phone call. I will promise you that this order will be approved by our bank before I hang up the phone."

"Mr. Curry, I will even give you eight hours if you can get this deal done for me."

"Please sit there while I make the call." I got up from my chair and went back around to the other side of my desk. I picked up my phone and called Kevin.

Kevin answered the call on the first ring. "Bob, what's up, buddy?"

"Kevin, I am going to put you on the speakerphone. Is that okay with you? I have Nancy with me here in my office."

"Sure, Bob." I pushed the speakerphone button, and Kevin and Nancy greeted each other.

I explained the reason for the call: "Nancy just brought a customer's purchase order to me for laptops and software from her big pharma customer. I need you to approve the order and finance the deal."

"Okay, who is the company, how big is the order, and who is the manufacturer of the laptops?"

Nancy handed me a copy of the customer's purchase order so that I could answer Kevin's questions. I told him the name of the client and that the laptops were ThinkPads.

"Bob, there is no problem with either that customer or the product, how much is the order?"

"The order is going to be approximately seventeen million dollars."

Kevin said, "What? How much did you say?"

Nancy spoke up and said, "Kevin, the customer is going to buy at least thirty-five hundred laptops, but the purchase order may go as high as four thousand. They also want to buy the newly released Microsoft operating system. The customer wants us to have the laptops shipped here, load the operating software onto the hard drive, and then download their company's proprietary software on each machine. After we are finished loading all the software, we are supposed to deliver the fully loaded computers to each of their six divisional locations. I do not have the second purchase order yet, but they also want to buy between twenty-five and thirty high-end servers. The total deal is going to be probably seventeen to eighteen-and-a-half million, with an estimated eleven or twelve percent gross profit. We are getting paid a hundred dollars per machine for loading the operating systems and their software. They also want to have laptops ordered for their European divisions. I charged them an extra hundred and fifty dollars per machine for the different power supplies for the European computers."

"When do they need all these laptops and servers?" Kevin asked.

"The customer would like the computers as soon as we can deliver them. Kevin, they have extra money in their capital budget that they have not spent yet, so they want to get the purchase order into this current year. If they don't spend their capital budget, the senior management reduces the budget for the following year. The purchasing manager does not want that to happen. Kevin, I have Alan, our purchasing manager, calling around to all the master distributors to see how much inventory each has of these ThinkPads in stock and when can they be shipped. I can get back to you probably within the hour with his findings. Kevin, the customer agreed to pay us a twenty-five percent deposit when their PO is signed, and another twenty-five percent when we have the product in our warehouse. The third installment of twenty-five percent is due when we deliver the laptops to the different divisions. The final payment for the balance is due within thirty days after delivery to their six divisional locations."

"Bob, we can set you up immediately with a temporary increase in your line of credit for ten million dollars for these orders," Kevin said. "With those payment terms, you will have over twelve million dollars in your checking account before the invoice is due to your suppliers. You probably will only need a seven- or eight-million-line increase, but we will make the temporary line of credit ten million to ensure that you have enough funds for the deal. We will segregate these purchase orders specifically for this temporary increase. Once you ship the orders, the customer pays their invoice in full, and you pay back the borrowed funds, the temporary line of credit will terminate. Bob, I will speak to Rick. He is in his office across the hall. After I talk to him, I will email you paperwork to sign and return."

Nancy's face lit up. She had walked into my office with a chip on her shoulder because she had just come from Craig's office, where she was told that we could not accept her customer's order. She met me for the first time, and I made her multimillion-dollar deal happen. These two customer orders were going to make Nancy's sales commission for this transaction approximately $400,000. I was equally as happy because the company was going to earn a net, after paying Nancy's commission, of $1.6 million gross profit on this transaction, less some expenses for staging and shipping the order. I looked at Nancy and said, "Nancy, for our first meeting, this turned out pretty good!"

She said, "Bob, I agree!"

"I am no longer Mr. Curry anymore?" I asked with a hint of a smile.

"Bob, not when you help me close my biggest deal ever. You are now, Bob, the 'Go-to Guy,' and Craig just became 'Craig Who?'"

"So, it is all about the money?"

"Yes, of course! What did you think?"

"Me, I thought . . . it is all about the money. Let's meet tomorrow morning with Alan to see how he did with sourcing the hardware and the logistics of this whole transaction. If they want these laptops loaded with software and shipped before year end, we are going to have to jump through some hoops to get this all done in time."

"Bob, they all don't have to be shipped before year end. I just said that to get Kevin cracking quickly with the order approval to provide us with the additional credit line and finish the appropriate paperwork."

Wow, I had just learned a lot about Nancy. She would say and do pretty much anything to take care of her customer and to increase her commission check. I just figured out how to turn around this business quickly: hire a couple more salespeople just like Nancy!

Later, I found out that the purchasing department had sourced 3,600 ThinkPad laptops nationwide from all our master distributors, and the customer had only wanted 3,500. There was a limited amount of inventory of these laptops because of the specifications of the machines needed by the client. These "souped-up" laptops were hard to find at times. I asked Nancy who her competition was for the purchase order. She said she did not know, but she was very close to the customer's purchasing manager, and she would give him a call. I asked her to find out from her contact at the company how many other distributors were bidding on the order. She called the customer and found out who was our competition. One other computer distributor was to receive the specifications for the purchase order in a meeting the day after next.

With our master distributor vendors, we could reserve inventory for seventy-two hours. At the end of the three days, we must have the product shipped, or terminate the reserve. I had the purchasing department commit to all 3,600 laptops so none of our competitors could source the hardware for this customer's PO. I called Nancy and told her that I could guarantee that she was going to get the order because we took the entire inventory of the product off the market. None of our competitors would be able to source and purchase the laptops. Nancy got all excited by the good news. It was quite apparent that she could feel her big commission check hitting her checking account soon.

I also told Nancy to talk to the customer and see if they wanted to increase the number of laptops because there were only a hundred remaining in the United States at the date of purchase. They probably could use additional machines for parts, loaners, and new hires. Nancy called the purchasing manager and told me that the customer wants the other hundred laptops. They would pay for the computers if we agreed to keep them in our warehouse and ship them when they needed them. That was not a problem with me, so I approved those terms for this deal. Nancy also found out on the call that they needed the product shipped by the first week in January.

According to Alan, each of the master distributors had a separate pricing department to call when the purchase was going to be more than $1 million. Alan and I called each master distributor and asked them to price all the fully loaded ThinkPads that they had in their inventory. Typically, they would reduce the total price by 5 percent if we purchased all the laptops they had in stock. They might even reduce the cost a little more since it was so close to year end. I told each of them that they needed to reduce the entire order by 7 to 8 percent, which included all the other server hardware and software on our customer's PO. I explained to each person that our customer had beat us up on price and we needed their help to make a little money on the deal.

The large order department managers who we spoke to could not approve the offer on the spot. Each said that they had to talk to their boss about the deal and get back to us. Each called us back in fifteen or twenty minutes. We learned that if we took their entire ThinkPad inventory, he would reduce the price by 7.5 percent off the whole purchase. The gross profit on Nancy's order had just increased by $1.36 million, and we had eliminated any other company from being able to buy the laptops to fulfill the purchase order.

We placed the purchase orders with all the vendors to buy 3,600 ThinkPad laptops, software, and thirty network servers. The total retail value increased to $18.2 million when we included the network servers. The gross profit on this deal would make our company profitable once the customer paid the invoices. I told Nancy and Alan that no one is to know about this transaction until the laptops showed up at the warehouse, so we could start staging them with the software. If for some unexplainable reason, this deal did not happen, the whole company would be in a state of depression. "Business as usual" until we start shipping the inventory. Even when we received the order in our warehouse, I wanted this transaction to remain confidential. Having that much product in our storage area was a security risk. We would have plenty of time to celebrate this order once we shipped all the computers to the customer and collected payment for the invoices.

We needed to contact our insurance agent to make sure that we had enough insurance coverage for the increase in our inventory while the laptops are in our warehouse. I went to see Darren to ask him how much property coverage we had for the stock in our building. He told me a total of $4 million. I told him to temporarily increase the coverage to $18 million in two weeks for one month.

Darren looked at me as if I was crazy. "Bob, you are not telling me something, huh?"

"Yes, Darren, I am not. I will talk to you later about the issue. Just please get the insurance coverage adjusted."

"Okay, but I do want to talk to you about our insurance agent."

"What's the problem?"

"Our insurance agent is Craig's cousin. Craig would not let me get other insurance agencies to quote on our policies to check his cousin's insurance premiums."

"Darren, when are the policies coming up for renewals?"

"Two and a half months from now."

"Okay, please have Patrick develop a spreadsheet of all our insurance policies, coverages, deductibles, and any critical endorsements. Let's get some agents in here to quote on the insurance coverages the week before Christmas. After Patrick finishes the schedules, we will give the insurance agents the information and let them go out to their markets and beat Craig's cousin's pricing."

"Bob, I have a feeling that we are getting screwed by that guy."

"Darren, I would not be surprised if you are right. Quoting the insurance policies with three new agencies will prove that either his pricing is at the market prices or that we are getting screwed by Craig's family again!"

I looked at my watch; I had ten minutes before my first management meeting, scheduled for 2:00 p.m. I rushed to my office and back to the conference room with plenty of time to spare—three minutes. I poured myself a cup of lousy coffee with a little cream and sat down at the table. My head was still spinning because I had just finished getting an $18.2 order approved, financed, and bought out in the last forty-five minutes. The gross profit on that order had taken the company from red to black and had kept Nancy secure in her job with this organization for a long time. Today was a fantastic day, and it was only 2:00 p.m. Now I had to bear down and focus on getting this management team fired up at the meeting.

I looked around the room, and the management team was all sitting at the table. Craig and Trish were not here for this first meeting. I was glad they did not show up. The less they mixed with this management team, the better. I asked Darren to close the door to the conference room so there would be no interruptions for the next hour.

I started the meeting by telling everyone about the rules of this and all future management meetings. My goal was to give everyone the rules, so they understood that management meetings were the most crucial hour of their workweek. These rules were:

- *There will be an agenda for the meeting distributed to everyone at least twenty-four hours in advance of the meeting. Whoever is chairing the meeting is responsible for creating the agenda. Everyone should be prepared to participate in all topics since each manager has one day to prepare for each issue discussed.*

- *Attendance for the complete management team is mandatory for all future meetings.*

- *Everyone attending should set their cellphones in silent mode to stop all phone interruptions. The management team may answer only emergency calls during the meeting.*

> I believe that it is critical for everyone in management to meet for at least one hour weekly to share information, so the company runs efficiently using an organized method of communication.

- *The meetings will be set for the same day and time each week, so members on the management team can post the meetings on their calendars for the balance of the year to ensure there are no scheduling conflicts for any meetings in the future.*

- *The meetings will start on time and last a maximum of one hour.*

- *We take meeting minutes at each meeting and distribute them immediately after.*

- *The first item on the agendas is the follow-up on any open tasks from the prior week.*

- *Finally, if anyone is late or does not attend the meeting, that person will put twenty dollars in the dish on the conference room table. The second time a manager is not on time, it will cost that person a hundred dollars benefiting a local charity. It would be an excellent idea for everyone never to be delinquent for a third meeting.*

I told the group that if they had any questions during the meeting, they should feel free to interrupt me at any time.

"The second item on the agenda is the chart of organization," I continued. "I am passing out copies of the chart of organization to share with the group. The revised chart showed that I had hired Chris as the new service manager."

I gave the team a brief recap of Chris's employment history and told them that he would be in the office Friday afternoon to attend the sales meeting at 2:00 p.m. and the service department meeting at 3:00 p.m. His official start day would be Monday, December 10. I told everyone at the meeting that Roger had done a great job holding the department together while we recruited and hired a new manager. I wanted to thank him for holding down the fort while we found an excellent candidate to fill the position. I also wanted everyone to know that I was not demoting or terminating Roger, but rather that Roger had asked me to hire a new service manager, so he could go back to his old senior technician position and work on servers and networks. Roger spoke up and told everyone that he hated the service manager position and had begged me to hire his replacement as soon as possible.

Roger looked across the table at me and said, "Thank you, Bob, I will forever be indebted to you for getting this service manager hiring transaction done so quickly."

I smiled at Roger's comment and moved on.

Next, I wanted the group to understand my goals for the company during the first thirty days—the month of December. I began a lengthy but informative monologue: "My first goal was to meet with each member of the management team to evaluate their skills and abilities. My second goal was to understand the problems that each manager is dealing with that are interfering with his or her effectiveness as a manager. I also wanted to know how those problems were affecting the profitability of the company. I met with each of you and was very impressed with this group. In our one-on-one meetings, I learned about several of the problems. Based on the information that I learned from each of you, I am now in the process of developing a plan on how to resolve to each of the problems. I am sorting the problems by the size of the financial impact that each has on the cash flow and profitability of the company. After finishing the process, I will then begin working with each of you to solve the most significant problems first, the second largest second, and so on.

"My next goal is to do a thorough evaluation of every member of the sales and service teams. Tom, you and I have already discussed this evaluation process with your salespeople, and I am going to ask Chris, with Roger's help, to do the same with the service department when he starts next week.

"My fourth goal is to grow sales in both the sales and service departments. I want our sales team to focus on calling on the corporations with more than a thousand employees in this geographical area. I am looking for the salespeople to bring in large orders from the bigger companies. I know that the sales cycle for those types of customers is much longer. The benefit is that larger customers issue higher dollar purchase orders compared to the smaller customers that our sales team has called on in the past, except for Nancy.

"I am passing out a task list form to everyone. Please use this form to list all the individual assignments that we have talked about in the last couple of days. This form will help you and me to keep track of the tasks and show your accomplishments as you check them off. For this turnaround to be successful, we all need to work hard and fix all the problems. I want this team on the same end of the rope and to all be pulling hard in the same direction. I trust that this group of managers can use all their skills and experience to fix this mess of a company. I will take the responsibility to do my part and resolve some of the major roadblocks. Then it is your job to manage your direct reports to work hard and be productive.

"We need to get to work on time and have our people do the same. Please focus on your job and support all the others who are sitting in this room. Turning around a company is not an easy job. Unfortunately, when a company is losing money, many employees get used to losing and eventually just give up. I will never get used to losing. I hope that each of you hates losing as much as I do. Stay close to your employees and push them hard in the right direction. When this company becomes profitable again, we all win."

"One of the problems in this company is that there has been no control or security over the inventory. Last year, there was a huge write-down of the inventory value after reconciling the physical inventory. Tim has developed a procedure and reporting form for any employee to request inventory from the warehouse. Tim, this is now your meeting, my friend."

"Thank you, Bob," Tim said, taking the lead. He had two stacks of papers in front of him. He grabbed both and handed them to Darren who was sitting to his right. Tim asked Darren to take one of each and pass the rest on so everyone has a copy. I could tell Tim was nervous, but he was doing a good job. He explained to the group that he had written the procedure for requesting inventory from the warehouse.

"This form is the document that will be used to record the transactions to the perpetual inventory and for the accounting records," he explained. "Therefore, how this works is, if you or one of your employees needs something from the warehouse, you must complete this form. There will be copies of the form sitting next to the warehouse door. We require the approval of the form by one of the managers in this room. The split door at the entrance to the warehouse is going to be open on the top and closed on the bottom of the door. Any inventory that leaves the warehouse in the future will need to have this form completed and signed, or I am not releasing the products to the employee. At five o'clock p.m. each day, I will be delivering the forms to Darren so he can make the appropriate journal entry to properly adjust the inventory counts and accounting records for the transaction." He paused, then asked, "Are there any questions or issues with this new policy?"

When no one said a word, I thanked Tim and turned to Donna. "Donna, you are up next."

"Okay, thank you, Bob. I am handing out to each of you a new performance review policy for this company and employee review forms. I know that no one in this company has had a performance review or salary adjustment in two years. That is about to change. I am also passing out to each of you a list of your employees in each of your departments. This list is confidential, so please be careful with the information. The list has every employee who reports to you, their salary, their date of hire, number of years employed with the company, date of last salary review, and the amount of the last salary review (see page 366).

"There is a column on the right side of the report for you to fill in your suggested compensation increase for each employee. The maximum raise for any employee right now is 5 percent, with the average for each department to be a maximum of 4 percent. Please do not tell any employee the amount of their raise until you receive the approved form back with Mr. Curry's signature. The performance reviews are due on Friday of next week. That is ten days from today. I know that is short notice, but if you want to give your people an increase beginning in January, you must prioritize this task and get it done. If any of you need my help with this, please see me as soon as possible. I will make myself available because this is a priority. Darren is going to plan for a four percent increase in the salaries for the budget for next year. Since we are still losing money now and year-to-date, the four percent average increase is the maximum we can afford right now. Are there any questions about this information?"

No one raised their hand or said a word.

"Thank you, Donna." I followed up Donna's comments with, "I want each of you managers to understand that we are going to be good to our employees in the future. We are going to treat them all with respect. Every employee in the company deserves to receive a performance review, so they all know what they are doing right and where they need to improve. I expect each of you to stay very close to all your employees. They are the ones who are doing the work to make this company profitable. Even though this company is losing money, we are still going to invest in our people. I want to send them a message that I reward employees who work hard and do a good job for this company."

"For the employees who are not working hard, have a bad attitude, and are not being productive, I want them out of here. If there are 'bad apples' in your department, they should *not* be here. They are the ones that are dragging this company down. I want everyone at ABC Computer Distributors to know that we care about our employees. We care about our employees, vendors, and customers. As managers, part of our responsibility is to reward the hardworking and productive workers by getting rid of the people who don't deserve to be part of this team. So please take what Donna just talked about as a priority and review all your employees by her requested deadline. Does anyone have any questions about this issue?"

My goal was to make this subject very clear to the group and judging by all the looks on their faces; I had accomplished my goal.

"The next topic on the agenda is the Christmas/Holiday party. Who would like to tell me what this company has done in the past years about having a party for the holidays?"

Donna said, "Bob, we have not had a Christmas party for this company because Craig said that we never had enough money to spend on a stupid holiday party, so we have never had a party."

"Thank you, Donna. It does not have to specifically be a Christmas party. Is this group interested in having a holiday party for our employees this year? I would like this company to have a party because it would be a great opportunity for us to thank all our employees for their hard work for the past twelve months. It would give us an opportunity to get all our employees excited about the New Year. Between now and the date of the party, we will have our next year's budget completed and can give everyone a state-of-the-company update. Soon, I believe, there are going to be several changes occurring within our organization. We can use this party to update our employees, so everyone knows where this company is going and what we expect from every employee in the next year. Everyone who agrees, please raise your hand."

Everyone on the management team raised his or her hands.

"Okay, who would like to assume the responsibility for coordinating the party?"

Tom stood up and said, "Donna and Darren, how about the three of us and Nancy get together and plan this party?"

Donna and Darren both said they would be happy to help.

"Bob, do you have any idea about a budget amount that we can spend for this party?" Tom asked.

"Tom, I will let the four of you determine how much you want to spend for this and when the party is going to be. When the controller of the company is on the committee for the party, I am sure that he can determine how much we can spend while keeping the company out of bankruptcy. I would suggest that you get together immediately because we need to give all the employees a date and time for when the party is scheduled so they can schedule babysitters, etcetera, for the party night."

"Thanks, Bob. I appreciate your confidence in us. Since it is much later than usual to find a location for this, maybe we can get a last-minute discount somewhere that needs the business."

"Tom, I like your attitude when you start talking about saving expenses."

No one has said much during the whole meeting until I brought up the holiday party topic. I was not sure why. Finally, Darren said, "Bob, I was waiting for the question and comments section to ask my questions. Is now a good time to ask our questions?" He had answered my question.

"Yes, Darren, go ahead! Ask away."

"My question is, where are Craig and Trish?"

"I have no idea," I said truthfully.

"Are they still a part of this management team?" he pressed.

"Obviously they don't think that they are, or they would have been at this meeting."

"Did you give them each an agenda yesterday when we received our agendas?"

"Yes, I did."

"Did either of them say that they were not going to attend this meeting?"

"No, neither Craig nor Trish said a word."

"Bob, what do you think about this?"

"Well, they both just made my job a lot easier."

"Okay, sir, you have answered all my questions, and I appreciate it. I knew that everyone in this room probably had the same question on their mind about those two, so that is why I asked."

"I will give you all an unambiguous message. I can see the actions and attitudes of everyone in this room that you are all interested in working hard and making this company successful. You have all just met me a few days ago. You are trying to understand who I am, what my plan for this company is, and how is it going to affect each of you. I am a very straightforward person. I do not hide my thoughts or actions about my mission here. I want this company to be successful. You are going to see me fight and claw to make it happen."

"My methods are simple. I hire the best people. I give them the tools to do their job. I encourage and reward those who are doing a good job, and I get rid of those who don't. I owe it to each of you to take care of the people who care about this company by doing a good job. I do not believe in investing the company's money in nonproductive people and bad apples. That makes no sense to me. I want to use the company's funds to reward those employees who are doing a great job. Does any of this make sense to this team?"

Everyone in the room nodded.

I continued, "So now you know who I am and what I am doing

here. You are all going to be able to predict my thoughts and actions in the future where there is a problem to resolve. I believe it will be rare if I surprise you. I am going to lead this company to be profitable and support each of you to accomplish that goal. I feel that you all deserve it and I am going to make it happen. Are then any other questions?"

There was silence.

"Okay, so everyone please remember to write down all your tasks on the forms I provided you by tomorrow morning and give me a copy. If you have any questions about this form, see me anytime. I want you to know that I am available to all of you as a resource to help you in any way that I can. My success at this company depends on each of your successes. You all have one last chance to ask any more questions before I end the meeting."

The room was silent.

"Okay, group!" I said. "GO WITH CONFIDENCE!" I looked at my watch, and it was 1:58 p.m. "Darren, are you ready to talk about receivables and payables?"

"Bob, let me run to my desk and get the reports. I will be back as quick as I can."

"Sure, we will meet back here in five minutes. I have a need to go get rid of all the coffee that I drank so far today."

* * *

A while later, Darren said, "Bob, this is the stack of invoices that are over ninety days old, sorted by customer. The entire backup is attached to the invoices documenting the receivables."

"Darren, were there invoices that you could not find the backup documentation for?"

"Yes, only five invoices that totaled under five hundred dollars. Bob, they were all service-related invoices."

"Did you check the service department files to find the backup?"

"Yes, I did, and we could not find anything."

"Are the service department files in good order or are they a mess?"

"They were okay. Not perfect, but not as bad as I expected."

"Have you written those invoices off yet?"

"No, sir, I have not."

"Okay, make a journal entry to write off those receivables, and I will sign the journal entry form. Darren, anytime you write off an asset for this company, I want to see and approve the journal entry."

"Okay, sir, no problem."

"Have you booked a monthly reserve for the write-off of accounts receivables and inventory?"

"Yes, I have. I have booked ten thousand dollars per month for the inventory and five thousand dollars for the receivables."

> I never want my financial person to have the ability to write off any assets of the company without my knowledge and approval of the write-off. That is why I told Darren I wanted to sign any journal entries to write off any receivables or inventory. This internal control procedure helps stop an employee from stealing inventory or cash and writing it off to hide the theft. It is not a fail-safe policy against internal theft, but it is a message to the financial manager that I am watching!

"Okay, Darren, it looks like there are six customers here in this stack. Is that right?"

"Yes, sir."

"Does the invoice show who the salesperson is for each customer?"

"Here, on the right side of the invoice, is the salesperson for each account."

I looked through the paperwork, and there was not one delinquent invoice for any of Nancy's accounts. "Darren, that is amazing. Nancy is responsible for fifty-five percent of the total sales of this company, and there is not one delinquent invoice for any of her customers."

"Nancy does not let any of her customers be delinquent with paying their invoices. If there is an invoice on a customer's accounts soon to be in the past-due column, she calls the customer and asks when we are going to receive payment. We do not pay sales commissions until the customer pays the invoice. If the invoice is over ninety days old, the salesperson loses their full commission for the sale. She does not permit any of her customers to let invoices go delinquent because it hurts her monthly commission check. Nancy's customers love her. She has a very nice business relationship with all her customers. She is an awesome salesperson. If we had one more Nancy in this company, we would be extremely profitable."

I agreed with that statement. "I have another question for you. Do you think that our customers would get very upset if we changed the payment terms on our invoices from net thirty days to net twenty days? I know that the change would materially improve our cash position. What do you think?"

"I do not think that it would be a problem to make the change."

"Good, I am going to bounce the issue off Tom and get his opinion also."

"Okay, Bob, and if you do decide to change the terms after you talk to Tom, let me know. All I would have to do is make a simple change in the billing system."

"Are there any problems with the payables?"

"No, sir."

"Well, then, thank you for your time, Darren. You have done a great job here, and I appreciate your efforts!"

"And, Bob, by the way, I called our insurance agent and told him to increase our inventory coverage from four million dollars to eighteen million dollars in two weeks for one month. He wanted to know why the increase, but I did not tell him, mostly because I did not know why myself."

I smiled because I knew that Darren was dying to know the reason for the significant increase in insurance coverage. I gave him the satisfaction of knowing that Nancy had a purchase order from one of her customers for over $18 million along with the rest of the details.

"What products are in this order?" Darren asked with a mix of excitement and alarm.

I told him about the 3,600 laptops, the thirty network servers, and the software.

"Bob, how are we going to finance this order?"

"Darren that is why I have been so secretive about this order. I am loaning the company eight million to do the deal."

"BOB, ARE YOU SERIOUS?"

"No, of course not, Darren!" I laughed. "The bank is giving us a ten-million-dollar temporary increase in our credit line for this deal."

"Bob, you had me going there! Well, anyway, Matthew is emailing me the endorsement of our policy. He told me that he would like to schedule an appointment to meet you. He wanted to know if you are a golfer."

"Darren, do you play golf?

"Yes, I do, sir."

"Okay, call him back and tell him that he can take you, Alan, and me out for a round of golf and lunch. We will let him spend some of those overcharged premium dollars on us. Please go see Alan and find out when he is available and then let me know."

"Are there any bad times for you?" Darren asked.

"No, not if we are going golfing! I take that back. Yes, there are some bad times. The three of us all have management meetings on Wednesday afternoons. I have service and sales meetings on Friday afternoons. Other than that, right now, I can adjust my schedule for a round of golf."

"Bob, thank you for including me."

"Darren, you and I are a team."

* * *

I took the stack of unpaid invoices that Darren had given me to see Tom in his office. "Tom, do you have a minute?"

"Sure, Bob, what's up?"

"Darren gave me this stack of delinquent invoices and the backup for each. Do you want to talk to the salesperson about these invoices, or should I?"

"Bob, I will handle them, if it is okay with you."

"Yes, that is fine! Please let me know the payment status of each by this Monday."

Tom pulled out his task list and wrote down to meet with the salesperson about the delinquent invoices and "notify Bob" after the salesperson has contacted each customer.

"Tom, one more question for you. Do you think that it would have a negative impact on our customers if we changed the payment terms from net thirty days to net twenty days?"

"No, not at all. I am okay with the change."

"Should we talk to Nancy about the change?"

"Bob, I will talk to her, but I am sure she will agree if it is good for our business right now."

> By changing our invoice payment terms from "Net 30 days" to "Net 20 days," the reduction of the accounts receivables reduced the company's loan balance by the same total. With the sales budget for the next being $120 million, this change in policy would reduce the average loan balance by ten days of sales or $3.3 million. **This reduction in our loan balance would reduce our interest expense by $148,000 for the year or a little more than $12,000 per month.**

"Please call Darren and tell him that we talked. Tell him to go ahead and make the change to the payment terms immediately. Do you think we should notify our customers of the change?"

"Yes, I do. I will take care of it, Bob. I will talk to Darren. We can put the message in the envelopes when we send out our invoices for the next month."

Glad that Tom was taking the lead on all those tasks, I went back to my office and sent an email to the management team with the minutes of the meeting. My notes were very brief because it had only been our first meeting. The only bullet point reminder was for everyone to complete their task forms and get them to me by the following morning. I also included a note in the email that I was changing the payment terms on our invoices from net thirty days to net twenty days. I decided that I was not going to send the email to Craig and Trish. Neither of them had said a word to me about not attending the meeting. Craig and Trish's lack of attendance confirmed to me again that they both should be gone this week.

I sent the email and noticed I had received an email from Kevin with the paperwork for the additional line of credit. I called my attorney and got his voicemail. I left him a message that I was for-warding him bank documents for a temporary increase in our line of credit. I asked him to review the paperwork immediately because I wanted to get this deal done before the bank changed their mind. I printed two copies of all the documents. I then called Kevin to ask him if he could stop by the office later this afternoon to pick up the paperwork and a copy of Nancy's customer purchase order.

Paul, my attorney, called me back in an hour and said that the documents were okay for me to sign. Then he asked, "Mr. Curry, help me understand this. You just started working for a distressed company on Monday and Wednesday; the bank increased your line of credit by ten million dollars? How did that happen?"

"Paul, it was easy. One of the women on the sales team, Nancy, came into my office today with a purchase order from one of her customers for over eighteen million dollars of laptops, servers, and software. The bank was happy to finance the deal. The gross profit on the deal is a little over three million dollars after paying the salesperson's commission."

"Okay, Bob, I get it. Congratulations!"

*　*　*

Once Kevin signed the loan documents for the increase in the line of credit, I told Nancy that she should get the formal purchase order signed by the customer, along with the check for the down payment as per the payment terms. Kevin stopped by the office at 4:00 p.m. and signed two copies of the loan documents, one for me and one for his files. With the paperwork taken care of, I told him that Nancy had first gone to Craig with the purchase order, and he had turned it down.

"Bob, you have got to be kidding! He did not even call me to see if we would finance the deal—that is crazy."

This company has just taken a significant step toward long-term profitability, I thought with satisfaction.

There was a light knock on my office door, and Charlie was standing there. I invited him in and introduced him to Kevin. I told Kevin all about Charlie's having been a cop for many years. He explained that he changed his career path after having been shot at twice on two different occasions in one night.

"Did the bullets hit you?" Kevin asked.

"No, the scumbags missed," Charlie replied.

I guessed that Kevin would have had more questions for Charlie but knowing that he had to get this paperwork back to his office before they closed, he took off.

Charlie and I walked into the warehouse so he could see how the security should be set up. We were there for about ten minutes when he said, "Okay, let's go to dinner."

We went to Ruth's Chris Steak House and Charlie, as promised, ordered the biggest steak on the menu. I knew the dinner check would be substantial, but I did not mind because Charlie always took care of my clients. Plus, he was the best storyteller. Charlie told me five different anecdotes during dinner, and I laughed so hard that my jaw hurt. At the end of the evening, he told me that he would have a layout for the security cameras and give me a total cost for the complete security system by noon the next day.

Chapter 7

THE NEW SALES GROWTH AND INCENTIVE PLAN

"I hire people brighter than me, and I get out of their way."

—LEE IACOCCA, AMERICAN AUTOMOBILE EXECUTIVE

THURSDAY, DECEMBER 7—DAY 4 OF WEEK 1

WHEN I ARRIVED AT THE OFFICE VERY EARLY IN THE MORNING, I noticed that Donna's, Tom's, Tim's, and Darren's cars were all in their parking spaces. Their enthusiasm was fantastic. The management team was beating me to work! I would have never predicted such passion from the group after Craig's comments about them that past Monday morning. Then when they had all walked into the conference room with the saddest looks on their faces to meet Rick, Kevin, and me, I thought they had all just come from a funeral. I would have never guessed that there was going to be so much energy and excitement, and I was so pleased with their positive progress.

When I got to my office, six tasks forms were sitting in a nice stack right in the middle of my desk. I picked them up and reviewed each one. All I could do was smile as I read each manager's list. My first thought was that these people were good at dealing with change. There was a significant difference between reporting to Craig and working for me. There was also a task report from Roger, even though he was not going to be the manager of the service department when Chris arrived. I was so pleased that each manager's list was right on point. I was almost overwhelmed by how well this week was going. I was no longer concerned that this turnaround was going to be successful. I had high confidence that this team—except for Craig and Trish—was going to work hard and do a great job.

Darren stopped by my office just before 7:00 a.m. and asked, "We are meeting in the conference room, right?"

I told him that sounded like a plan.

On the way, I walked past Donna's office, and she called out, "Bob, would you care for a good cup of coffee this morning?"

I turned back around. "Donna, you are the best! You have no idea how much I appreciate your coffee."

"Where are you going to be? I will bring it to you," she offered.

When I told her I would be in the conference room, she said she would have it there for me in a few minutes.

"You know that you do not have to do this for me," I said. I wanted to make sure that Donna did not feel obligated, but she assured me that she liked doing it.

"I like seeing you with a smile on your face," she added. "I know how much stress you are under with all the changes you are making here. If I can be responsible for getting you to smile every morning while enjoying a good cup of coffee, that makes me happy."

I expressed my sincere appreciation once more and headed to my meeting.

Darren was in the conference room when I got there. "If I remember correctly, you and I were to meet and talk about property and casualty insurance, health insurance, the year-end audit, taxes, and the return of Craig's Mercedes to the dealer."

"Bob, you have a good memory," Darren said with a smile. "Let's start with the last item first. Yesterday evening after work, Patrick followed me to the Mercedes dealer to return the car. You are not going to believe it, but they gave us our whole security deposit— seven thousand dollars—back. So, we now have no more monthly lease payments, plus we have seven thousand in the bank."

"Did you call the insurance agent to have the car removed from our auto insurance policy?"

"Bob, yes, I did while I was at the dealer."

> **Profit Improvement:** By returning Craig's vehicle to the dealer and terminating the lease, that transaction reduced our monthly expenses by $1,250 for the car lease and $250 for the insurance. **Annualized, we lowered our operating expenses by $18,000 and we received $7,000 back for the deposit.**

"Good, I am glad we resolved that problem. Darren, I would like you to arrange to take the sign down in Craig's old parking spot. I want the sign repainted to say, 'Employee of the Month.'"

"Where are you going to park, Bob?"

"In the parking lot with all the rest of the employees."

"But you are the president of the company! You deserve the special parking spot."

"I disagree. The employee who does something special during the month deserves that spot. Many good people work for this company. They have had to deal with poor leadership by the owner for years. I am here to deliver a new message. We reward employees who work hard and are productive. Those who do not work hard will not be part of this organization."

"That *is* an unambiguous message, Bob," Darren said. "Next, our good friend Matthew, the insurance agent, who is Craig's cousin, would like to host you, Alan, and me to a round of golf this Saturday morning at Aronamik Country Club. He would like us to be there at eight o'clock for a light breakfast, then hit some balls, practice some putts, and be on the tee of the first hole at nine o'clock. I am assuming that you are going to be able to be there in the morning, right?"

"Darren, if the weather is good, I would love to play. Have you checked with Alan to make sure he is available too?"

"Yes, sir, I did, and he is."

"Okay, great! This golf outing should be fun; I love Aronamik. Have you played with Matthew before?"

"Yes, I have, twice."

"What did he shoot?"

"He shot a ninety-two if I remember correctly, and that was a gift."

"What do you mean *a gift*?"

"Bob, he would drive the ball in the woods, not be able to find it, then drop another ball. He then would hit the next shot short in the rough, hack the next shot into the sand trap. It would take him two shots to get out of the sand and then three-putt the green. I would ask him what he had for that hole, and he would proudly say, 'a bogey five.' He had a bogey before he hacked the ball into the sand trap. Either Matthew has a short-term memory problem with remembering how many shots he took on that hole, or he had a terrible math teacher in grade school. This person will never be a good golfer. Wait until you see his swing. Honestly, I look away when he is swinging. If I don't, I break up laughing."

I chucked. "Are you serious?" I asked.

"Yes, Bob, you wait! I can't want to see your reaction when you see him swing at the ball."

After a little more kidding around with Darren, I refocused on the purpose of our meeting. "I would like to discuss how I want you to handle our insurance quoting process." Darren immediately pulled out his notebook and started taking notes. "We need three agents to bid on our insurance package, other than Matthew's agency. I would like you or Patrick to develop a spread schedule, as we talked about earlier. The report provides our current coverages, deductibles, policies limits, and any essential endorsements on each policy. We will give each agency this information and tell them that they are limited to three insurance companies for them to bid the coverages. Each agency will create a list of insurance companies that they are going to quote the business. We do not want any of the agencies going to ten different insurance carriers, therefore eliminating the other agents from being able to use those companies to get a legitimate bid for our company.

"Insurance companies will only give one agency a quote for a potential customer. If a second agency asks that insurance company to bid our company, they will not issue a second quote. We will tell each agent when our existing policies terminate, but we will give them a deadline to present their bid to us a month earlier. Agents try to give you their bid at the very last second before the prior policy expires, so you do not have time to negotiate with another agency. We will also tell them that if they do not submit their bid by our deadline date, they are not eligible to present their quote to us. We also will make them aware that they only get one chance to present their numbers. We are not going to negotiate. If they do not give us their best numbers on the first meeting, they do not get a second chance. They get one bite at the apple. So, Matthew gets his chance to retain the business if his numbers are the best, and if not, he is gone. Darren, do you have any insurance agents that you know other than Matthew? I am talking about both the property and casualty and health insurance agencies. Some agencies only focus on property and casualty or health insurance. It is not common for agencies to represent companies for both types of insurance."

"Getting three agencies to bid on both types of insurance will not be a problem," Darren assured me.

"Okay then, let's get the spread schedule done with our coverages this week. Let's schedule meetings with three agencies next week and give them deadlines for their presentations as of the last day of January. I know our policies terminate at the end of February. We are talking about both the property and casualty and the health insurance, right?"

"Yes, sir, you are right."

"I will mark on my calendar that I am going to be busy with our insurance coverages during the last week of January."

"Bob, this is going to kill Matthew when you tell him that we are bidding out all the insurance this year."

"Darren, it should not bother him if his numbers are good."

"That is my point. I don't think that the insurance premiums are good. I think that they are way high."

"Well, we will learn a lot about Matthew in the next couple months, won't we?" Then I added with good humor, "And I'm not just talking about his golf swing."

Darren laughed.

"Okay, now let's talk about our year-end audit. First, please give the partner at the accounting firm a call to come in to meet us very soon. Hmmm, the accounting firm—are they also related to Craig in any way?"

"No, Bob, they aren't. I will give them a call later to schedule a meeting."

"Yes, please do that right away so we can get this behind us as quickly as possible. Has this company been audited or reviewed in the past?"

"We have never been audited. We have had a review done for the past three years."

"Okay, that is fine. Here is what I suggest we do over the next couple of weeks to prepare for the accountants to come in and get their work done. If you and Patrick can have your general ledger analysis for the balance sheet up to date through the end of November's closing, we can invite their people to come in immediately and review the books through the end of November. Then they can come back maybe the third week of January to review December's activity. I believe that will work most efficiently and keep our costs down. We also need to schedule the counting of the physical inventory."

"Hmm, we have a little problem here. We are going to receive fifteen million dollars of computer hardware in our warehouse during the last week of December. I think that I would like to take the physical before that big order comes in and adjust the inventory by the 'after inventory' shipments received. Maybe we can ask the accountants to send someone in when we are receiving the large order and take the inventory then. I am sure that we will not be shipping much product during the week between Christmas and New Year's."

That sounded like a good plan to me. "Darren, I am comfortable with having you work out those details with the accounting firm.

You don't need my help. We can discuss that issue with the partner when we meet with him."

Darren agreed.

"Okay, so you call the accounting firm partner and schedule a meeting and let's get this year-end stuff behind us. We can talk about the income tax returns at the meeting with our accounting friends at the meeting. Since the company has lost money for the past two years, the tax returns are not going to be a priority."

Darren wrote down in his notebook to call the accounting firm to schedule a meeting.

"Bob, I will have Patrick create the insurance schedules immediately and schedule appointments with three different insurance agencies. We will meet and distribute the information and the deadlines that we have discussed today for them to provide us with insurance quotes for all our insurance policies. Once I set those appointments, I will be sure to let you know the dates and times, so you can participate if you so choose. I will also contact the partner for our accounting firm and get back to you as soon as I have an appointment booked."

"Thank you, Darren, and thank you for your time."

I returned to my office and closed the door. I decided to turn off my phone and not take any calls. I needed some quiet time to develop a new sales growth and incentive plan to generate more sales of hardware, software, and service.

My initial draft of the sales growth plan was as follows:

- *I am going to assign each salesperson ten target companies in the Philadelphia geographic area. These corporations are some of the most significant businesses in Pennsylvania and New Jersey. I researched and found the list of the top 300 companies in the Philadelphia geographic market listed in the Philadelphia Business Journal.*

- *Each salesperson will be responsible for contacting the purchasing and IT managers at the target companies to set up appointments with one, two, or as many executives in the companies who have the authority to purchase computers. The senior executives may be in the purchasing, IT,* engineering, or the sales departments. The more department managers that the salesperson contacts at the target companies, the better their chance to close a sale. Each salesperson should use LinkedIn to research the executives who work for their target companies. Once the research is done to discover which managers are responsible for purchasing the technology and computer service for the company, the salesperson should call and schedule an appointment(s) to introduce themselves. When a salesperson has a meeting time and date scheduled, then the salesperson should send the purchasing manager and any other executives an Outlook appointment email to confirm the meeting. Also, she should mail the executive a thank-you card with her business card enclosed to show appreciation to the person for the opportunity to meet with him or her to introduce themselves and our company.

- Once the salesperson has had the meeting with the purchasing manager, the salesperson should remember to ask if there is anyone else in the company who is responsible for purchasing computers or service contracts.

- Each salesperson will complete a Sales Call and Pipeline Report for each target list customer appointment (see pages 371 and 369).

My first draft of the new commission plan was as follows:

- The sales team will earn a 20% commission on the gross profit of their sales during the month on paid invoices within ninety days of the invoice date. We exclude paying any commissions on any invoices that are paid in ninety days old or more.

- For each target customer's first purchase order that is received, shipped, and fully paid for within ninety days of invoice date that is more than $5,000 gross profit, the salesperson will get a $500 cash bonus payment during the weekly sales meeting. If the first purchase from the target customer is more than $25,000 gross profit, the salesperson will receive a $2,500 cash bonus payment. Each sales rep is entitled to only one cash bonus payment for each of their ten target customers. The bonuses paid at the weekly sales meetings does not impact the *salesperson's monthly commissions earned. We consider the bonus pay-ments as "new customer" rewards.*

- *Each salesperson will earn 150% of the regular sales commissions rate for new service contracts sold for the next four months until the end of the first quarter of next year, starting immediately and ending at the end of March of next year.*

- *Each salesperson's commission rate will be cut by 20% (from 20% of the gross profit to 16%) for any month on sales of hardware and software if the salesperson does not sell a minimum of $25,000 in service con-tracts during that month.*

- *If the sales rep sells $25,000 or more of new service contracts, their commission rate on computers and software sales will increase by 20% (from 20% to 24%) for the month.*

- *Any salesman who sells more than $50,000 in service contracts in a month wins a four-day, three-night cruise for the salesperson and their spouse. If any salesperson sells $100,000 or more in new service con-tracts, the vacation trip will be for seven days, six nights.*

- *Any salesman who does not sell any service for the month goes on "my list." The goal of everyone on the sales staff is to not be on "my list" more than two times. I will let the salespeople figure out the impact on their job if they earn a spot on "my list" multiple times.*

When I finished my project for the sales meeting and looked at my watch, it was precisely noon. I decided to get a cup of coffee and then get some more work done before the weekend. I opened my office door, and Charlie was standing there. "Charlie, what are you doing here?"

"Bob, I told you that I would have the security plan information for you by noon today, and it is noon today." He held up his watch to show me the time.

"I know what time it is. My question is how you got past the receptionist to get back here unannounced?"

"I showed her my badge and told her that I was with the FBI."

"You don't have an FBI badge!"

"I know, but when I hold up a badge, most people are so intimidated that they don't know if I am from the FBI or Disney World! Bob, I told Tina that you were expecting me, and I have a proposal for you regarding the security plan. She just looked at me, smiled and sent me back here."

"Charlie, you are a piece of work!"

Charlie handed me an envelope with the information and told me that if I was going to be around this weekend, he would do the installation on Saturday afternoon.

"Charlie, how much is the proposal to protect the office and warehouse?"

"Bob, I gave you all the equipment at my cost, and I am doing the installation at the cost of a steak dinner. I promise you that you will not get a deal like this from any other security firm."

I said, "Charlie, I know that. Saturday afternoon would probably work out. What time do you want to meet here?"

"How about three p.m.?"

"Charlie, how long is it going to take to do the installation?"

"Only two to three hours. It goes fast. These are battery-powered cameras, so there is minimal wiring to do."

"Okay, Saturday at three p.m., I will be here."

"Bob, if you have some time right now, I will take you out for lunch."

"Charlie, are you saying that you are going to take me out to lunch and pay for both of us?"

"No, are you kidding? I will take you out, but you are going to pay. I quoted the security system at my cost, so I am not going to make any money on this deal except for last night's dinner and today's lunch."

"Okay, Charlie, let's go!"

As we were walking out, we passed Darren in the hallway. I introduced Darren to Charlie, and the two of them shook hands.

Charlie said, "I am taking Bob out to lunch, Darren, and he's paying. Would you like to join us?"

Darren cracked a smile and looked at me to see if it was okay. I told him he was welcome to join us, and he followed us to Charlie's big pick-up truck.

When we returned to the office after lunch, Charlie dropped Darren and me off because he had to go to another appointment. Darren asked me where I had met Charlie. I explained that Charlie had done a security job for another company I used to work for, and we became friends after he finished the project."

"Bob, Charlie is a funny guy."

"Yes, he is, Darren."

"Are you going to have him install a security system here?"

"Yes. We are going to have eighteen million dollars of computers in our warehouse soon. I thought that it might be a good idea to have some security to protect our inventory."

"Sounds like a good idea to me! Bob, thanks for lunch."

"No problem, my friend!"

I went to my office and got the copies of the sales and service meeting agendas. I took the sales agendas over to Tom and asked him to pass them out to the salespeople. Then I went over to see Roger and asked him to give all the techs a copy of the service meeting agenda. Then, I went to see Donna. I found her sitting at her desk in her office.

"Donna, I would like you to come up with a policy for the management team to name an employee of the month. The employee of the month should be someone who has done something extraordinary for the company. I would suggest that the management team have a monthly meeting to nominate candidates for the employee of the month and then they all vote to determine the winner. The employee will receive a plaque they can hang in their office. The employee will be able to park their car in Craig's old parking spot and will receive a gift card for dinner for two. We will acknowledge the employee for winning the award in front of the whole company. I also want to order a big plaque to be hung in the reception area listing the current employee of the month and all the previous winners of the award."

"Bob, I love the idea! It will not take me long to come up with the policy. But I thought that you would be parking in Craig's old parking spot since you are the president of the company after all."

"Donna, I would rather use that parking spot as a reward for the employee of the month. Alan told me a story when I had my one-on-one meeting with him. He said that every employee in the company walked past that parking spot every morning coming to work with that hundred-thousand-dollar Mercedes parked there and hated it. I want every employee who walks past that spot in the future to want their car parked there as the new employee of the month. I am going to turn a liability into an asset for the company."

"Bob, my level of respect grows for you when I hear you say things like that. That is awesome."

"Thank you, Donna. I appreciate that. When you say things like that, I know we are going in the right direction. I do have several other ideas that I would like to discuss with you that I want to do for our employees when you have the time."

> When an employee goes above and beyond their job responsibility to do a good job, I acknowledge and reward that employee. If done properly, it will encourage others to do the same. This practice creates a "team corporate culture" in the company, and it just keeps getting better.

"Now is a good time, Bob, if you also have the time," she offered.

"Okay, first, I want to fund a college scholarship for a disadvantaged high school senior who has the intelligence, the grades, and the maturity to go to college, but does not have the funds to afford the tuition. I would like to have the management team form a committee to search and find the perfect candidate for us to raise money to pay for the student to go to college. I want to locate the high school senior who would go college but cannot because of money. I want us to pay for the student's tuition, room and board, books, and travel expenses to and from college. I want to provide money for the individual to afford clothes and look like every other kid at the university. I want to give an opportunity to someone who knows that there is no way he or she can go to college because of their lousy home environment. When we fund this student, I want someone here to be his or her sponsor and stay in touch weekly or monthly. I want us to be there for the student to help get the individual through the rough times in college and support this kid's success. I would like for us to be responsible for taking a young high school student who has no future because of his or her home environment and give that person the opportunity to become a doctor, lawyer, or the future president of ABC Computer Distributors!"

> Every company that I have ever managed, I always tried
> to management the business well enough to afford to give
> back something significant to the community where the
> company was located. I have always felt that providing funds
> for a student to go to college was a great "give back."

Donna's eyes filled up with happy tears. "Bob, I can hardly believe we are discussing a scholarship program. Before you joined this company, I did not believe we would still be in business come January. It was like someone pulled the plug and everything was quickly going down the drain."

"Donna, when I took this engagement, I decided that this was a good company with bad leadership. I recently worked for a good company with good leadership, so I know what can happen when you hire the best people in the area, treat them with respect, give them the tools to do their job, provide them an excellent environment to work in and compensate them fairly. When you use this 'secret formula' in business, your company will be successful every time. Well, it is my goal to use this business formula and make this company extremely successful. When this company is successful, we are going to take care of the management team and the employees who were responsible for making this company a success. In addition to the management team and the employees, I would like to take care of some kids that have it tough right now. I would like to make their lives better because all of this company's employees kicked butt and made a ton of money. I also want to encourage some of our vendors and customers to add to our funds to help some high school kids."

I could tell that Donna was really on board with this, and I wanted her to know that I genuinely believed in the company's ability to be profitable. "This company was failing because of one individual. This company is going to be very profitable because of fifty people. All we need to do is get them all working together and pulling the rope hard in the same direction. The secret formula works. It is going to work and make fifty people in this company very happy. Then these fifty employees are going to make some high school students even happier and help give them to a very bright future. Donna, I am hoping that this scholarship program will motivate our employees to work a little bit harder because not only will it benefit our company, but it will give some kids a chance who do not have the opportunity now to make it in life without our help."

"How are we going to start this scholarship program?" Donna asked.

"I am not sure right now," I admitted, "but I do plan on doing some research to figure out how to do it right. I do not want to start such a project and fail. For this to be successful, we are going to need every employee in this company to endorse this. We need every single employee to work hard to make this company successful so that this organization can do the same for some high school students."

Donna offered to help, so I asked her to call some of the local colleges and universities in the area to see if they knew of any other companies that were providing scholarships for students. If so, I said we should contact those companies and get some expert advice. "I don't want to make any mistakes with this program," I told her. "When we start the program, I want it to get better and better as time goes on. Let's keep this confidential until we have our I's dotted and our T's crossed. I would like to announce the program to the company at our holiday party if we can get this all accomplished by then."

Donna wiped her eyes with the back of her hand. She was very touched. "Bob, first, I want to thank you for including me with this idea of yours. I want to scream with excitement. Second, I want to thank you for having such a positive vision for this company and its employees. There are many very wonderful people working here, and I did not want to see them hurt. Craig was leading this company and its employees to pain, failure, and bankruptcy. Then you get here with an attitude that nothing is going to interfere with our success. Nothing is going to get in our way of helping our employees and even some high school kids who need help. It is so hard to believe that this much can change within one week."

"Donna, it is not going to be a week for another day and a half! I have confidence that we can do this. It is not going to be easy, but nothing that good is going to be easy. If it were easy, everyone would be doing it."

"I will make you a solemn promise, Bob," Donna said. "I will do everything I can to make this scholarship idea successful."

"It is going to happen! In fact, I can see the look in the college graduate's eyes when he or she walks up on the stage to get the diploma. We all need to keep our eye on *that* prize."

There was a soft knock on Donna's door. I stood up and opened the door. Darren walked in and looked at us both with concern. "Is everything okay?" he asked.

"Yes, why would you ask?"

"Because Donna looks like she has been crying."

"These are happy tears," she said, easing Darren's concerns.

Darren smiled wide. "Is Bob spreading some of his magic again?"

"Yes, he is!"

"Is it anything that you want to share with me?" he asked curiously.

Her eyes flew to me than back to Darren. "No, I can't, it's confidential."

Darren looked disappointed, then turned to me and said, "Bob, the managing partner of our accounting firm stopped in to talk about the year-end schedule. Do you have some time to talk to him?"

"Sure, where is he?"

"He is in the conference room waiting for us."

"Okay, let's go see him." I started to follow Darren out into the hall but turned back and told Donna it would be okay to talk to Darren about the program so he could help her where possible.

Darren's eyes lit up. "I will be back as soon as this meeting is over to hear about it. Don't go anywhere!" he said.

"I won't," she assured him. "I have too much work to do! Our new boss is a slave driver!"

I looked at Donna. "Donna, am I a slave driver?"

Donna laughed. "Bob, you are the best slave driver a company could ever have!"

* * *

Darren and I walked into the conference room, and there were three "suits" sitting at the table. They all stood up, and Darren introduced Fred, the managing partner; Steve, the tax partner; and Russell, the manager in charge of our account. We all exchanged business cards and sat back down to talk.

Fred said, "Darren tells us that you are running this company now. I was shocked to hear that Craig had hired someone to manage his company."

"Fred, Craig did not hire me, our floor-planning bank hired me. I believe that they were concerned that their outstanding loan was at risk under Craig's leadership."

"That was going to be the subject of our conversation today. We are concerned that since the company has lost money for two years now, we are going to have a problem with giving a 'going concern' opinion in our year-end report."

"Fred, that is not going to be a problem here."

"Really, why is that?"

"We have plans to grow the company aggressively. We are making several changes to the organization to turn around the results of operations very quickly."

"Bob, can you share some of what you are talking about because we came here today to talk to Craig about helping him to find a bankruptcy attorney and file a Chapter 11 bankruptcy."

"Fred, neither Craig nor I will need your help with filing for bankruptcy protection. Yesterday, we received approval for a ten-million-dollar increase in our line of credit. I am planning on record sales for December and January. In January, we should do more than twenty-five million dollars."

"What are the company's sales going to be this current year?"

"Probably between forty-nine million and fifty-two million."

"So, you are telling me that the company is going to report twenty-five million dollars in sales in the first month of next year?"

"Yes, plus we are going to achieve those results with thirty percent fewer employees working for ABC Computer Distributors."

"Bob, with all due respect, may I ask how you are going to achieve those results?"

"Fred, yes, you can ask, but that is not why we are meeting. Darren and I talked about getting the year-end work done as quickly as possible, so we can move on with making money. Darren will soon have November's general ledger analysis completed for your review. If you can have one of your people review the books through the end of November that would work well for us. Then, by the second week of January, you can update your work papers for December's activities. We will be ready to do the physical inventory before Christmas. One of my goals is to have the inventory as low as possible by then. I plan to operate this business next year with zero inventory in the warehouse. I am going to get rid of the inventory and pay down the loan balance, which will reduce our interest expense by approximately twenty-three thousand per month."

"Bob, good decision. I never understood why Craig had inventory, too much risk."

"I agree. It's been a pleasure meeting you. I must run to another meeting. I will let you work out all the details with Darren. Darren is a superstar, and he does not need my help."

"Bob, I know that Darren is a superstar, but we need to talk more about this company. We are concerned about this company's future. That will affect how we go about our work over the next couple of months."

"Fred, I appreciate your concern. As I said, I am not in the market for a bankruptcy attorney. I am not concerned about a receiving a 'going concern' opinion from your firm. I trust Darren to make good decisions about working with our accounting firm regarding our year-end work. If the two of you cannot work out a schedule to do the year-end work, then I need either a new controller or a new accounting firm. As I said to you earlier, Darren is a superstar. So, thank you again for your time, and please stay in touch. There is one issue that you should be prepared to talk about, and that is your fee. Darren is going to ask you to review your work schedule to see where you can reduce your time, and therefore, lower our cost for your services."

This time Steve spoke up. "Mr. Curry, would you be interested in talking about the tax situation for this company?"

"Thank you, Steve, but no I would not. I know that this company lost a lot of money last year and did not make much money two years ago. So, therefore, I am assuming that we will not be paying any taxes this year, nor will we be getting any refunds from prior years."

Steve said, "That is all true."

"With extensions, the tax returns are not due for another nine and a half months, right?"

"Mr. Curry, yes, that is true also."

"Then, Steve, thank you for coming here today. I appreciate meeting all the senior members of your firm. We should talk again after the first quarter of next year. We are going to show a substantial profit for the first three months next year, so I am sure that we are going to have to make a tax deposit. We will need your help at that time, okay?"

"Yes sir, thank you!"

With that, I stood up, shook their hands, thanked them for their time, and left the conference room to go back to my office.

A half an hour later, Darren showed up at my office door. "Bob, do you have a minute?"

"Sure, Darren, what's up?"

"First, thank you for calling me a superstar!"

"Darren, you deserve it, you *are* a superstar."

"Second, I appreciate your letting me handle the issues in my area. I know that you were a controller and CFO and you could do my job blindfolded. I enjoy learning from you, and I appreciate that you are here. I was concerned when I heard that your background was in finance that maybe I should start looking for a new job. But much to my surprise, it is just the opposite."

"Darren, you are very valuable to this company and me. If you are concerned about me doing your job because I was a controller too, that will never happen. If I am doing your job every day, then I am not doing my job. I think that it is more important right now for me to focus on being the president of this organization rather than backing up my controller. So, did you get everything squared away with our accounting firm friends?"

"Yes, I did. After you left the conference room, Fred's first question was about your background. Then he asked me if you were smoking dope before you came into the conference room. I told him that he should not doubt your projections. I also told them that you are a no-nonsense person. I suggested to him that they raise their level of respect or there probably will be a new accounting firm here within a week doing the year-end work. They got real serious then and adjusted their attitude. We then moved on to discuss the year-end schedule."

"Good, Darren, I am proud of you for standing up to those guys."

"Bob, it seemed to me that you did not like Fred within the first five minutes of meeting him, is that true?"

"Darren, Fred gave me a funny look when I told him that we were going to do twenty-five million dollars in January. When I told him that Rick and Kevin had just approved a ten-million-dollar increase in our line of credit, he should have put one and one together and figured out that we have a huge customer order to ship in January. He focused on his preconceptions and did not hear a word I said. As soon as I figured that out, I left the meeting. When someone is not listening, why meet?"

"Bob, you intimidated Fred when he tried to control the meeting, and he was no match for you! Then when you asked him to lower his fee, he was speechless. Then you walked out of the meeting, and his level of frustration maxed out."

I wanted Darren to understand what had transpired. "Let me share with you how I feel. We do not need Fred's firm to make this company successful. They offer a service that is available by many other accounting firms in this city. We could fire his firm today and have another accounting firm here tomorrow. If Fred was going to add value to our organization in the meeting, I would have stuck around. For him to come here and not listen first before he started talking about a bankruptcy attorney, my patience ended there. I got out of the room and decided that I had a great controller to handle the situation. I used my intelligence rather than my emotions."

"See, Bob . . . I just learned another lesson from you."

Chapter 8

BLACK FRIDAY

*"Letting the wrong people hang around is unfair to all the
right people, as they inevitably find themselves compensating for
the inadequacies of the wrong people. Worse, it can drive away
the best people. Strong performers are intrinsically motivated
by performance, and when they see their efforts impeded by
carrying extra weight, they eventually become frustrated."*

—JAMES C. COLLINS, AMERICAN BUSINESS
CONSULTANT, AUTHOR, AND LECTURER

FRIDAY, DECEMBER 8—DAY 5 OF WEEK 1

ON FRIDAY MORNING, I WAS UP EARLY AND WENT TO HAVE
breakfast at the local diner before I went into the office. Darren was
there sitting at a table in the back corner of the restaurant. I walked
over to see if I might join him. He stood up when he saw me, shook
my hand, and asked me to join him. The server came over and took
my order after she poured me a cup of coffee. Darren told me that
his wife was still out of town with the kids visiting her family and
that he loved to have breakfast in the morning before work.

"So, Bob, how has your first week at ABC Computer Distributors
been?"

"Darren, it has only been four days, but it has not been as hard
as I expected. Plus, I think that it is going to get much better."

"What do you mean?"

"At four o'clock today, I am informing Craig and Trish that today is their last day working for this company."

"It is hard to believe that this day came so soon. By the way, speaking about Craig and Trish, I have those schedules you asked me to create listing all their reimbursed non-business-related expenses."

"Good, please get with Donna first thing when we get to the office, so she can do the paperwork for their final paycheck deducting all those personal expenses reimbursed."

"Okay, I will do that." Darren pulled a small notebook out of his pocket and made a note. "Bob, I also have the year-to-date productivity schedules for the service department—the technician billings. And also for the sales department—sales by salesperson. You are not going to like the information once you see the report."

"Why is that?" I asked, then sipped my coffee. It was almost as good as the coffee Donna made me.

"The billings for the service department are terrible when you look at it by technician. Several technicians have billed less than ten thousand dollars for the whole year."

"What do they do all day?"

"When I was done creating the report, I talked to Roger about the issue. He said that when the service calls are slow, he doubles up the teams, and sends out two technicians on each service call. Then when you see the sales by salesman report, you are not going to like that one either."

"Okay, go ahead, tell me why."

"Three salespeople have sold less than sixty thousand dollars in hardware and software year-to-date. Then several salespeople have zero sales in service contracts. I will put the reports on your desk when we get to the office."

"Okay, thank you. I look forward to reviewing the information."

"What else can I do to help?"

"I want you and Donna to meet me in the conference room for the meeting with Craig and Trish at four p.m. After I terminate them, you can help Craig and Donna can help Trish clean out their offices."

"Bob, you have made my day. I would love to accompany Craig on his way out. Is it okay if I kick him in the butt as he walks out the front door? I never thought that this day would happen. I only met you a week ago, but it feels like I have known you for months."

"Darren, I am pleased that you are part of the team here. You are a valuable member, and I am going to depend on you to take on more responsibility after you get everything in your financial department buttoned up and running smoothly."

Darren straightened up, obviously feeling proud that he had made such a good impression on me.

"When I joined my former company eight years ago, I was the CFO," I told him. "That company was *the* best. It was in good shape when I started there, but I still upgraded everything in my department so that it could run efficiently even without me in the building. The owners noticed how well my department ran so they promoted me to be the chief operating officer also. The promotion made me responsible for managing the total organization. Initially, I thought that it was going to be a struggle to take on more responsibility, but I was wrong. It was much easier because I could manage all the executives with good coordination and communication. I miss my old team; they were the best. I intend to reproduce it as closely as possible."

"Well, Bob, you have me pumped. I quit this job three times in the past year because I did not trust Craig, and rightfully so. He would have thrown me under the bus in a heartbeat if I had signed that borrowing base report with the overstated numbers he sent to the bank. I hope that we work together for a long time, Bob. I know that I will learn a lot from you. I have already in just four days. Within a short period, I also know I can trust you."

"Darren, stay close and pay attention. If you provide me the support I need to fix this company, we will be very successful together." With a big smile on my face, I said, "I think finance people are the smartest people in the world. I also think that salespeople pay my salary, so I treat them well too. Life is good, my friend. Breakfast in on me! Let's get to the office . . . we have a lot of work to do!"

"Agreed but breakfast is my treat. As I said earlier, you have made my day. The least I could do is buy you breakfast!"

* * *

When I arrived at the office and sat down at my desk, Donna showed up at my door with a cup of coffee for me in her hand and a smile on her face. "Bob, I figured that you are going to need this to start your day." I thanked her and asked her to have a seat. I got up, and as I was closing my office door, Darren showed up and handed me the reports we talked about at breakfast.

"Darren, why don't you join us, I want to talk about our meeting at the end of the day, today."

"Yes, sir."

"Donna, I am going to terminate Craig and Trish today. Because you have a good relationship with both people, I would like you to arrange the meeting with Craig and Trish at four o'clock in the conference room."

"Okay, I can handle that."

"I am going to explain that their employment here ends today, and then you can talk to them about the COBRA benefits and anything else you need to cover with an exit interview. Also, Donna, Darren created a schedule of Craig's and Trish's reimbursed personal expenses charged to the company. We are going to adjust their final paychecks by the amount that is on each schedule."

Donna asked, "Bob if we are going to be kicking their butts out today, why are we going through the hassle of adjusting their paychecks?"

> **Profit Improvement:** The expenses from Darren's schedule were more than the final check for both Craig and Trish. Rather than attempt to collect the whole balance that they had charged the company, I reduced their paycheck down to $100 and ignored the balance. **Cost savings: $12,035.**

"Donna, good question. I did it because it is the right thing to do!"

"Yes, you are right, I agree."

"After you finish, you can go with Trish to clean out her stuff from her office, and Darren will do the same with Craig."

"Darren, you are going to have to get on the network and change their passwords immediately before the four o'clock meeting. I also want to change the locks on the outside doors once they are gone today."

"Bob, I will call the locksmith and have him here at five o'clock today."

Donna asked, "Bob, what is the reason that you are firing them?"

"Craig is getting fired because there are three sexual harassment complaints filed against him this week. Then, I am going to tell Trish that we are discontinuing selling training for the company, so her position is being eliminated and will not be replaced."

Donna commented, "Good, we now have a plan. Getting this transaction behind us is exciting! The atmosphere in this company is going to change quickly. It is going to be a new company starting Monday morning with those two gone."

I got a call from Tina, the receptionist, to tell me that our bank officers were in the front lobby. I asked Darren to get them and meet me in the conference room.

On my way to the meeting, I stopped by Tom's office to talk to him briefly about the year-to-date sales by salesperson report I had just received. I wanted to show him how his sales team was doing. Tom reviewed the information on the report and shook his head as if he could not believe the numbers.

"Tom, I want to call your attention to the bottom half of the report. I have a meeting right now with some bankers. After I finish, if you have a few minutes, I would like to review the information with you."

"Sure, Bob, I will be here until eleven o'clock."

"Thanks, Tom."

"Bob, I will have some recommendations for you by the time you come back from your meeting."

"Thank you, sir, see you in a few."

I went to the conference room where Darren and the two bankers sat. Darren introduced me to Stan, the vice president/loan officer, and Glen, the branch manager. I sat down at the table and handed both my business card. "Gentlemen, I know you both must have hectic schedules, so I will not keep you here long. It is my understanding that this company has used your bank for several years now. Unfortunately, I am not familiar with your bank, but that is not important right now. I wanted to introduce myself and let you know that I am now the president of ABC Computer Distributors. I am in the process of looking at every functional area of the business to improve the profitability of the company. Cash and cash management is important to me. I know that we are not using any of your treasury services at the bank right now. We have cash sitting idle in our checking account and the only people making money on our funds is your bank. So, I would like you to meet with Darren and share with him how our company can work with your bank more efficiently to maximize our return on the funds sitting in our checking accounts."

"Mr. Curry, we have several different options for your company to invest your idle funds. Could I share them with you now?" Glen offered.

Profit Improvement: Better cash management will save the company in interest expense just by making this simple change of paying down the loan balance daily rather than weekly. **Estimated savings: $52,000 for the next 12 months.**

"Glen, you can share them with Darren, he is much better at this stuff than I am. However, I must warn you, Darren does not want to hear about several different options, he only wants to hear about the best option. Our goal, sir, is to pay down our line of credit daily with the available funds because our rate of interest that we are paying our floor-planning company is much higher than any interest income that we could earn at your bank. I believe that Darren is going to tell you that we would like our money moved to pay down our line of credit the quickest, cheapest, and most efficient way daily. Therefore, I would like to thank you for coming in to meet me, and I look forward to a long mutually successful business relationship between our two companies. Darren, please do not forget to share with these men that we are planning to double our sales next year, which means that our cash deposits are going to double also. Darren would like to fix our current banking relationship now before our volume doubles."

I stood up, shook their hands, and left the room.

* * *

I went back to Tom's office to talk again about the report I had given him ten minutes earlier. I knocked gently on his open office door and walked in.

Tom looked up said, "That was a fast meeting!"

"It was with bankers. I usually don't like bankers."

Tom laughed and said, "I hope you like sales managers!"

"Tom, I do, salespeople pay my salary, and I always treat salespeople well, if they sell!"

"Well, Bob, it looks like we have one superstar, five salespeople who are doing fine, eight people who need to wake up quickly, and three people who should be gone. The bottom three are heavy baggage that we do not need. I will put together a PIP (Performance Improvement Plan) immediately to light a fire under the eight salespeople who need to get moving with selling product or get moving out the door. Either way, I will get them moving!"

"Tom, I think that salespeople will get a wake-up call at the sales meeting today. I also think that if we make three nonproducing salespeople disappear, that will give the rest of the group a wake-up call."

"How do you suggest we deal with the bottom three?"

"How do *you* suggest we deal with the bottom three people in *your* department?"

"Hmm, good question, Bob. I will talk to Donna and ask her to have an exit interview with all three after I terminate them before noon today. Are you okay with that plan?"

"I am, but let me ask you a question: do you think that one of the two women on your bottom three could be moved over to the sales support department and be an asset to the company there?"

Tom's eyes lit up. "Bob, I did not even think about that option! It's a great idea."

"I will let you figure out who you want to keep and who you want to terminate. Make sure to adjust the salary of whomever you transfer over to sales support to fit with that department's salary structure."

"I will get with Donna right now and take care of these terminations and the transfer. Bob, I think that I have already decided, Charlene is going to move over to sales support, assuming she agrees to the transfer. Otherwise, she will be terminated with the others."

"Please speak to Darren to remove their passwords from the computer system and make sure that the people you are terminating do not take anything with them that is company property, such as a customer list."

"Bob, you do know that the bottom person on the list is Craig's cousin, Frank. Frank was hired by Craig to sell service. The only thing he does around here is chasing the sales girls around. He is worse than Craig."

> When an employee performance review is below acceptable performance, it is always extremely important that the review be written up in detail, signed, and dated by both parties—the employee and the supervisor. It takes a little time to write up the review, but it takes a long time and a lot of money to defend a wrongful termination lawsuit.

"Tom, please tell Donna and Darren to check the old employee manual to see if there is a severance policy. If there is one, comply with whatever it says. If there is not one, pay everyone two weeks salary. And if there is not a severance policy, please ask Donna to draft one and email it to me."

"Okay, Bob will do."

"Tom, terminations of employees should take you less than five minutes to accomplish. You terminate them for nonperformance issues, and they are going to receive two weeks salary as severance. Tom, how long have these people worked for the company?"

"Too long, all three less than two years. I have talked to each of them several times."

> **Profit Improvement:** One of the essential action items I accomplish first when I do a turnaround is identify the non-performing managers and employees and deal with the problems. Terminating Frank and the other salesperson reduced the payroll and benefits cost to get the company closer to breakeven. **Estimated savings: $132,500 for the next 12 months.**

"Did you put anything in their personnel files after your one-on-one meetings?"

"Yes, I documented their nonperformance several times and added the information to their personnel files."

"Good, then we are not in a risky position for terminating them and then one of them suing us for wrongful termination."

As I was leaving, Nancy walked in and grabbed my hand to pull me back into Tom's office. I had no idea what was going on.

Nancy said, "Bob, please sit down." Nancy closed Tom's office door and turned around.

She told us that she had just come from visiting her customer this morning, and he had given her a purchase order for $18.2 million. He also gave her a $4.5 million check. She pulled out the PO and the check from her briefcase and handed them to me. She had a smile on her face that she could not control. Tom stood up from his chair behind the desk and gave Nancy a big hug and a kiss on the cheek, which was permissible in the office because they were married.

"Stand up, Bob, you get a hug too," Nancy said with that smile still plastered on her face. "You are responsible, too, for getting this deal done with the financing. You also negotiated the special pricing to increase the gross profit!" The increase was precisely $1,365,000.

I stood up, and Nancy gave me a big hug.

"Life is good!" I said, and Nancy and Tom wholeheartedly agreed.

I took the purchase order and the customer's deposit check to Darren and asked him to have Patrick deliver the funds to the bank immediately after he made copies and put the documents into the customer's file. I told Darren to transfer the funds as soon as they were available to pay down the line of credit. I also asked Darren to give a copy of the PO to Alan in purchasing so he could begin creating purchase orders to our suppliers to buy all the hardware and software. I requested Darren to schedule a meeting with Tom, Nancy, Alan, and Tim on Monday at noon in the conference room.

"Darren, I would like to talk about the coordination of the purchasing all the laptops, servers, and software," I told him. "We need to plan for receiving the inventory, staging the complete order, then shipping everything to the customer on time during the first week of January."

Darren wrote down all my instructions, and then he read them back to me to make sure that he did not miss anything. After I confirmed that he captured all my instructions, he got up from his desk and started to see everyone about scheduling the meeting.

I went to find Roger; he was in his office. I wanted to understand why he would double up the technicians on service calls. He told me he had two choices, double them up or send several of the technicians home due to lack of service call demand. I said, "Roger, the second option sure would have saved the company some payroll dollars when there are no service calls for these guys."

"Bob, the decision was not mine; Craig tied my hands and made the decision."

"I figured that was the case. Craig said he would talk to all the salespeople to start selling more service to get the service department busy again."

"How long ago was that?"

"Since June, there has not been an increase in service at all since then."

"Thank you for your time, Roger."

"Bob, is there anything else I can do to help you?"

"Yes, there is, Roger, now that I think about it. How well do you know the skills and abilities of all the technicians?"

"I know all these guys, Bob; I know them all very well."

"Okay, then, I want you to write a list of everyone in the department and then rate each technician from a one to ten, one meaning terrible and ten meaning excellent. I want you to rate their skills and abilities on their overall skills to handle our average service call for our customers."

"Bob, if you have a few minutes, I will do it for you right now."

"Okay, Roger, I will make time for this."

Roger wrote down the twenty names on a tablet of all the service techs and started to rate each one as requested. As I was watching him, there was no hesitation in his decisions about assessing each of the technicians. There were ten on the list that Roger rated with an eight, nine, or ten. Surprisingly, there was not one tech with a four, five, six, or seven. There were a bunch of threes; one technician was a two and two were ones. As I scanned the list, I started feeling sick to my stomach. I looked at Roger and asked him if he was confident about these ratings for each technician.

"Bob, I am very confident. Look at your year-to-date revenue schedule for the techs that Darren created for you. Now check where the lowest-rated technicians are on your list. Every technician rated with a three, two, or one were at the bottom of the list for billable hours."

"Okay, Roger, I trust you with your ratings. But your scorings do beg the question, why are these people still on the payroll for this company?"

"Bob, Craig would not let me terminate any of the technicians."

"Thank you for your time and help, Roger. You have helped me make another important decision today, and I appreciate it."

"Bob, can you give me an idea of what you are planning to do with these guys, especially the ones on the bottom of the list who are rated poorly?"

"Not right now, but I will give you an update as soon as I finish my plan."

"Thank you, sir."

* * *

It was 10:00 a.m., and I received a call from the receptionist, Tina.

"Mr. Curry, there is a very tall man out here named Chris who wants to see you."

I was surprised. "Please tell Chris to have a seat, and I will be out in a minute."

When I walked out, Chris stood up, shook my hand, and hugged me. "Bob, I am so glad to be here. I am looking forward to working together."

"Chris, you are not as happy as I am to get you started. But I did not expect to see you until one o'clock today."

"I could not wait until one o'clock," Chris said unabashedly, "so I got dressed and came in now. And, as you requested, here is the signed and dated job offer letter!"

I took the letter from him and said, "Thank you for remembering, Chris. Okay, good, please follow me to my office."

Once we were in my office, I gave Chris a copy of the agenda for both the sales and service meetings. He read them both and commented, "Bob, you are trying to motivate these salespeople to get out there and get some sales, huh?"

"Chris, the sales team's successes are what pays our salaries. I am going to motivate and fire these people up to get out them to run through walls to grow our sales volume. I plan to do the same thing with the service department. I want to motivate them to provide outstanding service and refer sales from the customers to the sales department. I am going to pay the service department referral fees for sales that they find and pass on to the salespeople."

"I like that idea, Bob. My old employer did not do that, but I like it."

"Chris, I have a philosophy, everyone should be a salesperson, which includes you and me. This company sells other company's products and services them to make a profit. The more hardware we sell, the more service calls your department will have. The more service calls your department has, the more money we are going to make. It is an easy equation. Chris, I am going to focus on getting more sales with the sales team. I need you to concentrate on delivering quality service to keep our customers and keep them all very happy."

> I firmly believe that anyone who works for a company that sells services and/or products should be a salesperson for that company regardless of their position in the company.

"That will not be a problem," Chris assured me. "I have laid out a plan on how to hit the ground running once I start."

"That is great, Chris. When we first talked about your working here, I knew that you were the right person for the job!"

I then gave Chris a copy of the rating sheet that Roger had just written for me about the service technicians and the year-to-date billings recap per technician. He looked at it and said, "This is ridiculous. If these technicians are not billing, what are they doing all day?"

"My controller just gave me this report, and a few minutes ago, Roger informally rated all the service department technicians. I almost lost my breakfast when I saw both schedules."

> **Profit Improvement:** Terminating the ten service technicians accomplished some significant goals. These ten people were on the payroll due to poor hiring practices by the company. All ten were unproductive and a burden to the organization. The employees who were not terminated received a crystal-clear message on Black Friday: if you are not a productive employee, you are not going to be employed by this company very long. **The terminations reduced the payroll burden by $550,000. The reduction in staff improved the company to cash flow breakeven.**

Chris looked at the two lists and said that he knew some of the techs on the top of the list.

"Well, Chris, you may not get a chance to know some of them. I was planning on terminating all the guys at the bottom of the list."

"Bob, you do not have to do that, I will handle it."

"Are you serious, Chris?"

"Sure, I have no problem getting rid of clowns who are doing nothing but dragging the company down."

"Okay, good, then I will introduce you to Roger. You get with him and have Roger call the employees who rated as a one, two, or three on this list. Have them come to the office as soon as possible. You and Roger can do the terminations. I will talk to Donna and Darren to get all their final paychecks ready. Chris, make it brief. Tell them that we do not have enough work for the number of technicians we have in the department, so we are laying off the techs to match the current workload. That is all you need to say, nothing else."

"Okay, Bob, I get it!"

"Please tell Roger also to stay on script."

"I will keep him under control. We will take care of this, I promise!"

I immediately went to update Donna and Darren. A laugh escaped my lips when I told them that Chris was here and that he and Roger were in the process of firing ten technicians. What was humorous was that Chris was now the company "hatchet man" and was not even on the payroll yet. I handed Donna the list of the ten employees about to be terminated and said, "Please add Chris to the payroll as of today." The least I could do was pay him for the day since he was getting rid of half the service department.

"Darren and I will handle everything, we have it covered," Donna confirmed.

"Just to recap these personnel moves, so we are on the same page: Today, we are terminating Craig, Trish, two salespeople, and ten service technicians, and we are hiring Chris. We are transferring one salesperson over to the sales support department."

"Who is that, Bob?"

"I believe it was Charlene, but please check with Tom, as he made that decision earlier. Please clarify with him who is staying and who is going. But I know for sure that we decided to terminate Frank."

"Bob, I now have the total list of payroll changes, and we"— she looked over at Darren, who nodded at her— "agree with your decisions."

"Okay, good!" I said, then I turned my attention to other matters.

* * *

Profit Improvement: Cash management for a company is usually an easy function to improve, and the rewards can be immediate reduction of the loan balance and interest expense. In this case, **we reduced our interest expense by $52,000.**

"Darren, how did your meeting go with the bankers?" I asked.

"Bob, it went well. We are now going to 'ACH' the funds from our bank account to pay down the line of credit Monday through Friday at four p.m. I was concerned that Kevin's company would not credit our paydown until the next day, but that is not the case. (In banking, "ACH" stands for Automated Clearing House, which is a network used for electronic payments and money transfers. ACH is a way to move money between banks without using paper checks, wire transfers, credit card networks, or cash.) The new cash management procedures will save us approximately fifty-two thousand dollars for the year in interest expense just by making this simple change. And, Bob—Glen, and Stan commented about you after you left the meeting. They said, 'Boy, Bob is a no-nonsense guy,'"

When working to improve the profit performance of a company, it has been my experience that it is not a case of one thing being 100 percent wrong with the company. Rather, it is 100 things are 1 percent wrong. When you keep clean up the one-percenters, the business becomes more profitable.

"What did you reply?" I asked.

Darren smiled. "I told our friendly bankers that I have never known anyone who could accomplish so much so quickly. I don't know anyone who could go at your pace, Bob. You have materially changed this business in five days. I would not have thought that it would be possible. And, to top it off, you have done it with a distressed company with extremely limited funds."

"Well, thank you, Darren, but we have a long way to go before we can relax and catch our breath."

*   *   *

The time for our first sales meeting was fast approaching. I knew the outcome of this meeting would be critical to the success of the turnaround of this company. Most of the employees who worked for this organization were either salespeople or service technicians. Those were all the "revenue generators" for this business. If I could manage them properly and make each salesperson productive, I could accomplish this turnaround a lot faster. I just needed to pump them up, get them excited, and show them that they all have a great future with this company!

It occurred to me that this task was going to be difficult because the former president of this organization—Craig—had been sexually harassing the women on the sales team, which meant that this sales group had minimal to no trust in the management team. Most of them thought that Tom supported Nancy and only Nancy. While Craig's leadership goal was to get as many of the women in this company into his bedroom, my goal was to show each salesperson how they could be successful. I wanted them to know that I was going to support them by eliminating any roadblocks in their way.

I already had a feeling that Tom had turned the page to a new chapter in the last few days by being proactive and riding with the salespeople to attend sales calls. I knew that I had Nancy on my team after I helped her close that $18.2 million-plus deal. I felt great because I was able to recruit and hire Chris to clean up the service department. Now it was my responsibility to fire up this group of salespeople to start closing big deals and selling service contracts.

When I walked into the sales conference room at 1:55, I was very impressed. Everyone who was supposed to attend the meeting was there with a notepad and pen in front of them ready to take notes during the meeting. I was sure that Tom had shared the meeting rules he learned at Wednesday's management meeting with everyone here. Tom stood up and told me that he would like to start our sales meeting by introducing everyone in the room.

I said, "Tom, thank you, I would appreciate that, go for it."

Tom began with the salesperson on his left, Sandi. He told me how long she had been working for the company. Then he shared a humorous story about how she had once spilled coffee all over herself right before a meeting with a client. Sandi didn't look embarrassed. The group, I found out later, had agreed to let Tom share these blunders with me to break the ice.

Tom flawlessly introduced every salesperson, the sales support employees, and Alan from purchasing with one of these short stories after giving the factual details of their employment. Again, I was very impressed. After Tom had completed the introductions, he shared a funny story about himself. As he told it, he had flipped over backward in a conference room chair while sitting with a client on a sales call. He did add that he had closed that deal despite looking like a fool. I was sure that it had not been easy for him to get back up *and* close the deal after that fall.

Pleased with how Tom had started this meeting, I introduced myself and shared my professional and personal background. I told the group about why I was here at ABC Computer Distributors and my list of short-term goals. Then I shared one of my own humbling experiences since Tom had done such a great job sharing all the others.

"I was working for a public accounting firm right out of college. I assisted in an audit of a company in Virginia. My sister lived very close to the client company we were auditing, so I stayed at her home during the three weeks I was on the audit. My sister had two large

Great Danes (Thor and Jaws), which she had rescued earlier that year. I knew with two large dogs with names like Thor and Jaws; there was going to be trouble! I was staying in a spare bedroom on the second floor. When I went to bed the first night, I closed my bedroom door and got into bed under the covers. Jaws jumped up on the bedroom door and pushed it open. He came into the room and crawled up to the bottom of the bed. It was a double bed, so if he was on the opposite of the bed, I was okay with him being there. Besides, as big as he was, I did not want him mad at me."

"The next morning when I woke up, Jaws was gone, and so was one of my dress shoes. I had only one pair with me for work. As soon as I noticed that one of my shoes was missing, I immediately jumped out of bed and ran to find Jaws. I found him downstairs in the kitchen eating my shoe. I grabbed it off him, but not before the whole backside of my shoe was gone. He bit it off and ate it. As I was walking back upstairs to my bedroom, my sister was coming down the steps and said, 'Be careful to keep your shoes away from the dogs; they will eat them.' So, I showed her the shoe and said, 'You are a day late with your advice.'

"I had to be at the client's job site to start the audit at eight a.m. There was no way that I would be able to find an open shoe store before I had to report to the company for my first day of the audit as a junior auditor. Therefore, I went to work with one shoe that was okay, and the other shoe was a 'slip-on' because Jaws ate the back with one big bite. I walked funny the whole morning dragging my left foot trying to keep the shoe on. Everyone at the company thought that I had a leg injury. I was so embarrassed because I did not want to call attention to my damaged shoe. At lunch, I went out to a local mall and purchased a new pair of shoes." I showed everyone in the room how I walked with the mangled shoe. Everyone was laughing at my story. I was pleased that the meeting was going so well.

Then I said, "Okay, now it's time to get down to business." I first explained to the group that the bank had hired me to turn the company around. "My task is to implement several changes to the firm to make it cash flow positive again," I explained. "Over the past week, I have reviewed the financial statements for the last two years. I have a list of problems that I am planning to resolve. I have a mission right now to get this company to a breakeven point as quickly as possible. I am planning to make several changes to improve the financial status of this business. I am going to share some of them with this group right now. The reason I am sharing this information is that everyone in this room is an intricate part of the profit improvement plan. I am looking for an increased effort from every salesperson in this conference room today to double your sales volume in the next three months compared to your last three months. If you accomplish this, I promise you that the rewards for your sales efforts will be much better than before I joined the company. We are going to support each of you to be successful for as long as you work hard for this company. I would like to talk now about a couple of immediate changes beyond the revisions to the commission plan. I believe you will be pleased with each of them."

I began a monologue that was sure to keep them all interested:

"We are going to hire another employee to work in the sales support department. We are anticipating an increase in sales volume by the sales department shortly. Therefore, they are going to need help to stay current with processing sale orders.

"Tom is going to be riding with each salesperson over the next three weeks to assist each of you on the sales call to close more sales."

"Tom and I will be helping each of you if you run into any roadblocks during the sales process. For example, one of the sales staff in the room recently landed a more than eighteen-million-dollar customer order. To fulfill this sale, we needed an increase in our line of credit from the bank. As of yesterday, our bank has increased our credit line by ten million dollars because they trust that this company's sales volume is going to skyrocket immediately. I would love to have to call our banker every hour to get an increase in our loan because of additional ten-million- or fifteen-million-dollar orders from the salespeople in this meeting today!

"Next, I have hired a new service manager, who is with us today attending this meeting. I am going to introduce you to Chris in a minute, but I first want to finish my explanation about how Tom and I plan to support this sales team."

"I am handing out to each salesperson a list of ten different target companies that are in the Philadelphia geographic area. No one from this organization has ever sold any hardware, software, or service to any of these corporations. It is now your responsibility to contact each of the ten target companies on your list to schedule an appointment to sell each of them our products and services. Please be aware that businesses like the ones on your list usually have several people in their organization who have the authority to sign purchase orders to buy the types of products and services that we sell."

"Every salesperson should be aware that at each of the next four sales meetings, we will be reviewing the results of your efforts on each of your ten target companies assigned. I want you all to know that I expect every salesperson to have contacted all ten businesses to schedule appointments with their managers who purchase computer hardware, software, and service. Please don't let me down with this mission. I want you all to be prepared for our meeting next week to have several of your targets contacted and appointments scheduled."

When I completed my monologue, the new sales reporting system was next on my agenda. Currently, the whiteboard created for this purpose was hidden under a big white sheet. At noon that day, I had given all the target lists to Amanda, Traci, and Vicki from the sales support department. I asked them to draw a grid on the whiteboard in the conference room. On the left side of the whiteboard from top to bottom was one through ten. On the top of the whiteboard were the names of the fourteen salespeople. Below each salesperson's name, they listed the ten target companies assigned to that salesperson: "the customer target list."

The fourteen salespeople's names on the top of the board were listed alphabetically and in different colored markers as were the names of the target companies listed below them.

Amanda, Traci, and Vicki also purchased markers with whiteboard magnets to report each salesperson's progress with their newly assigned customer targets. The markers would indicate one of the following stages achieved with the customer:

1. Appt. Made

2. PO Received

3. Invoice Paid

4. BONUS PAID!

Besides the fact that it looked like a work of art, my goal for creating such a reporting system was to motivate the salespeople to progress through the sales process with their new target customers to sell computers and service contracts. It would be exciting to report each salesperson's progress publicly on a whiteboard in the sales conference room. The sales manager and every salesperson could see how they were doing compared to the other thirteen salespeople.

In the military, when soldiers do something noteworthy, they earn medals that they wear on their chest of the uniforms for everyone to see. Our system rewards the salespeople by posting their new customer sales on the whiteboard for everyone in the sales department to see plus we bonus them either $500 or $2,500 in addition to their commission for closing deals with their target customers.

This system was a great idea because each week at the sales meeting, I would pay the salesperson the bonus and that salesperson could post the magnet on the whiteboard indicating the BONUS PAID. Each week, everyone at the meeting could see who was doing the best job of getting appointments and closing a sale with at least $5,000 or $25,000 in gross profit.

Later, at the end of the sales meeting, I gave Amanda, Traci, and Vicki each a gift card for dinner for two at Ruth's Chris Steak House as a thank-you for doing such a great job on the whiteboard. They were thrilled.

Next, I said, "I am distributing a copy of our new sales commission plan. This incentive program will start on Monday morning." Then I spoke about each point on the plan:

"Since my goal is for each of you to start selling more service contracts, I am increasing the commission rate on the sales of all service contracts until the end of March of next year. The old commission rate was twenty percent of the gross profit. The new rate will be thirty percent for the next three and a half months."

"Each salesperson's commission rate will be cut by twenty percent from twenty percent of the gross profit to sixteen percent—for any month on sales of hardware and software if the salesperson does not sell a minimum of twenty-five thousand in service contracts during that month. If the sales rep sells twenty-five thousand or more of new service contracts, their commission rate on computers and software sales will increase by twenty percent—from twenty percent to twenty-four percent for the month."

"Any salesperson who sells more than fifty thousand in service contracts in a month wins a four-day, three-night cruise for the salesperson and their spouse. If any salesperson sells one hundred thousand or more in new service contracts, the vacation trip will be for seven days, six nights."

"Any salesperson who does *not* sell any service for the month goes on my list."

The goal of everyone on the sales staff was to not be on "my list" more than two times. I decided that I would let the salespeople figure out the impact on their job if they were a sales rep who earned a spot on "my list" multiple times.

I could tell by the expressions on everyone's faces that they were both excited and intimidated by my plan. Then I covered the next item:

"Right now, there are fourteen salespeople in this conference room, and as of the first of April, I am only going to need twelve salespeople. The top twelve salespeople, those with the highest gross profit dollars for the next three and a half months, get to stay. The other two will need to look for new jobs."

This last item caused quite a few raised eyebrows, but I wanted to send these salespeople a message that it was time to buckle down, get out there, and sell. I planned to reward the top producers much better than in the past. I did not need or want anyone who was not motivated, willing to work hard, and do their job working for this organization.

"Everyone, please read the plan, and if you have any questions, I will answer all questions at the end of this meeting."

I told them to please pay attention to the bonuses paid for the *first* purchase from each of the target customers with over $5,000 and $25,000 in gross profit. If the first sale to one of their target customers is more than $5,000 but less than $25,000 gross profit, the salesperson will receive a $500 cash bonus at the next sales meeting following the customer's payment of the invoice. If the gross profit is more than $25,000, the salesperson will receive $2,500.

When I was sure that was clear, I told them that we were going to have a sales contest for the last three weeks of December. The salesperson who sold the most service contracts from now until December 31 would win an iPad. A few of the salespeople expressed their interest in winning.

Next, I told them that Tom and I would be setting a sales quota for every salesperson in the department. With a few exceptions, the quarterly sales quota, starting January 1, would be $1.6 million for hardware and software sales and $150,000 for service contracts. I added, "If each of you does what your potential is, your annual income will be approximately three to four times what it was for this year. I want you all to know that I respect our salespeople. Your sales pay the salaries of everyone in this company. If we do not have sales, we can shut down the company right now."

Satisfied with all that I had covered so far in this meeting, I said, "I would like to complement each of you for being on time for this sales meeting. I was impressed. I have a few rules about the sales, service, and management meetings with organizations that I lead. I set a regular weekly date and time for future management meetings. After the meetings are set and on everyone's calendar, I expect everyone to attend and be on time without exception. Effective communication and the efficient use of time are critical when a company is in the process of going from losing money to being profitable."

I passed out the meeting rules for this sales department (see page 372) and added, "Attendance of the sales manager, the complete sales team, the sales support department, and the purchasing department manager is mandatory at all future meetings. The sales meetings are every Friday at two o'clock. Post the meetings on your calendar for the balance of the year and the first quarter of next year to ensure that there are no scheduling conflicts for any of the meetings in the future. If the Friday falls on a holiday, Tom will notify the schedule change at least a week in advance."

I noticed Chris straightening his jacket because he surmised that it was time for his introduction, and he was right. "Next, I would like to introduce our new service department manager. His name is Chris, and I am very excited to have him here as part of our team. I have known Chris for many years, and he has quite a solid reputation in our industry. He was to be formally starting with our company on Monday, but he was so excited about joining our organization, he came to work today. Chris, welcome to ABC Computer Distributors."

There was a polite round of applause.

"Thank you, Bob," Chris said in a clear and confident voice. "It is nice to meet you all, and I look forward to meeting with each of you to talk one on one. I know that this service department is crucial to the success of this company's profitability. I can promise you that I am committed to improving the delivery of technical services to this company's customers. I am going to be interviewing each person in the service department to develop a schedule of technological skills by technician. I can better assign the service calls to the technicians based on the customer's problem. Once we have this list of competencies developed, we will be scheduling training for each of the weaknesses of every technician, so everyone on the team is qualified to handle every call."

"To improve the quality of the service technicians' efforts to the customers, I am going to implement a new Customer Survey Program. This post-service customer survey procedure will verify the completed service call and determine if the customers were happy with the outcome of the technician's work. The goal is to improve the service department's production in revenue and the quality of the service. I will be contacting each salesperson to get on your calendar so that we can sit down together and talk about any issues you may have with the service department. I am here to help you become more successful in selling service contracts. The more service contracts you sell, the more money you and the rest of the company makes. Thank you to everyone here for your time. Please feel free to contact me anytime, which is why I am here, to support you and manage the service department."

"Thank you, Chris!" I said cheerfully, knowing full well that I had hired the right person for the job.

The last item on the agenda was for questions and answers. I told everyone, "I have covered a great deal of information in a one hour. I know that there are many changes. I am sure everyone here understands why I have made all these changes. If not, I assure you that each change is to make this company profitable again. Now, I am opening the floor to any questions you may have. Please do not hold back anything. I didn't!"

"Mr. Curry, if you don't remember, I am Jenna. My question is what happens if a salesperson does not make their monthly quota?"

"Jenna, please call me Bob. I believe that salespeople not making their quota will not be an issue with this company in the future. There are several reasons for this. The first reason is that I have increased the commission structure for the sales department, which, I hope, will motivate everyone. Second, I have hired who I believe is a quality manager to oversee the service department. It is these reasons that will give every salesperson the confidence now to sell service contracts. You can now trust that the service department is going to do a great job for your customers. The third reason is that we have a salesperson in the room, and I will not name any names, will I Nancy, who will close this year with over twenty-seven million dollars in sales. I am not asking every salesperson to match our top salesperson's performance, only achieve a sales quota equal to twenty-six percent of her sales total. I will also tell this sales depart-ment that if you start selling the way I know you can, I will add several more employees to the sales support department, as well as to the purchasing department. I will give the sales team in this company all the support they need. My goal is to motivate every salesperson to spend more time in the field with their customers and less time doing the paperwork to make the customer order happen timely. Jenna, did I answer your question?"

"No, you did not," she said.

"Hmm, you are right, my apologies. Let me try again. Jenna, if there is a salesperson or several people in the sales department not making their sales quota, then I have made some bad decisions personally, and I will review everything I have done to figure out where I have failed. There are not many people in the world who hate to fail more than I do. If you are not making your monthly sales quota, Tom and I will be reviewing the details of why you are not making it. We will help you accomplish your sales quota and our overall all sales goals."

"May I ask what you are planning as the sales goal for this company for next year?" she asked next.

"Sure, Jenna, a very nice round number—one hundred twenty million dollars. We are in the process of breaking down the sales of hardware, software, and service, but we will have those numbers within the next week. Are there any other questions?"

The room was silent.

"No, well then, thank you, each one of you! With the support of every single employee in this company, the sales department is the team that will make this business successful again. GO WITH CONFIDENCE!"

* * *

Feeling great about the sales meeting, Chris and I walked into the service department conference room at 2:58 p.m. and every service technician was already there waiting for us. As Chris and I sat down at the table, five of the technicians got up and walked over to shake Chris's hand.

"Gentlemen," I said, "please talk among yourselves for a few minutes, and help yourself to some coffee. Chris and I have a few things to go over." I had some questions for Chris, and I didn't want to be overheard.

"Chris, do you know some of these guys?" I asked for his ears only.

"Bob, computer technicians, are like bankers, they move around from one company to another for a dollar-an-hour raise. Those guys worked for me between three and five years ago."

"Were they any good back then?"

"Since I let them go without trying to talk them into staying, they obviously were not computer service experts. And, Bob, aren't you going to thank me for being your 'hatchet man' today and getting rid of those ten pieces of deadwood ... I mean those ten unproductive service technicians?"

"Chris, I cannot thank you enough for taking care of that. It is appreciated. Tom made two salespeople 'disappear' at lunch today, and at right after this meeting, at four o'clock, Craig and Trish are going to bite the dust too."

"Boy, Bob, you must have quite a reputation. Are you going to have someone else in the company start your car today—just in case one of the fourteen ex-employees rigs it to blow up as you turn the key?"

"Here are my car keys, Chris. Can we meet at five o'clock today out in the parking lot?"

"I am not getting anywhere close to your car today, Bob. In fact, I am going to move my car away from yours to avoid damage from the explosion."

I didn't take our lighthearted banter seriously at all, but it was time to get serious. As the talk among the techs died down and those who had gotten coffee returned to their seats, I could tell the group was feeling stress. After all, we had cut the department in half at lunchtime by terminating ten technicians.

I started the meeting. "Gentlemen, thank you for being here on time. I passed out an agenda for the meeting yesterday that I hope you all received. If you did not, we have additional copies up here (see page 362). I hope that you all have a notebook to take notes because we have lots of information to review today."

All at the same time, they held up their notebooks. Roger must have also talked to the group about the meeting rules he had learned at Wednesday's management meeting.

"As everyone is probably aware, the company has not been doing well financially. My name is Bob Curry, and I am the new president and CEO of the corporation. The bank has hired me to turn the company around to be profitable again in the future. I would like to accomplish several goals in the next three to six months. The service department is going to play a huge role in the profit improvement of this organization. That is the purpose of this meeting."

"My goals for the next ninety days are to make this company cash flow breakeven by aggressively growing the hardware, software, and service revenue. I also want to improve the quality of the service this department delivers to our customers. I believe that if we, as a team, accomplish these two simple goals, this company will be profitable very soon. These tasks are not going to be easy, but I know that if we all work together, we can accomplish them."

"To achieve these two goals, the first thing I have done was recruit and hire a new service manager who has several years of experience managing a very successful computer service department. He has an excellent reputation and the talent to manage this service organization profitably. Some of you already know Chris and have worked for him in the past. Therefore, you also know his no-nonsense management style. In a few minutes, I am going to ask him to talk to this group and share some of his goals for this department. But, first, I want to discuss some of the changes I plan to make, most of which you will benefit from and appreciate."

"I want everyone to know that nothing negative is going to happen to Roger. He is still going to be part of the service team. Craig promoted Roger on a temporary basis to manage the department until we could replace the service manager position. As of today, Roger is going to be doing service calls again for our customers, which is where he wants to be."

"This company has lacked any productivity reporting for the sales and service departments. I am going to ask the controller, Darren, to provide me a monthly report that is updated weekly. He will be creating reports documenting the billable hours by a service technician for the week- and month-to-date (see page 365). We are going to install a large whiteboard on the wall in the service department that will show the same information as my report. On the whiteboard, we will post the month-to-date revenue for each technician in this department. This way, every technician will be able to see his billable hours each week and for the month. For this department to contribute to the success and profitability of this company, each technician should invoice a total of ten thousand to fifteen thousand dollars every thirty days. For your information, that is not happening right now. By the way, gentlemen, please feel free to interrupt me to ask any questions that you may have as I am going over this information."

"Bob, I have a question," asked Rob.

"Thank you, Rob, what is your question?"

"What if we are not assigned service calls for the day or very few for the week?"

"Good question. First, the better your skills, the more calls you will be assigned. Second, we are planning training sessions you can attend to improve your skills. The better your technical skills, the more service calls you can accomplish, and therefore, the more you can invoice for the month. Chris will meet with each of you and develop a schedule of skills by technician so that he can properly assign the right technician to the service call according to his skill level in that technical area. Chris will test each of you to determine which service calls you can handle most efficiently. When Chris assigns you to the proper service calls based upon your level of skills, that gives you a better chance to be successful. I hope that answered your question."

Rob said he understood, and I continued, "Also, I am going to immediately incentivize the sales department with one and one-half times their standard commission rate to sell more service contracts.

I believe that the service department will soon be very active with many more service contracts to keep you all very busy. My goal is to at least double the average monthly service revenue in the next ninety days and then increase the revenue again by two hundred percent during the next ninety days."

"Those are some aggressive goals," Chris said matter-of-factly.

"Yes, Chris, they are, but I have always set my goals high so that when I accomplish them, it feels good, and the success is very evident to everyone. I am going to challenge you and this service department to achieve the goal of doubling the service revenue—the fourth quarter of this year compared to the first quarter of next year. I am going to fire up the sales department to get them productive with their sales of new customer service contracts. I need you all ready to handle those service contracts with exceptional service delivery!"

The technicians all seemed on board, and I was pleased by how carefully they were listening and how some of them were taking notes. I continued, "To turn around the financial situation of this company, I feel that it is important that I do everything necessary to improve the quality of the service for our clients. My goals are to increase the revenue production for the department as well as improve the quality of the service calls by the technicians. We are implementing a Customer Survey Program to report, analyze, and improve the service quality to each of our clients. This new survey is going to start next week. I am passing out a copy of the survey letter that is going to be given to every one of our clients after the completion of the service call, without exception (see page 364). As you can see, the survey asks the customer to answer six questions concerning the service call. The survey requests that the client rate the technician in six different areas. There are a few blank lines where the customer can write in their comments about the service call and the service technician."

"When assigning a service request to the technician for a client, he will also be given the customer's survey letter with a stamped envelope addressed to the president/CEO of the company. The survey letter will have the name of the client, service request number, the date, and the name of the technician already noted on the form. Each form has a serial number so that the service department can account for all forms during the month. After completing each service call successfully, the technician will give the survey and envelope to the customer. He will request that the customer complete all the questions, write a comment if they so desire, and then put the letter in the mail. When I receive the surveys in the mail, I will review each and hand them to the administrative assistant, Gina, in the service department. If there are any poor ratings on a survey from a customer, I will give a copy of the survey to Chris to ensure that he is aware of any customer problems."

Chris added, "And, gentlemen, I suggest you do your service calls with care, so the customers are not writing poor scores on the surveys. I hear that the new president of this company is ruthless when dealing with employees who upset our customers because of poor performance. Isn't that right, Bob?"

"Chris, I also heard the same comment somewhere. At the end of each month, Gina will follow up on any customer surveys that were not received back from the clients. After accounting for all the surveys, the accounting department will issue a report and distributed to Chris, me, and each service technician in the department. The report will include the following information: service order number, the date assigned, customer number, customer name, customer's employee requesting service, date service completed, hours invoiced, date customer survey received, and total customer survey rating (see page 365). We will be reviewing the reports during our weekly service department meeting on Fridays and rewarding technicians who receive the highest ratings from our customers. We will also discuss the problems when a technician receives a bad rating."

"The monthly report will list the number of service orders completed by a technician for the month and their average rating of the customer surveys for the month (see page 368). Two different reports, one by service technician showing the details by service order and the other listing each technician with a total of all the service calls and the average customer rating. This monthly report will show the total revenue for the whole department. This report will be sorted by the highest survey rating to the lowest by a technician."

"One of the positive changes that we are going to implement is, effective the first of January; the service department will be rewarding the top three technicians with the highest revenue for the month. At the end of January, the highest revenue-producing technicians will receive a gift card for dinner for two at the Ruth's Chris Steak House."

"Mr. Curry, just put the gift card in my locker at the end of January because I am going to win that contest!" said Troy.

I laughed. "Troy, I hope that you *do* win with a huge revenue total and that the other guys in the department are equal to you. I hope I have to give *everyone* a gift card because everyone doubles their billings every month!"

All the technicians shared in the laughter, but they looked determined now, like Troy.

"Also, effective in January, we will be rewarding the top-three technicians with the highest average rating from the service customer surveys. Please note that the technicians can win only one reward per month."

This system would create healthy competition among the techs; everyone would strive to be in the top three in the monthly report as well as the highest producer. And, for obvious reasons, none of them would want to be in the bottom five.

"In the near future, Chris will be meeting with each of you to discuss your technical skills to determine your strengths and weaknesses. He will then create a training schedule to upgrade your skills in various areas of computer service as needed. These training classes will be scheduled for Saturday mornings starting at nine and will finish no later than noon. There will be a technical test on that subject at the end of each class. Chris will issue certificates of completion to all the techs who pass the test. Technicians who are qualified enough in a certain technical subject to do the training for the other techs in the department will be paid for their time and rewarded for upgrading the skills of the other technicians in the department. We are paying the techs their hourly rate for attending the training classes."

I heard some sighs of relief in response to my statement that they would be paid to attend these classes. Giving up a Saturday morning for work is a big deal, especially if you're not getting paid, even if it will benefit you in the long run.

"Effective the first of January, the company will pay a one-thousand-dollar referral fee to any employee who refers a tech candidate to the company who is then interviewed, hired, and is still working for the company six months later."

Chris leaned forward and asked, "Does that include me, Bob?"

"Yes, Chris, it does. It includes *every* employee who works for this company."

Chris smiled wide because he already had several techs to refer.

I went on, "Effective immediately, the company will pay any employee a sales commission for referring lucrative sales opportunities to our sales department. I firmly believe everyone in this company should be a salesperson, even employees who work in the service department, sales support, and the receptionist. The sales commission will be equal to 5 percent of the gross profit on each order for that customer for one year."

One of the techs raised his hand, and at my nod, he asked, "How do you keep track of that? If I introduce a potential customer to someone on the sales team, the salespeople can just take the credit, can't they?

"Good question," I said, and then explained, "The employee who plans to make a referral should fill out a referral form and give it to Chris, who will then give a copy to sales manager and the controller. The sales manager will assign the referral to one of the salespeople, and the referring employee makes the introduction. The controller will register the referring employee on the commission schedule so that a commission check is issued for every sale to that customer and invoice paid in full. I have designed a form for each of you to use that will register you to receive the commissions when you refer a potential customer. If, in the future, you have a referral, complete the form, sign, date it, and give it to Chris. I hope that every one of you will be getting big monthly commission checks in the future. In fact, I hope that your commission checks are more than your salaries. Does anyone have any other questions about this referral program?"

> Whether or not they are in sales, every employee in a company should talk to every one of their friends, family, and associates to make them all aware that they work for a company with quality products and/or services to offer— in this case, a computer distributor that sells computer hardware, software, and IT services. To help motivate our employees to promote ABC Computer Distributors, I planned to pay referral fees and commissions to anyone who made a referral that turned into a profitable sale.

"I have a question," one of the techs said. "Do our current service-call customers qualify for a referral commission by the service technician?"

"Yes, but let me explain: assume you are on a service call at a customer's location and you find out that they are planning to quote a big computer order soon. If you bring that information back to the company and complete the referral form, you will receive a commission for that order if the salesperson did not already know the customer was going to make a purchase. If none of our sales staff has visited that client in the past thirty days, you will receive a commission on the order. I will handle disputes that arise between any salesperson and the referring employee, but there should not be any because the salesperson will still receive the full commission with or without the other employee's commission. In fact, I am sure they will encourage you all to find future orders. It is a 'win-win' situation for both parties and the company."

"We have recently ordered ABC Computer Distributors logoed thank-you note cards and envelopes, which will be available to everyone in the organization to use, including the service department. Unfortunately, the use of thank-you cards has almost disappeared from the business world. I believe that sending a thank-you note to a customer has a positive impact on the salesperson's business relationship with that customer."

Another tech raised his hand. At my nod, he asked, "What are some of the reasons you would suggest sending a thank-you note?"

I told him that was a good question, and suggested the following reasons:

- If the employee receives a customer referral from a client.

- If the customer placed a computer or service order with our company.

- For using your services to fix the customer's network server, etc.

I summed up this topic with, "If you write a nice thank-you message on a card, include your business card in the envelope; it only takes a few minutes. Receiving the thank-you note will put a big smile on your customer's face!"

> Sending thank-you notes is a relationship-building exercise that improves your relationship with your customers, which is extremely important for continued business. People will do business with people they like. If your customers do not like you, they will figure out how to get rid of you. My advice: focus on building a relationship with all your customers as well as with your potential customers.

I was eager to get those custom cards in hand so that I could encourage our employees to start using them. Next, I brought up the subject of professionalism during a service call.

"Gentlemen, I would now like to describe to you what I believe is the ideal customer service experience. Maybe you already have some of these guidelines in place, but in case you do not, I will go over each aspect carefully."

"First, the technician should be dressed professionally and be well-groomed. *Well-groomed* means that facial hair is kept neatly trimmed and the tech is wearing a clean and pressed ABC Computer Distributors logoed shirt tucked into clean khaki pants with a brown belt and brown shoes that have been shined. The company will be purchasing these logoed shirts for the service department, and each tech will receive three shirts." I took a moment then to ask Chris to make a list of everyone's shirt sizes so we could place an order for the shirts immediately. Then I added, "Technicians are not permitted to smoke cigarettes, electronic cigarettes, pipes, or cigars before or during a customer service call. We do not want our technicians smelling like an ashtray when calling on our customers." I was not sure if any of this had been a problem in the past, but I wanted to make sure it would not be in the future.

"When the technician receives his customer service from the service manager's administrative assistant, he should review each order and estimate how long each repair order is going to take. He should then organize the service orders by the most efficient traveling route from the company to the customer's locations. After organizing the orders, the technician should call each customer and schedule the visits. Do not be too aggressive scheduling the service calls to avoid falling behind. If you see that you may be running late for your next service call, phone the customer well in advance, making him or her aware that you are going to be late and give your client a new estimated time of arrival. Then, once you arrive at the location, record the actual time of arrival on the service order paperwork."

"Always greet the customer politely and pay close attention to his or her explanation of the problem and note this on the service order. If possible, work on the computer in an area away from the customer's desk. Be very careful to keep your work area clean and organized. Always keep the tools in your case; do not spread them all over the work area."

"When you determine the problem, inform the customer how long the repair will take. If you need to order parts, call the office immediately to see if the parts are in our inventory. Discuss the problem with the customer if you cannot repair the computer onsite. Ask the customer if he or she needs a replacement computer while we are making the repairs. If they do need a replacement, call and speak to Chris to issue them a loaner after loading the proper software. One of our employees will deliver the loaner and bring the broken machine back to the office for repair. The technician must carefully document this whole transaction and have the client sign the paperwork at the end of the service call. Be sure to record the time on the service order before the customer signs the paperwork.

"After the customer signs the service order, provide the customer a copy of the service order and the customer survey form with the pre-addressed envelope. Then politely ask the customer to complete the survey and drop it in the mail as soon as possible."

"Before you leave the client's location, make sure that the area where you worked on the computer is clean. Check to make sure you have all your tools in your bag, and always say goodbye to the client before you leave. All technicians should leave the customer a business card and always ask for the client's business card so we can build a database of our clients. All paperwork for service calls must be turned in daily so we can invoice daily. If the customer gives you a purchase order number for the service call, be sure to record PO number on our service order paperwork."

I was concluding what I wanted to say to this group technicians. Being the fact that this was our first service department meeting, I wanted to be sure I covered all the bases. I had just a few more things I wanted them to note: "Chris, your department manager; Tom, the sales manager; and Alan, the purchasing department manager will be inviting some of our vendors in from time to time for a Lunch and Learn seminar. I will make sure that the schedules for these seminars are distributed to the service department at least a week in advance, so everyone can try to attend. I suggest that everyone attend as many as of these presentations as possible. You will get a free lunch because the vendor will be paying for the lunch for all attendees. Many of the Lunch and Learns will be quite educational, which will give you better knowledge about their products. We also ask the vendor to bring door prizes to be raffled off and given to a lucky person attending. The last Lunch and Learn I attended, I was picked to receive the door prize, which was a new iPad. I ended up re-gifting it to my secretary at the time for all her wonderful assistance."

"And last, the service department weekly meetings are every Friday at three p.m. If Friday falls on a holiday, the meeting will be the prior Thursday at three p.m. The meetings are mandatory, and please don't be late. Chris will explain to you all later what happens to employees who arrive late for meetings."

That was my segue into formally introducing Chris to the group. I made the introduction, and Chris stood up and walked around the table and shook every one of the technician's hands.

Once back in his seat, he said encouragingly, "We cannot change the past, but we sure can change the future and make it better. Each person in this department is going to be accountable for their time and production. I believe that production reporting is important for accountability; therefore, each of you will meet with me monthly to discuss the results of your week and month. Please do not consider these meetings as a threat to your job. It is my contribution to help you become more productive and successful. Because this company has been losing money, your jobs *are* at risk."

"At lunch today, Roger and I had the difficult task of terminating ten unproductive technicians. That was one of the primary reasons this company has been losing money. You are sitting in this meeting today because we believe you are the best in the department. I know that each of you can grow and become a much better computer technician. Please raise your hand if you disagree with me!"

There was not one raised hand in the room.

"Okay, good! Bob has covered a lot of information over the past half hour about his procedures and regulations to improve the performance of this department. Now I am asking each of you, what are *you* going to do to improve your performance?"

Chris paused, waiting for an answer for quite some time. I surmised that the techs were too nervous to respond.

Finally, Troy spoke up. "I know that everyone in this department can raise their production levels and improve customer relations. I know that I, for one, am going to show you two gentlemen that I am going to kick butt, make my numbers, and every customer who sends in a customer survey about my work will rate it excellent. I love what I do for a living, and I do not want to be number eleven looking for a new job! I know I speak for all of us. Raise your hand if you agree." Every tech raised their hand. Troy's comments eased the tension enough for one of the techs, Brandon, to add to the discussion.

"I can tell you that I believe that you have this whole group in this department on your side," Brandon said. "Craig ignored our department, and our old service manager's behavior was similar to Craig's. We had no real leadership, but the message you two shared today is crystal clear, and I appreciate it. You are going to take care of us, but demand that we do our job and do it right. I agree with Troy. You will not have any problem with my billing numbers in the future, and I am going to do everything I can do to make every one of my customers happy with my work."

Chris thanked both of the techs for their contribution to the morale of the department. "The new customer surveys and the service department production reports are my tools to measure your performance and supervise you. I am a straightforward manager. I take care of employees who work hard, are productive, and treat our customers well. Any employee who goes above and beyond their job description will be rewarded. I promise you that if you do your job well, you will love working here! I know I will!"

I looked at my watch, and it was a 3:45. I asked the group for any questions.

Troy raised his hand and asked, "Mr. Curry, would you like me to show you my locker's location, so you know where to put those top service technician gift cards?"

Everyone at the meeting laughed at Troy's comments.

I told Chris I had another "expense reduction" meeting to run to, and I was officially turning the group over to him.

"Aw, Bob, I'll miss seeing you in action at your next 'meeting'—I could learn a thing or two!"

I shook Chris's hand. "Welcome aboard, my friend! Take care of this group—they are the revenue generators whose services pay our salaries!"

Chris laughed again and assured me he had it all under control, and I was confident he did. I walked around the table shaking the technicians' hands and thanked them for their hard work. Then I was off to deal with the Craig and Trish issue.

* * *

At 4:00, I walked into the conference room. Craig, Trish, Donna, and Darren were already there. I sat down opposite from Craig and Trish and noted their sullen expressions. I decided that this would be a short and sweet meeting.

I said, "Craig, I want you to pack up your belongings and leave. We have had three sexual harassment claims filed against you this week, and I cannot have you in this office anymore."

Craig made no denial; in fact, Craig just sat there without saying a word.

"Who filed the claims?" Trish demanded.

I reminded her that that type of information is confidential. "But I am sure that Craig can fill you in on the details."

Trish stood up and looked down at Craig. "You pig!" she shouted and headed toward the door.

"Trish, please sit down," I urged. "I also need to talk to you."

"What, what do you want with me?" she asked, turning back and taking her seat.

"This company has not sold a training contract in over six months, so I am going to terminate the training business, and therefore, we will no longer need a training manager. Today will be your last day here also."

Donna handed me two envelopes containing Craig's and Trish's severance checks. I continued, "Donna will be talking to you about your health insurance and other relevant matters as soon as I finish what I have to say. Then Darren and Donna will accompany you to your offices. Tim put a couple of boxes in your offices to pack up your personal items. I must ask you both for your office and building keys now."

They both pulled out the keys and placed them on the table.

> **Profit Improvement:** The controller had provided me with all the reporting I needed to identify the weak employees in the organization. I acted quickly by terminating Craig, the former president, and Trish, the training manager. Craig's poor leadership was a cancer to the company. Worse yet, he had been using his ownership position to sexually harass several employees. Trish was just a bad hire with a horrible attitude and had absolutely no value to the company. **These two terminations reduced the expenses by $260,000, bringing the company closer to the cash flow breakeven point.**

"Craig, if you would like to meet from time to time to discuss our progress in the business, I would be happy to do that at your convenience. I hope that there are not any hard feelings. This is a business decision that I must make to keep this business on the trail to be profitable soon."

Trish bit out, "I don't know about Mr. Piggy here, but I hated you the moment we met, Mr. Curry."

"Well, Trish, I am sorry you feel that way. I wish you the best in the future."

I reached out to shake Craig's hand, not knowing if he would accept the offer. He stood up and reached across the table for the handshake, which pleased me, and said, "Bob, I hope you kick butt here. There are a bunch of good people working for this company. I do hope you can save the company because these people deserve to work for a good, healthy company."

I shook Craig's hand and asked him to please keep in touch. Meanwhile, Trish would not raise her eyes to look at me, let alone shake my hand. I said goodbye and left the room.

It was short and sweet, just as I had planned. I went to my office feeling glad that meeting was over. It had lasted only five minutes, but it felt like five hours. A half-hour later, Donna and Darren came to my office.

Darren said, "Who here is ready for happy hour?"

"I will be ready as soon as I prepare the new chart of organization," I said (see page 205). "And, Darren, did you call the locksmith to change the locks?"

"Yes, sir, I did," he replied. "He just texted me and will be here in five minutes."

"Great," I said. "Where is a good happy hour?"

In unison, Donna and Darren replied, "Carrabba's!" Then Donna added, "The vodka tonics with lime are four dollars each, and all the appetizers are half price."

"Sounds great! Gather the troops, and I will meet you and anyone else who wants to join us at five thirty. I must warn you, though, I am limiting us all to one alcoholic drink, and then we are all cut off. I do not want to have to bail anyone out of jail for driving under the influence!"

"Should I ask Chris to come?" Donna asked.

"Yes, of course. Chris has had a very stressful day here for his first day, terminating ten technicians. Chris is officially part of the team now!"

There was another bit of business I needed to discuss: "Darren, you now have the information for the payroll budget. We terminated fourteen people today, transferred one salesperson, Charlene, to sales support and added one service manager, Chris."

Darren sat down and pulled out a small notebook from his back pocket. "Bob, I have learned to keep a notebook with me at all times now. Every time we are together, I need to write stuff down."

"Darren, you are a smart man!"

* * *

At 5:30, when I walked in Carrabba's, Tom, Nancy, Chris, Alan, Donna, and Darren sat around a big table in the bar area with drinks.

ABC Computer Distributors
New Chart of Organization
After "Black Friday"

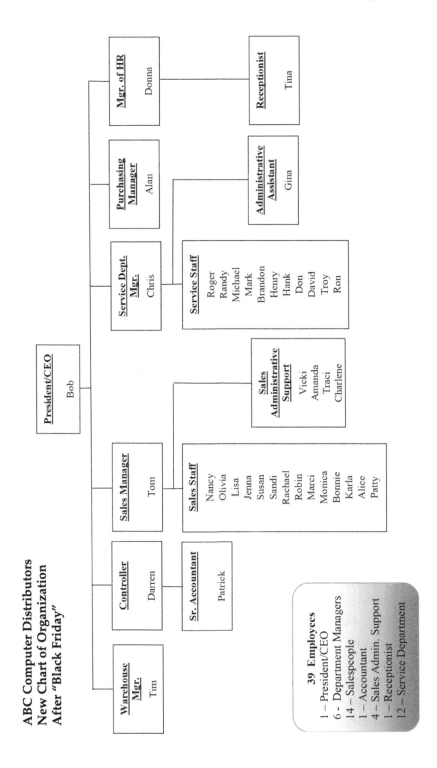

President/CEO
Bob

Mgr. of HR
Donna

Receptionist
Tina

Purchasing Manager
Alan

Administrative Assistant
Gina

Service Dept. Mgr.
Chris

Service Staff
Roger
Randy
Michael
Mark
Brandon
Henry
Hank
Don
David
Troy
Ron

Sales Manager
Tom

Sales Administrative Support
Vicki
Amanda
Traci
Charlene

Sales Staff
Nancy
Olivia
Lisa
Jenna
Susan
Sandi
Rachael
Robin
Marci
Monica
Bonnie
Karla
Alice
Patty

Controller
Darren

Sr. Accountant
Patrick

Warehouse Mgr.
Tim

39 Employees
1 – President/CEO
6 - Department Managers
14 – Salespeople
1 – Accountant
4 – Sales Admin. Support
1 – Receptionist
12 – Service Department

Tom pointed to an empty place at the table where a drink was waiting for me. "That is your drink there—vodka tonic with a bunch of limes. Did I get it right?"

> During my first week at ABC Computer Distributors, I was rarely in my office. I was either meeting with the management team as a group or individually, the sales department, the service department, the customers, the vendors, the insurance agency, the accounting firm, the floor-planning company (Rick and Kevin), or the bank. Unfortunately, many companies are not profitable because the president or owner does not manage his or her direct reports. Too many senior managers spend too much time in their offices and not enough time where the action of the company takes place.

"Yes, my friend, you got it right!"

Nancy stood up and gave me a big hug.

I asked, "What was that for?"

"Bob, you got rid of the two people I vehemently disliked in this company, and you did it all in one day. Thank you!"

I did not need to ask; I knew two people who she passionately disliked.

I told Chris, "When I started my car, it did not blow up!"

Chris laughed. "That surprises me. I beat it out of the parking lot to avoid damage to *my* car."

"What are you two talking about?" Tom asked, seemingly aware that we were kidding around.

I explained the joke to Tom, then said, "No explosions today, but I did get on my hands and knees in the parking lot to look under the car for a bomb before I got into the car!"

The group laughed, but everyone knew that there were some crazy people out there who would do such a thing. Fortunately, although those fourteen ex-employees were hardly the cream of the crop, they were all relatively decent human beings according to their former coworkers.

Everyone had a "Craig and Trish story" to share, and the telling took an hour. I listened while I nursed that one drink and ate an order of chicken wings.

I also learned something new about Tom and Nancy. When they were relaxed, they were two of the funniest people I had ever met. I laughed so hard; I had tears running down my cheeks several times over the hour.

When my last chicken wing was nothing but bones, I gave my credit card to the waitress to pay the check for the group. I walked around the table to say my goodbyes, offering handshakes and hugs.

Before I left, I warned, "If you have more than one drink, Lyft is going to be your ride home tonight." Then I turned to Darren and Alan. "I will see you in the morning at the golf course." And to Tom, I said, "I am holding you accountable for this group!"

"Bob, why would you do something *that* terrible? I thought you liked me!"

I gave them all a big smile. "Good night, group! Each of you had an awesome week . . . my compliments!"

It had been a long, stressful week. Once I got home, I sat in my recliner, turned on the television. My wife knew that I had a tough week, so she covered me with a blanket knowing that I would promptly fall asleep. She was right.

Chapter 9

USE YOUR BRAINS, NOT YOUR EMOTIONS

*"If you do not have control over your mouth,
you will not have control over your future."*

—GERMANY KENT, AMERICAN PRINT AND TELEVISION JOURNALIST

SATURDAY, DECEMBER 9—DAY 6 OF WEEK 1

I PULLED UP TO THE "BAG DROP" AREA AT ARONAMIK COUNTRY Club at 7:30 to drop off my clubs, and then I parked my car. It was a beautiful Saturday morning, not a cloud in the sky, sixty-five degrees, and just a slight breeze. I walked into the clubhouse, and Matthew was there waiting for me. We shook hands, and I thanked him for the invitation to play a round of golf today. He invited me to follow him to the restaurant, where Alan and Darren were already enjoying a cup of coffee. I shook their hands, sat down, and the waitress poured me a hot cup of coffee.

There were windows almost from the floor to the ceiling around the whole inside of the restaurant with a beautiful view of the eighteenth hole. Matthew was chattering on about something, but I did not lose my focus on the view. It looked like a beautiful, unframed picture. The eighteenth hole could not have been any more picturesque.

I knew the only reason I had been invited to play golf today was that Matthew did not want to lose our account. He probably knew by now that I had fired Craig, and he no longer had his "rubber stamp" (Craig) running the company to approve and pay for his high insurance premiums from now on. Matthew seemed like a nice guy, but he was a little too plastic with his syrupy sweet compliments. I was there to enjoy a nice round of golf on an incredible golf course in perfect weather and have some fun. I worked hard all week and had to deal with stressful situations daily, one after another. Today, on the golf course, would not be about work, and I hoped Matthew realized it.

Matthew said, "So, Bob, Darren tells me that you are a good golfer?"

"Darren and I have not played golf together before. He must have me confused with someone else."

"Well, are you a good golfer?"

"I used to be good at one time when I was in college. Unfortunately, since then, I have not practiced or played enough to shoot low scores like I used to. I work too many hours to be a good golfer. I believe to be a good golfer it is like anything else: you must focus on the game, practice regularly, and be committed to the game . . . How is your golf game?"

"Bob, I am an average golfer, like you. I also don't practice enough. So, guys, let's get a little breakfast, hit some balls, and play a nice round of golf. What do you say?"

We all had a light breakfast and went to the range to hit some practice balls.

On the way to the driving range, Darren said for my ears only, "Bob, you in for a treat."

I knew he was referring to Matthew's swing, and I could not wait to experience for myself what Darren found so amusing.

On the practice range, I started with my sand wedge, hit five balls, then hit five more balls with each club in my bag, progressing up to the driver. I looked over at Matthew, and his swing was slightly strange but not as bad as Darren had described it. I figured he must have been taking lessons since Darren last played with him.

When I finished practicing, I carried my bag back and put it on the golf cart. Matthew was right behind me and put his clubs on the same golf cart so that we would be riding together. I closed my eyes and prayed I did not have an insurance salesman trying to sell me insurance for eighteen holes. I walked over to the putting green to practice some putts, and Matthew followed me. I was getting a little uncomfortable because, as I was putting, he was almost in my personal space, yacking in my ear about something. I paid zero attention to what he was saying. Finally, we were done practicing and off to the first tee right in time for our 9:07 tee time.

On the first tee, Matthew asked if we wanted to throw up the balls to pick the teams. I knew that I was going to end up with Matthew as a partner. Everyone always says, "The match is won or lost in the first tee." As I guessed, Matthew and I were partners competing against Darren and Alan. I figured that we had no chance to beat them—I mean zero chance! Therefore, I knew that my wallet was going to be just a little lighter when we finished the eighteen holes.

Darren and Alan were up first and hit their drives down the middle of the fairway and long. Matthew was next to hit. Darren walked over and stood next to me before Matthew hit his drive.

Darren whispered in my ear, "Watch this."

Matthew stood over the ball, drew his driver back, and swung the club as hard as he could. His swing looked nothing like what I had just seen on the driving range. He connected with the ball but almost fell over from turning so hard on the swing. The ball was a low liner about six feet off the ground that started off slicing to the right and then sliced further deep into the woods.

Matthew looked at the three of us and said, "Breakfast Ball."

He then teed up another ball. (For those non-golfers, a "breakfast ball" is like a mulligan on the first tee. If you don't like your initial drive on the first tee, you can hit a second ball without any penalty.) Matthew's second shot went much further to the right than the initial drive. The second ball was gone deep in the woods, one that you don't even bother to search for, especially on the first hole. Based on those two shots, I knew it was going to be a very long day on the golf course.

Matthew said, "I am sure we will find that first shot."

After Matthew walked off the first tee, I hit my drive in between Alan's and Darren's in the fairway. We spent the next ten minutes looking for Matthew's ball until he finally conceded and dropped another ball. The swing Matthew used on the first tee, he used consistently for the next 110 shots, not including his putter. I kept the scorecard, so I knew that Matthew did not get creative with his scoring as Darren had suggested he might be. I never once asked Matthew his score on a hole. I just added up his strokes myself and recorded his score on the card. I did not want to embarrass Matthew by asking him what he had on a hole and then correct him with the "real" number of strokes for that hole.

After the first nine holes, we were down five holes with Darren and Alan's team. The whole day, Matthew was either in the woods looking for his drive or pulling out his ball retriever to pick his ball out of a lake. He always took his time when he had his ball retriever searching to pick out three or four other golf balls out of the lake.

He commented, "Golfers at *Aronamik* only use the best balls and never pick their balls out of the lakes. I am not that proud. I will pick anyone's ball out of the water and use it."

I just shook my head and laughed.

On the back nine, Matthew and I came back to tie up the match. I was shocked because Matthew was all over the course with his shots. I think Darren and Alan were so amused that they lost their focus.

After the match, we all went to the restaurant to have some lunch. I was fortunate that Matthew did not once try to talk about business on the golf course. I was not so lucky in the restaurant.

"Bob, do you know that my firm has been ABC Computer Distributors' insurance agent for the past nine years?"

"Yes, I did hear that from Darren."

"We are like family with your company."

"Matthew, that is great. I think relationships are important in business. But, Matthew, I have told Darren that we are going to bid the insurance this year."

"Bob, what do you mean? We will bid out the insurance with as many carriers as you want."

"Please do not take this personally," I said, "but I have been hired to get this company profitable. I reviewed our insurance premiums this past week, and they seem to be very high for this business. I am responsible for lowering the costs, and the only way I know how to do that is to invite three other agencies to bid on the business."

"Well, Bob, I *do* take offense to that. You are not treating my firm or me like family at all. I invested all that time and effort doing right by your company for the past nine years, and you are going to treat me like this?"

"Again, please do not take this personally. I am only doing my job. Since you are the incumbent agency with nine years of experience writing the insurance policies for our company, you have the advantage over any other agencies to continue to win the business again."

"Bob, if I had known you were going to bid out the insurance and treat me like any other insurance agent, I would have never invited you here today."

Darren and Alan said not a word, but I could tell by their expressions that they were shocked by Matthew's comments.

"Okay, Matthew, I am sorry that you feel that way, but thank you for the wonderful day." Right then, I could hear my father's voice in my head: *"Bob, use your brains, not your emotions."* I pulled $450 out of my wallet and put it on the table to pay for Darren's, Alan's, and my share of the food and golf.

Matthew seemed flummoxed, but he accepted my hand for a handshake. Then I told Darren and Alan I would see them Monday morning. I left to get my golf clubs, put them in my car, and drove home.

Darren called me on my cell phone a few minutes later. "How are you doing, are you mad?"

"No, why?"

"Well, when Matthew made that stupid comment, I thought you were going to knock him off his chair, but you remained cool, calm, and collected."

"What did Matthew say after I left?"

"He told me that he was very offended by your attitude. He

thought that after nine years of serving our company, he's entitled to our business this year. He said that telling him that we were going to bid the insurance coverages was rude."

> Employees who believe they are entitled to anything because they have been with the company for a specified period or are related to the owner of the company offend me. My father taught me a long time ago that if you work hard for two weeks, you are entitled to your paycheck. Then if you work hard for two more weeks, you get your next paycheck. When an employee believes he or she is entitled to their paycheck *before* they work hard, that is their message to me that they want to be in the unemployment line with other "entitled" individuals.

I just started laughing. "Darren, what did you tell him?"

"I said that he just killed any chance of retaining us as a customer." I could hear the laughter in his voice.

"It is funny. Another relative of Craig's in the sales department, Frank, displayed that same entitlement attitude with me on Wednesday, and Friday I fired him."

"An entitlement attitude from an employee, or in this case, an insurance agent does not sit well with you," Darren said, stating the obvious.

"Darren, I think that you are right. On Monday, please start scheduling meetings with other insurance agencies."

"Should we include Matthew on the bid list?" he asked.

"Matthew who?"

"Okay, Bob, enjoy your Saturday."

"You too, Darren. See you Monday, my friend!"

* * *

I knew I had to be at the office at 3:00 p.m. for the security system installation. It was already 2:00 p.m., so I decided to go directly to the office even though I needed a shower after that round of golf. Charlie was in his own world anyway and would probably not even notice if I smelled like a rose or a skunk. When I arrived, he was there sitting in his big pick-up truck.

"Charlie, you are here early," I said with surprise as he got out of his vehicle.

"I finished my last job early, so I came over in case you were already here. And, look at that, here you are!"

"Okay, let's go get this done," I told him. "I need a shower."

"You are not kidding, Bob. You *do* need a shower."

In what seemed like no time at all, Charlie had mounted twelve cameras—two outside pointed at the warehouse garage and the entrance door, two pointed at the door going into the office, and one in the office pointed at the door and the other in the warehouse. He mounted the other eight cameras in the corners of the room, and then the other four equally spaced between the cameras in the corners. Charlie installed a box on the outside of the warehouse door to turn the system on or off. He explained that the code (1, 2, 3, 4) was entered there to set or turn the system off.

"Let's go to your office," he said when he was all done. "I will show you how to view the cameras on your computer. The system will record everything from any camera that is activated when the system is on. The cameras will turn on with any movement within 150 feet of the camera."

"Charlie, this is perfect," I complimented. "You did a great job. I appreciate your work, as always."

"Bob, give me your cell phone," he said, sticking his hand out.

"Why?" I asked.

"I will set it up so that you can see what the cameras capture right on your phone."

I handed my cell phone over, and a few minutes later he said, "Okay, you are all set. If someone goes in the warehouse after setting the alarm, the alarm will go off. It will sound like a police siren. The system will notify the security service, and your phone will start beeping."

I hoped my phone would never beep for that reason.

Chapter 10

WOW, WHAT A WEEK!

"The best way to predict your future is to create it."

—PETER F. DRUCKER, AUSTRIAN-BORN AMERICAN
MANAGEMENT CONSULTANT, EDUCATOR, AND AUTHOR

SUNDAY, DECEMBER 10—DAY 7 OF WEEK 1

I WOKE UP EARLY SUNDAY MORNING THINKING ABOUT
what had happened to me and my life over the past two weeks.
I had had the best job of my career at H&N Construction, which
ended when Hal and Nick sold the company. After the settlement,
I planned to travel and play golf at the top courses in the nation.
I had postponed my dream trip after playing a round of golf with
Kevin, and he talked me into doing my first turnaround, at ABC
Computer Distributors.

During this past week, I met with Craig, the owner of the company, and his management team. Between Monday and Friday, I
had interviewed each department manager one-on-one to evaluate
who on the management team was qualified to help me manage this
company in the future, and more importantly, who should *not* be on
this management team. The quality of the management team was
especially important because I was planning to quickly grow this
company from $50 million and losing money to $120 million and
being extraordinarily profitable starting January. My business logic

told me that if one salesperson (Nancy) in the sales department can do $27 million in sales in a year in a poorly managed, financially distressed company, then fourteen salespeople should be able to do at least $120 million in sales next year. In the past week, we had made some sweeping changes to this business, including:

- I terminated the company's owner (Craig), his girlfriend (Trish), who was the manager of the training department, two salespeople, and ten service techs, thereby reducing the annual payroll burden by over one million dollars. Those changes alone brought the company to its breakeven point.

- We terminated Craig's Mercedes car lease and returned the vehicle to the car dealership. We reduced the company's annual expenses by $18,000 for the year and received the security deposit back ($7,000) on the car.

- I asked Tom to transfer one of the non-productive employees (Charlene) from the sales department to work as part of the sales support group to help clean up the backlog of work plus handle the anticipated increase in sales.

- I hired a new service manager (Chris) and transferred the old service manager (Roger) to be a senior service technician again, which was where Roger best belonged.

- I asked Darren to create new financial and operational reporting for the sales and service departments, which provides accurate information about the individual employee's and department's weekly and monthly performance.

- We held the company's first weekly management, sales, and service department meetings to create positive lines of communication within and between all departments of the business.

- I revised the sales commission program to reward the sales team to start focusing on growing their sales and increase the sale of service contracts.

- I provided each salesperson with a list of ten target companies to go after to solicit new business. These target companies have many more employees compared to our company's current customer base.

- We received approval from our floor-planning bank for a $10 million temporary increase to our credit line to fund the purchase order received from one of our top salesperson's customers.

- Alan and I negotiated with our suppliers better pricing, payment terms, and the delivery schedule for Nancy's $18.2 million customer order, which increased the gross profit by $1,365,000.

- Darren and I met with our operating bank to set up a cash management procedure to efficiently use the company's idle cash in the checking accounts to pay down our line of credit daily and reduce our interest expense by over $50,000 per year.

- We changed our invoice payment terms from net thirty days to net twenty days. The reduction of the accounts receivables balance would reduce the company's loan balance by the same total. With the sales budget for the new year, this change in policy would reduce the average loan balance by ten days of sales or $3.3 million. This reduction in our loan balance would reduce our interest expense by $148,000 for the year.

- I implemented a sales spiff program to incentivize the sales department to sell the products in our warehouse inventory with a goal to reduce the warehouse stock down to zero as soon as possible. When the company no longer had an inventory investment, the change would reduce our balance in the credit line by $4 million, thereby reducing our annual interest expense by $180,000. Not having computers in the warehouse would also reduce the inventory shrinkage experienced the prior year by $155,000 and reduce the cost of the property insurance by approximately $10,000.

- Chris and I implemented a customer survey program for our customers to report to our management team how the service technicians were performing during their service calls. The goal of this program was to improve the quality of service by the techs to our customers.

- We implemented incentive programs in the service department to reward the techs for quality service to our customers, the most billable hours by a service tech in a month and referring sales leads to our sales department.

- We met with the outside public accounting firm managing partner to discuss the year-end review of our financial statements, the reduction of our costs, and having the work done as quickly as possible.

- We met with our property and causality insurance agent, who was Craig's cousin, to inform him that we were going to bid our insurance coverages to three other agencies to ensure that we were paying market rates for our insurance policies, and not a penny more.

- Darren and I started the budgeting process for the following year to plan the profitability of the business by implementing all the changes as listed above.

> I learned that you could have a company with a great product in a fantastic location with a growing industry during a healthy economy, and still lose money if you have a weak management team. Or you can have a business with a bad product, in a terrible location, in a declining industry, with a weak economy, and still be profitable if you have a strong management team. The common denominator is the management team. When you have a quality management team, the company will be successful.

Now, after being involved with this company for a week and making all these changes, my next step was to plan for the following week, month, and new year.

I got out of bed, made my first cup of coffee of the day, and sat in my recliner to better organize my thoughts about the future of this business. After I finished my coffee, it was clear what was necessary for me to accomplish soon. The critical issues for this company were strong leadership, a solid management team, and a healthy corporate culture for the business.

I thought back to my eight years at H&N Construction Company. Hal and Nick's leadership, the management team they hired, and the corporate culture of the business all were, in my opinion, the best. Hal and Nick were responsible for the success of all three. They were excellent leaders. They went to great lengths to hire an outstanding management team, and Hal and Nick created a corporate culture within the organization that was second to none. Every employee who worked for that company loved their job and did it well. I decided right then that I was going to attempt to model this company's corporate culture as close to H&N Construction as possible. Even if I couldn't match it, getting it close would make this business very successful.

Strong management teams have excellent managers in every position, including sales, service, finance, human resources, purchasing, and warehouse/inventory management. If one manager is weak, the company is weak and vulnerable. It is like having a chair with three strong legs and one weak leg. The weak leg will cause you to fall even with three strong legs unless you fix the weak one and make the chair stable again.

In the past seven days, I had terminated two executives, demoted one, and hired a great service manager. The relationships of the current management team so far were excellent and on the way to being even better. I was happy with Tom, Alan, Darren, and Donna. Unfortunately, Tim's role as the warehouse manager might become obsolete once the sales team managed to sell through all the inventory in the warehouse. For Tim to continue to be a valuable contributor to the group, he would likely end up in the purchasing department as an assistant to Alan, but that would be Alan's decision to make in the future. I had known Chris, my new service department manager for many years, and my opinion of him was that he was a star.

It was my most significant responsibility to continue to build and maintain a quality management team for the company. Every one of my direct reports needed to be a leader in their position, and I would evaluate each manager quarterly. Regular evaluations are especially critical when a company is losing money, like ABC Computer Distributors. I have never believed that sticking my head in the sand and ignoring a problem would resolve anything. Not dealing with weak managers sends a message to the other managers and every employee in the company that it is okay to be a C- or D-level player. Unfortunately, most business owners take the easy way out—the nonconfrontational route—and don't do anything about the weak managers. Truthfully, a business owner who does not deal with this type of issue is a more significant problem than having a poorly performing manager on the management team.

I pulled my notebook out and made some notes to plan for what I needed to accomplish that upcoming week to continue the forward momentum with this turnaround:

- *First, meet with Donna and deal with the sexual harassment complaints against Craig and make some decisions regarding the employee manual and all the other HR forms, policies, and procedures.*

- *Next, meet with Darren and Patrick and finalize next year's operating budget.*

- *Then, meet with Alan, Tom, Nancy, and Tim regarding the logistics of Nancy's big order.*

- *Finally, interview the group of techs from Chris's old company that he wants to hire as soon as possible.*

I reviewed the list and decided that if I could accomplish all these issues, I will have had a very productive week!

I enjoyed the rest of my Sunday and did not think any more about ABC Computer Distributors.

Chapter 11

$120 MILLION IS POSSIBLE UNDER IDEAL CONDITIONS

"The purpose of business is to create and keep a customer."

—PETER F. DRUCKER, AUSTRIAN-BORN AMERICAN
MANAGEMENT CONSULTANT, EDUCATOR, AND AUTHOR

MONDAY, DECEMBER 11—DAY 8 OF WEEK 2

MONDAY MORNING WHEN I ARRIVED AT WORK, I WENT straight to my office. Donna walked in with a cup of coffee and placed it on a coaster next to my phone.

"Donna, you are a lifesaver with your special stash of coffee. I am officially authorizing you to purchase an ample supply of that coffee and replace the crap in the breakroom. Maybe everyone in the whole company will be a little more efficient with your brand of coffee than the other stuff, so it offsets the additional cost."

She smiled. "The good news is that this coffee costs less than the coffee in the breakroom."

"Okay, my decision is made and confirmed. Your brand of coffee is now the company's brand of coffee from this day forward and thank you!"

When she left, I saw that there was a sealed white envelope on my chair bearing my name. Curious about what was inside, I opened it to find copies of the three sexual harassment complaints.

I read each in detail. I went to Donna's office with my coffee and the harassment complaints.

"Donna, do you know what happened to these women to make them file these complaints?"

"Yes, I do. Apparently, the three ladies were at a bar last Tuesday night, and Craig showed up. He offered them a bonus in their next paycheck if they went to a local motel together and had some fun as a foursome. He told them that their second option would be to go find a new job."

All I could do is shake my head in disbelief.

"Bob, according to the women, Craig was drunk and obnoxious. They did not know if he was kidding or not. But, to say the least, they were all intimidated."

"Okay, Donna, I understand. Since I made Craig go away Friday, do you think these complaints will go away?" I asked hopefully.

"Yes, I do. All three women came to talk to me after your first sales meeting. Apparently, you have them all pumped up from your speech at the meeting. They said they want to continue to work for this company if you could get Craig straightened out. Then after you terminated him, they happily agreed to drop their harassment complaints. They love you for pulling the trigger and getting rid of Craig—and Trish."

I turned that information over in my mind and asked, "Will they write a statement formally dropping their complaint now that Craig is no longer working for the company?"

"Yes, I think that I could make that happen. And, Bob, I forgot to tell you, last week, I started ordering the employee manual, a bunch of HR policies, and forms from the website you suggested. When I saw the total, I decided that it was too much money to spend right now. I called the company's customer service department, and they discounted the order by 40 percent if I placed it over the phone. Suddenly, the cost of the order went from fairly expensive to very reasonable!"

"Great job, Donna. I learned a long time ago that everything is negotiable."

"Friday, late afternoon, Tim brought in the big box from the HR company. When I opened the box and reviewed everything, I saw that they had double shipped the order. So, we have an inventory of HR forms now and employee manuals for every employee, plus a stack of extras for new hires in the future. I called the company and informed them of the over shipment, and they told me just to keep the forms. I would have felt guilty if I just kept the stuff. And, Bob, thank you for letting me update everything in the HR department. I no longer need to feel embarrassed if I don't have an employee manual for an employee who wants to review our company policies."

"Good for you, Donna, I am proud of you! By the way, would you please follow-up with the management team concerning their performance reviews for all their employees? They are all due by this Friday. That reminds me—I want all new hires to sign a non-compete, non-solicitation agreement as part of the hiring package."

"I have samples of each agreement; do you want me to send them to you to review?" she asked.

"Sure, that would be fine."

> A non-compete agreement blocks a former employee from competing against a former employer for a specified amount of time. The non-solicitation agreement is a less restrictive contract and is intended to legally prevent an employee from soliciting his or her former employer's employees or clients.

Donna opened the notebook on her desk to write down the two tasks she was assigned.

While she had her notebook open, I said, "Donna, I have one additional request. Please talk to each of the managers and ask them to develop at least three to five goals they believe they need to accomplish next year for it to be a successful year for them and their departments."

"I will be happy to convey the message to everyone, but if they have any questions, I am going to refer them to you, okay?"

"Yes, of course."

"Should they have these goals ready to discuss by when, Friday morning?"

"Yes, Friday is good. Thank you again, Donna."

Tom walked into Donna's office with a stack of papers under his arm.

"Good morning Tom, how are you doing, my friend?" I asked.

Tom looked chipper. "Fantastic, and good morning to you both!"

"What's that stack of papers?"

"Those are all the invoices you gave me on Wednesday afternoon. Bob, the delinquent invoices are all paid in full. The three salespeople for those accounts took the invoices to visit the customers, and they got a check for payment for each of the past due invoices. Plus, they came back from the visit with purchase orders for four of the six customers who had over ninety-day receivables."

"That is wonderful. If we did not pay attention to those invoices as we did, those bills would have ended up being written off, and instead, we get to deposit over twenty thousand dollars into our checking account and process four customer orders. Please make sure these salespeople watch their customers closely, so the new orders received do not fall into the delinquent category again. Plus, they should be aware that the new payment terms are net twenty rather than net thirty days."

Tom nodded, but he looked like he was ready to burst. "There is a bonus to the story, Bob. Of the four orders, three were hardware and software, and one was a service contract for sixty-five thousand dollars. The computers on the PO's were for three hundred eighty-five thousand, and all the product is in our warehouse to ship immediately. Bob, you have only been here for a week, and a half and ABC Computer Distributors feels like a different company!"

"Well, Tom, I hope that is a good thing! And, honestly, filling Craig's shoes would not have been a big challenge for anyone considering the past eighteen months!"

Tom laughed, then said more seriously, "It is almost unbelievable how one person can join an organization and change everything, including the attitudes of the management team and every employee, in just a week."

"We still have a lot of work to do to get this company turned around," I told him.

"I know, but the morale around here is hugely improved. Everything seems much better," Tom said with passion in his voice.

"Well, wait until tomorrow, Tom, everything is going to be even better than it is today."

"How is that, Bob?" Tom asked.

I motioned over to Donna, who looked at me expectantly.

"Donna is going over to Costco to purchase *good* coffee for the breakroom."

"You have got to be kidding me!" Tom said with a big smile.

"No, I am not! Tell him, Donna!"

Donna just smiled.

My cell phone started to vibrate in my pocket. It was 8:50, and there was a reminder on my phone that I had a budget meeting with Darren and Patrick in the conference room from 9:00 to 11:00, this morning. I thought, *Did I really schedule a two-hour meeting with these guys? That is out of character!*

I went to my office, picked up my notebook off my desk, and headed over to the conference room. Darren and Patrick entered the conference room, each holding a tablet and a big binder marked BUDGETS.

Darren said, "I hope you don't mind that I brought my budget expert with me today."

"You can bring Patrick to any meeting. When you have an asset in the company like Patrick, you should not keep him locked up in his office all day. Good morning, Patrick!"

"Good morning, and thank you for your faith in my work," Patrick said, and the two men took their seats.

"Okay, gentlemen, let's talk budgets! First, I thought we should put together a list of assumptions for next year's budget that will be distributed to the management team so they can do their budgets for their departments. These are my thoughts, and please, if you disagree with anything, speak up. I do not want this to be *my* budget; I want it to be the management team's budget."

Darren gave me a knowing look. "I have already learned that you do not want a bunch of puppets working for you on your management team!"

"You are exactly right, my friend! Let's first start with sales."

I told Darren and Patrick that I thought we should set the total sales budget at $120 million. Since the company was going to end this year with only $50 million in sales and this new sales budget was 240 percent over the current sales total, Darren asked, "Do you think that we can grow this financially distressed company's sales by that much?"

I assured him that I did and that if we could motivate the balance of the salespeople to be one-quarter as productive as Nancy, just 25 percent, the company would do $135 million in sales next year. I also reminded him that we would be starting the year with over $18.2 million to be shipped in the first week of January and that if we did $25 million in January, that only left $95 million for the balance of the remaining eleven months.

"Bob, when you state it that way, it is hard to argue with the numbers. Still, ninety-five is a lot when we only did fifty this year."

"I understand, Darren, but until last week, Craig was managing this company. Now it is my turn to motivate the sales team and make these people more productive."

Darren agreed that it might be obtainable under ideal conditions, but it was still a massive jump from $50 million.

"I understand what you're saying," I said, "but let me explain to you why my view is so different from yours. I believe that there is one person on the sales team who is self-motivated and is genuinely driven to be successful. She is going to end this year with more in sales than the other sixteen salespeople combined. The other people on the team do not have Nancy's drive, motivation, or confidence. I believe that the rest of the sales team can be motivated and managed to be substantially more productive than they are today. I believe there are several changes we can make to improve their sales productivity. We can direct them to customers. We should train each salesperson on the team to use proper selling techniques, much like Nancy uses. Management can measure and report their weekly, monthly, and quarterly productivity to motivate each of them. The company can reward them for their successes. Tom and I can attend sales calls with each salesperson, and then later show them what they are doing wrong and what they are doing right. We can have monthly and quarterly sales contests to motivate the team.

"I firmly believe that most of the sales force can achieve close to Nancy's sales level. I plan to have her share with the rest of the sales department her selling secrets and skills that make her numbers so strong. As I said, if the rest of the salespeople are one-quarter as productive as Nancy, we will do one hundred thirty-five million in sales next year. The only number I think is not accurate with my estimate is the 'one-quarter' as productive as Nancy. I think that they will do much better than that."

I went on to tell Darren that the breakdown of sales would be $116 million in hardware and software and $4 million in service. Darren expressed concern that this represented a 200 percent increase in service sales over this year's totals. I reminded him that we did not have Chris as the manager of the service department. Did I think that Chris would sign up to produce $4 million in revenue next year for his department? I told Darren that my best guess was that Chris would increase that number closer to $4.5 million without my even pushing him. Not only would he sign up for $4 million, but he would likely achieve it by October next year.

"Gentlemen, Chris is a much better manager than I am and more competitive," I told them. "His team will work hard for him because they will not want to let him down. I want you both to know that I would never hire a manager to join this company if that person was not much better than I am."

"Bob, it is going to be hard to find managers who have your passion and leadership skills," Darren said admiringly.

"Thank you, Darren, but that was a true statement. I will hire only the best!"

Next, I wanted to talk about the cost of sales sold and the gross profit. I explained that if the gross profit on hardware and software was 15 percent, the $116 million in sales would generate $17.4 million in gross profit. The $4 million in service would generate $2.4 million in gross profit for a total of $19.8 million.

"Patrick, are you following me with these figures?" I asked.

"Yes, sir, I am with you, and I agree with your estimates. I believe if you continue to light a fire under these people's fannies, you will be able to generate the sales that you are talking about."

"Patrick, I told Darren that I liked you the first time I met you!"

Darren smiled and said, "That is right, Patrick, he did!"

Patrick's face flushed from the compliment. "Thank you, sir, I appreciate that!"

"Payroll, next. Let's review the assumptions of payroll department by department. But first, add a four percent increase to all salaries effective the first of January and another four percent on the first of July. This whole company has not had a raise for a couple of years. These employees deserve an increase in compensation."

Both men wrote in their notebooks, and I could tell they were happy about the 4 percent increase. I continued, "I want to keep the sales staff at fifteen people—the sales manager and fourteen salespeople—for the year, but increase the sales support to six employees by the middle of the year. Plan on one new hire in March and another one in June. Calculate the monthly sales commissions at twenty-two percent of the gross profit. The commission rate for the sales staff is twenty percent and then add another two percent of sales contests and incentives to motivate the staff."

I moved on to the service department. "We have eleven techs in the department right now, and there will be five more hired before the first of the year, then five more probably by the second week of January. By the end of the first quarter, I expect Chris to hire another five technicians, who would bring the department up to twenty-six techs, with another four more new hires at the end of the second quarter. We will plan the service department on ending the year with Chris, the department manager, Gina, the administrative assistant, and thirty technicians. Let's assume that all the new hires will start with a sixty-thousand-dollar salary.

"Patrick, please create a schedule that calculates the sales for each existing and new hires. When a new technician starts, he will generate two and a half times his salary in revenue. Therefore, the technician will cost us five thousand in salary per month, and he will produce twelve thousand five hundred in monthly revenue. Please let me know when you finish the calculated annual sales total. I would like to review the numbers as soon as possible.

"But, mark my words, Chris is going to come up with his service department's revenue using the same method. Please add a commission expense line item to the service department's general ledger. I am going to pay commissions to the service techs or anyone else in the company for referring sales to the sales team. Add sixty thousand to the budget for commissions for the service team, five thousand per month."

"Next, the purchasing department. We are going to need to get Alan some help if we are going to bombard him with an enormous increase in sales next year. Add an assistant buyer salaried at sixty thousand at the end of January and an administrative support employee at the end of April salaried at forty thousand.

"Administrative departments. That covers everyone except Donna, Tim, Tina, you two gentlemen, and me. First, with everything that I am dumping on your department, I think you will need to add an accountant to do some of the number crunching for all the reporting. I do not want the two of you working sixty-hour workweeks. I want to staff the finance department properly, so I don't walk into your office and find you asleep on your desk."

A look of relief appeared on Darren's face. "I sincerely appreciate your giving us a budget to hire some additional help."

I told them that we were planning to drive this company to generate $120 million next year, so we were going to need some quality employees back at the office to take control of all that money and other responsibilities. "As for all the rest of the line items on the income statement, I am going to ask you to generate the budgets. I want you to create your list of assumptions to justify each budgeted number. Are we all square with this budget process now? Do you have any questions?"

Darren had one. He wanted to know if I was serious about budgeting sales at $120 million for the following year. My response was "Yes, but if you think that it is going to be higher, I can move it up based on your advice."

Darren shifted in his seat and said he thought $75 million might be more realistic.

Again, I explained that we would already have somewhere around $25 million in sales in January alone. To reach $75 million, we would only have to do twice that total for the next eleven months. I added that these people should be able to do $75 million just by working on the weekends.

"In fact, I will make you and Patrick a wager. If we do not reach my projected target in sales by November 1, I will treat you and Patrick to dinner at Ruth's Chris Steak House. But, if we do reach it, you and Patrick have to pull out your credit cards for *my* dinner."

Darren waved his hand. "I am never going to bet against you again—not after our golf game when you managed to tie our score even with Matthew on your team. Anyway, even if we don't exactly reach your projected target, this is probably going to be one of the most profitable computer distributors in the United States next year."

Well, it looked like I wouldn't be getting a dinner out of these two, and I said, "Okay, let's recap what we talked about before we end this meeting. We need to have a spread schedule that shows the actual monthly financial statements for the past twelve months—December, last year and January through November this year—with the totals for the year. The last two columns should show the average of those twelve months and the totals as a percentage of sales."

"Patrick already has that schedule done," Darren said.

"Good, this schedule will be valuable for all the managers to do their budgets. I would like you to generate a worksheet for payroll by the department that includes the new hires as we discussed. Then we will need a schedule for the sales commissions, and one for the hardware/software sales and service department sales by month. I want a one-page list of all the assumptions we discussed so you can hand Tom, Chris, and Alan a sheet of paper that explains my thoughts on how we are going to turn this company around in the next twelve months. Tom is going to be responsible for the sales of hardware and software, cost of sales, and gross profit budgets. He will also be responsible for the budgets for the sales staff payroll, commissions, and all sales related expenses." I added that I would not let Tom submit anything less than $120 million in sales.

"Bob, I hate to keep asking, but are you serious?" Darren asked.

I told him that I would like to plan for $150 million, but if Tom signed up for $120 million, I would approve his sales goal. Then I said, "I would like to have a spread schedule for each expense category for each department, so these managers do not have to do too many of the details. I want them to write down their assumptions, and you and Patrick crunch the numbers."

Darren agreed and said that he and Patrick would set up all the schedules and give me a list of their assumptions. He added, "I am assuming that you want to see their assumptions before Patrick and I update the schedules."

"Yes, I do. And I almost forgot. There are two additional items for the budget that I want to add that are the possibly the *most* important line items. First, I want to accrue ten thousand dollars per month for a scholarship fund."

"Scholarship fund for who?" Darren asked.

"We will discuss that in detail later, as I am not yet done developing my plan. Second, I want to accrue thirty-three percent of the monthly profits to fund a management bonus to be paid quarterly to the management team."

"Bob, you are full of surprises!" Darren exclaimed.

"I told you about the company I used to work for before I joined this organization. The two owners of the company distributed twenty-five percent of the profits to the management team and twenty-five percent of the profits to the balance of the employees. I am a strong believer that all employees should receive bonuses based on the success of the company. I would do the same fifty percent profit bonus, but first I want to build up the balance sheet to keep the company secure."

Darren looked like he wanted to give me a high five. Instead, he said, "Patrick and I now have a strong incentive to calculate the budget to determine the management bonus figures!"

I turned to Patrick. "I know you are not officially a member of the management team, but I will ensure that we do not forget you when it comes to passing out bonuses."

"That is very kind of you to do that," Patrick said, putting down his pen for a moment.

"I am going to tell you what I told Darren already. I think finance people are the smartest people in the world, you included."

Patrick blushed again.

Well, gentlemen, that is all I have, any questions?"

"Yes, when do you expect us to have the first draft completed for your review?" Darren asked.

"Do you think that you can have this all done by Tuesday evening, the twenty-third?"

Darren looked at Patrick to answer the question.

"I have most of the schedules almost finished," he replied. "There will be a few minor changes per this discussion today that I need to make. I then can have all the budget information distributed to Tom, Chris, and Alan tomorrow morning, which will give them the weekend to work on the numbers. As you said, with all the schedules we have for them, they will have very little detail work to do."

"Darren and I can meet with them this Thursday afternoon if they are available. I can do all the other line items that we are responsible for the budget this week. Monday night, we should have a first draft for you, no later than Tuesday morning."

"I gave you two weeks, Patrick, and you are telling me that you will have the first draft of the budget in seven days? Do I understand you correctly?"

"Yes, sir."

"Darren, are you okay with Patrick's schedule?"

"Bob, knowing Patrick as well as I know him, he will have the work done before Monday night, and it will be accurate. I am okay with his schedule."

"Gentlemen, I am pleased!"

Darren asked, "Why?"

"Because this meeting only lasted fifty-five minutes even though we scheduled it for two hours. I hate meetings that last longer than one hour. Darren, we have a meeting scheduled for noon today about Nancy's big order. Do you think we should order in lunch for the meeting?"

"Bob, that is a good idea, I will take care of it, okay?"

"Yes, and thank you for your time, Gentlemen! GO WITH CONFIDENCE!"

* * *

When I walked into the conference room at noon, everyone was there—Tom, Nancy, Alan, Darren, and Tim—already serving themselves some lunch. I got in the back of the line and eventually filled up my plate with a turkey sandwich, coleslaw, a bag of potato chips, and a bottle of Diet Coke. I decided not to start the meeting until everyone finished eating their lunch, so no one was talking with their mouth full of food . . . including me!

When everyone finished, I asked, "Who is chairing this meeting?"

Nancy said, "Bob, I will chair the meeting since it is my order."

"Okay, Nancy, I have my notebook here to take the minutes of the meeting."

"Bob, I am assuming that our credit line with Kevin is all done, and both parties signed the documents, right?"

"Yes, Nancy, they are, everything is good with the money for the transaction."

"Alan, are we all coordinated with the master distributors we purchased all the hardware and software from?"

Alan said, "Nancy, I issued purchase orders the day Bob finished up with the line of credit increase. Everything is in order with our negotiated prices and the schedule of the delivery dates. Bob that reminds me, all three vendors offered us a half percent discount if we sent them a fifty percent payment on the order before Friday. Actually, that is not true. One vendor called me and made the offer, and then I called the other two to see if they wanted their money early for a discount also."

"Alan, our purchase orders with the vendors total approximately fourteen million, is that right?" I asked. When he confirmed that was correct, I did the math out loud: They were going to give us a half a point on $14 million or $70,000 to pay them $7 million approximately forty-five days early. The $7 million on our line of credit was going to cost us 4.5 percent interest, or $39,375 for that month and a half. We would get a $70,000 discount on our purchase price if we paid them early, which was going to cost us roughly $40,000.

"Hmm . . . tough management decision, what do you think, Darren?"

"I would do that deal seven days a week!" Darren exclaimed.

"Okay, Alan, tell your three contacts to send us an invoice, and we will wire them the money on Friday. That was fun; we just made an additional thirty thousand dollars today. That money should pay for this lunch, right?"

> **Profit Improvement:** When a company has managed their cash and loan balance properly, there may be deals they can take advantage of and pay the vendor early. In this case, we earned a quick **$30,000 of unplanned profit.**

"This deal keeps getting better!" Nancy said, retaking the lead. "Tim, are you ready in the warehouse to receive all these computers, stage them within one week, and deliver them to the customer the first week in January?"

"Yes, Nancy, we are all ready to receive the computers, download all the software required, do the diagnostics testing, pack the laptops back up, and deliver them to your customer on schedule. Three college students who are home for the holidays are going to help us."

I chimed in, "Tim, please talk to Donna about doing background checks on these three students. I don't want them coming in here, working on the laptops, and then we find out that thirty computers disappear before we ship the hardware in January."

Tim pulled out a small notebook from his pocket and took some notes. "Bob, consider it done immediately after the meeting. All three of the guys have been here already to fill out an employment application. Donna already has all the information she needs to do the background checks right away."

Nancy asked, "Bob, am I forgetting anything?"

"Only one thing, probably the most important issue of all," I said.

"What is that?" she asked, looking a bit concerned.

"You need to talk to that salesperson who closed this big deal to go pick up all those big checks when payment comes due!"

"Bob, you do not have to worry about that," she said. "I have that covered. I talked to my customer, and we developed a schedule to have the checks ready on the agreed-upon dates. I already have those dates scheduled on my calendar."

"As do I, Nancy, just as a backup!" I said.

Nancy smiled at me. "You never miss anything, Bob, do you?"

"I try not to forget the big issues! This deal is too big to drop any balls."

Everyone agreed with nods and smiles. No one had anything left to say about the sale, so I said, "Okay, let's make this deal happen without any problems. This meeting has ended. GO WITH CONFIDENCE!"

* * *

Monday was Chris's first full day at ABC Computer Distributors, and I had not seen him yet. I went over to his office to see what he was doing. I stood at his office door, and I was amazed. He had several pictures hung on the walls along with his college diploma. There were trophies from golf tournaments and about ten photos on his desk and credenza of his wife and children. The office looked like he had worked for the company for several years, not just one morning. He had a whole bookshelf of computer manuals, none of which I had read. I wasn't a computer technician, nor did I want to be one.

"Chris, your office looks great. What did you do, get to the office at 4:00 a.m. to set all this up?"

"No, my wife and Gina did all this. All I had to do is carry everything in from my car."

"Chris, your wife was here, and you did not introduce me?"

"Bob, you were in meetings all morning, and I did not want to bother you, nor did she. She is a little shy at first, but when she gets to know you, she has no filters."

"What you are telling me is that she is a lot like you— no filters at all. Well, Chris, I am looking forward to meeting her."

"She will be back sometime, but today she insisted on coming here to clean my office, hang pictures, and set everything up."

"She *cleaned* it?"

"Yes. My wife is a bit of a clean freak. She scrubbed the rugs, polished all the furniture, and cleaned the glass next to the door. Before she hung the pictures, she cleaned the glass and polished the frames."

"Chris, your house must be spotless."

"Bob, you would not believe it. If I get up to go to the bathroom in the middle of the night, she makes my side of the bed before I get back. But, enough about my wife, do you want to ride with me to go visit some of the technicians at our customer locations?"

"Chris, I would love to! How soon do you want to leave?"

"As soon as possible. I would like to hit at least four locations this afternoon. I did not tell the guys I was going out into the field today, so it should be an interesting afternoon. Do you think any of them will be surprised when they see the president of the company and their new boss show up at their location unannounced? I have the addresses of the four customers, and I have mapped out the route."

"You are very wise, Chris! I will enjoy the afternoon riding with you. By the way, you should stop over to see Donna before we leave.

She has your business cards. We ordered them immediately after you accepted the job. We had them overnighted so they would be here on time for your start date."

"That is impressive, Bob."

"Chris, when you showed up to work early on Friday and agreed to fire ten deadbeat technicians, that was the least that I could do for you!"

"The least is not what I am expecting from you because I am going to get the most out of you!"

I laughed. "Every employee in this company is going to get the most out of me, but you probably knew that already."

"Sure did. Let's get going!"

Five minutes later, I met Chris in the parking lot and got in his Lexus SUV. We were at the first customer's location in about fifteen minutes. We walked in the front door of the office building and gave the receptionist our business cards. Chris asked if we could see Troy, the technician from ABC Computer Distributors.

The receptionist said, "Sure, follow me, I will take you back. By the way, Mr. Curry, we love Troy. He is awesome. He might be the funniest guy on earth, and Mr. Jones, the head of IT also likes and trusts Troy."

The receptionist took us to Troy's work area. When we walked in, Troy was shocked to see us. "What are you doing here?" was the first thing to come out of his mouth. Then he corrected himself. "Ah, I mean, welcome, did I do something wrong?"

"Not that I am aware of," Chris replied. "Did you do anything wrong I should know about?"

"I am the least of your worries in the whole service department," he answered confidently.

"Are there any problems with this client?" Chris pressed.

Troy looked confused. "No, these people are the best."

"How long do you think you will be working here for this customer?"

"Hopefully full time for the rest of my career. I am here about four and a half days a week. The only time I am not here is when one of the other technicians has a problem they cannot solve. They call me, and I go fix the issue."

Chris barely acknowledged Troy's statement, then said, "Okay, we are out of here."

Troy still looked confused. "Chris, why did you come here?"

"To see if you were working."

"Your second day on the job and you have to check on me?"

"Troy, I already have you on my schedule to come check on you daily!"

"No, sir!"

"See you later, Troy. I am warning you, if you call any of the other technicians to give them a heads up that we are going to their job site to check on them, I am going to fire your butt when you get back to the office."

"Chris, I would never do that."

"Yes, you would, and we both know it. I am going to check your phone when you get back to the office to make sure you did not call anyone."

"You do not need to do that; I am very trustworthy."

"Yeah, okay, see you at the office and have your phone ready for me to check it!"

It occurred to me that Chris was giving Troy a tough time, and I wondered why. I supposed that he had his reasons. I asked Troy how he was doing.

"Good, until you hired Chris. I used to work for him two years ago, and he fired me."

"He fired you, why?"

"Just kidding. I joined ABC because Craig offered me a bigger salary."

Chris chimed in sarcastically, "Yeah, a buck a day, big raise!"

"Chris, it was two dollars an hour," Troy said.

Just as we were leaving, the client's IT manager, Mike, walked into the room, introduced himself, and handed us one of his business cards. Chris and I did likewise.

"How is Troy doing here, okay?" I asked.

Mike said, "Troy does a great job for us. I would like to talk to you about having him stationed here full time if that is possible."

"I think that we can make that happen," Chris agreed readily. "When I get back to the office, I will draw you up a contract and email it over to you for signature. Okay?"

"Yes, Chris, I am glad that you stopped by to visit Troy. I have meant to give your company a call for a while. I think we need to purchase some servers for our network. Who do I talk to about buying hardware from your company?"

"Who is your salesperson from our company?" I asked.

Mike took a moment to think. "Gee, Bob, I don't know. Maybe the person who called on us in the past no longer works for your company. I have not heard from anyone in quite a while."

"Well, now Chris and I each have an assignment to follow up on: a service contract and a salesperson for you."

Mike said he would appreciate that, and added, "Nice meeting you. I have to run to a meeting. Maybe we can get together sometime soon for lunch and talk business."

"That would be great," I said. "I will give you a call, and maybe we can go grab lunch together later next week?"

Mike said he looked forward to my call and headed for his meeting.

As Chris and I returned to his car, I said, "We went to visit one customer and got a sale of a service contract and a request from the customer to sell them some hardware. Sales in this industry is not a hard thing to do. And, Chris, you were pretty hard on Troy, weren't you?"

"Bob, that joker is my brother-in-law. He worked for me at my old company for five years before he came to ABC two years ago. I see him every other week at my house. What you saw is soft compared to how I usually treat that clown."

"But he is a pretty good tech, right?"

"He is excellent. Troy and Roger are the best in the department of all the technicians I know. We need to determine how good or bad the other guys are with their customers, which is why we are out here right now. If I am in the office all the time, I am not making us any money. Out here in the field is where the action is, as you know."

"I could not agree with you more," I said buckling my seatbelt. "We are now one for one, Chris."

Chris started the car. "I have a plan to visit each of my customers from my old company by the end of January. They all love me and don't even know my ex-boss, the owner, because he never left his office, so there will be no loyalty to him. Right now, you and I have more customer visits together today than I had with my old boss in nine years."

> Too many senior executives of companies spend too much time in their office and not enough time with their employees, customers, and vendors. The way to make money in business is spend less time on your office and more time with your team, customers and suppliers.

Chris and I visited three more customers that afternoon. At each visit, we were able to meet with our technician, as well as with the IT and purchasing manager at each company. I scheduled lunches with two of the purchasing managers. Chris planned to return to each customer to meet with the IT manager to discuss service issues and annual contracts. I received two requests to have a salesperson visit the company because they wanted to place orders for hardware to use their current year's capital budget before the year ended.

> In most organizations, the president is the best salesperson in the company because customers love to meet the owner and talk business. The owner can make pricing decisions on the spot and resolve problems when necessary. It is very important that the owner/president of a company gets out to meet with customers and understands what is going on in the field.

We arrived back at the office at 4:45 p.m. I went to meet with Tom to pass on my messages to get salespeople out to those customers.

Tom and I also talked about some of our customers who did not have a salesperson assigned to the account. Tom said that he was not aware we had a problem with unassigned customers, but he would investigate the issue, and have it solved immediately. He also assured me that he would get a salesperson out to those four customers tomorrow.

"Tom, I learned a lot today."

"What did you learn, Bob?"

"First, there is a huge demand out there for good service technicians."

"I agree, but our problem has been that Craig did all the hiring of the service department. He had no idea how to hire the right people. The ten technicians that Chris and Roger fired on Friday were Craig's last ten hires."

I shared my other lesson for the day: "I also learned that there are companies out there who have money in the capital budget and need to spend the money before the end of the year. If they have the money in the budget, they need to spend the balance remaining, or they will lose it at the end of December. Tom, we need our salespeople to visit every single one of our customers *immediately* to get those purchase orders."

Tom took a deep breath. "I will call an emergency sales meeting tomorrow and take care of that problem immediately."

"It is not a problem; it is an opportunity!" I corrected him. "The last thing I learned today was that the four technicians we visited at the customer locations were all awesome. Each of the customer's IT managers told Chris and me that they loved their assigned technicians."

"That is great news," Tom agreed. "Now, all we need are more technicians like those four."

I nodded. "I know, that is my next project. My first project was to get Chris hired. Now my next task is to get more quality technicians hired. Tom, I have to run. Monday nights are my men's basketball night at the YMCA."

"Enjoy your evening, and I will see you in the morning," Tom said.

"Thanks, and please send my regards to Nancy when you get home and find her slaving over a hot stove cooking your dinner."

"You are a funny guy, Bob!"

* * *

After our basketball game, Chris told me that I had to join him at Duffy's because he had invited five technicians from his old company to meet us there. That was not a problem because only six guys from our team showed up for the game. Therefore, I was exhausted. I had to stay on the court most of the game.

When Chris and I arrived at Duffy's, the five technicians were sitting around a big table in the corner of the restaurant. They each had a beer in front of them, and a massive stack of wings was in the middle of the table for all to share.

Chris and I walked around the table as he introduced me to the guys. This group seemed like a different sort compared with the technicians at ABC Computer Distributors. They were all young in their mid-twenties and early thirties, resembling young executives rather than computer nerds. Their appearance impressed me.

After my introductions to the "young executives," Chris and I sat at the table for a while to chat with them. We each ordered a beer. I got the impression that Chris had hired a bunch of technicians at his old company who were very similar to him. They all were very personable, dressed nice, groomed professionally, confident, and polished. I knew after an hour that I would hire any of them in a heartbeat, assuming they passed the background check and drug test. If they did, these guys were the epitome of the type of employee I wanted at ABC Computer Distributors.

Chris asked, "Bob, do you think that we have any room in our company for any of these clowns?"

"If you are vouching for these techs, I am okay with hiring them. They are going to be working in your department, so you are the one accountable for their production and results."

"All of these guys are stationed one hundred percent of the time at their customer's locations. You will rarely see their faces other than at the holiday party once a year. Or if they screw up something at the job site, then I have to bring them into the office and beat them up some."

Chris' language about his former employees was a little rough around the edges, but every one of them loved Chris and would follow him anywhere. It appeared to me that he was not a good manager, he was a great service manager, and I was lucky to have him on my team. "Did you share with them that they must pass background and drug tests?"

"I did, and it was not a problem with any of these guys."

"Okay, good, then the second issue. Are the customers for the techs going to approve of moving the service contract over to our company?"

"Bob, that is not a problem either. They have all talked to their customers' IT managers and told them that I had moved over to ABC Computer Distributors recently, and they were considering making the move also. They asked the IT managers if it would be okay if I presented them with a new service contract for the new year. They all got an affirmative answer."

I looked at the group sitting at the table and asked, "Gentlemen, is all this true?"

They confirmed that it was. I also asked if any of them had signed a non-compete, non-solicitation agreement with their current company. They had not.

"If we hire them, Chris, I assume they need to give their present company two weeks' notice."

"Yes, but I know from personal experience that the owner will cut them loose as soon as they give notice. Bob, I have already talked to the customers they are servicing, and they know this transaction is going to happen."

"And all five told you, Chris, that they would sign a new contract immediately and they would be okay with receiving their invoices from us in the future?"

"Bob, five for five!"

Of course, the techs were listening to this exchange since it was tight quarters at the table.

"Mr. Curry, my name is Greg," one of the young men said. "There are at least ten other technicians at the company who would be very happy to jump over to your company now that Chris is working for you. We all like and respect Chris and enjoy having him as our manager. He is one of the good guys. Unfortunately, the owner of our company is not. None of us out in the field hardly even know him because we are only numbers to him, but that is not how Chris treats us. He always has our backs if there is a problem at the customer's location."

I looked at Chris with mock disbelief. "How much did you pay him to say all that?"

Chris just smiled and said, "These guys are the best of the best. They require very little supervision, do an excellent job, and their customers love them."

"I guess you cannot ask for any more than that. You have my approval to go ahead with this transaction. Chris, have them all answer our ad in the Philadelphia Inquirer, so we do not get in trouble with your old employer. I am okay with pulling the trigger with these guys immediately."

> Chris is the type of manager that would have fit in well with H&N Construction Company with Hal and Nick. He hired the best people, treated them with respect and paid the fairly. Just as Greg stated, Chris *had their backs*, but the owner did not. When it comes to the corporate culture that I am trying to generate, Chris was the perfect hire for ABC Computer Distributors.

"I knew you would agree with me to hire these guys, Bob, so that is why over the weekend, I drew up service contracts for the five customers. I already talked to Donna this morning and gave her the five resumes. She gave me dates and times to have each technician come in to meet with her and get all the paperwork done. After they meet with Donna, they are scheduled to go to the clinic for the drug test. This week, I am going to visit each customer to present the new service contract and get it signed immediately. These guys have already written the letter of resignation and are going to hand it in this week. Are you okay with all of this? I know that this is all happening very fast, but I did not want to lose these particular technicians to one of our other competitors. Because you are such a good businessperson, I knew you would recognize that this is a profitable transaction for our company."

"Chris, two things. First, I trust you, but I think that you should partner with me on future decisions, just because the two of us can make better decisions than just one."

Chris shook his head yes and said, "No problem, I understand! What is the second thing, Bob?"

"Make it happen!"

"You will not regret it!" Chris said enthusiastically.

The guys around the table look excited too.

"Hiring these guys will turn out to be a great move for our company! This decision will turn out much better than most of those shots you took tonight on the basketball court!" Chris joked.

I gave him a sideways glance. "Chris, did you notice that when I shot foul shots, the ball made it all the way to the rim? That is required if you ever want to make a free throw. But when you are on the foul line to shoot two, you are *never* going to be able to make the shot if you don't shoot the ball and make it all the way to the rim. I bet that was embarrassing for you!"

"Bob, you know that was the first time that ever happened," he said with a playful bump on the shoulder.

"You are right—not since the last time!"

I finished my beer, stood up, and walked around the table and shook hands with each of the guys and welcomed them to the company. Each of them thanked me and told me that they were looking forward to working with Chris again—and now with me.

"Gentlemen, I need to ask you all a favor. When you come in to meet with Donna to complete the paperwork, please see Tom, our sales manager. Once you join the company, I would like you to introduce one of our salespeople to meet with the purchasing manager to sell the company hardware and software. And, by the way, our company pays every employee in the company a commission for a customer referral. You will receive five percent of the gross profit as a referral fee on every order for one year."

The guys seemed pumped by this good news. "Chris," one of the guys said, "you mentioned nothing about referral fees. Were you going to keep all the money for yourself?"

"Guys," he chided, "today was my first day at work. Sue me for not having all the benefits memorized yet."

"That is bull," another joked. "When it comes to money, you have *all* the rules memorized!"

"Gentlemen, welcome to ABC Computer Distributors." I gave each one my business card. "If you have any questions, please call me anytime."

I left and drove home, feeling great. Building up the service department with talented technicians was yet another positive transaction in the matter of ABC Computer Distributors.

Chapter 12

"MR. BEST
IN THE COUNTRY"

*"If you hire people just because they can do a job, they'll work
for your money. But if you hire people who believe what you
believe, they'll work for you with blood and sweat and tears."*

—SIMON SINEK, BRITISH/AMERICAN AUTHOR, MOTIVATIONAL
SPEAKER AND MARKETING CONSULTANT

TUESDAY, DECEMBER 12—DAY 9 OF WEEK 2

DARREN KNOCKED ON MY OFFICE DOOR AT 7:30 A.M. WITH
a big smile on his face. He handed me a report on an Excel spreadsheet showing the monthly invoices by serial number sorted by technician with a total at the bottom of the page for the current month. I
reviewed the information and found a few problems. Several serial
numbers were missing from the report, but Darren had no idea why
they were missing. Then there were vast differences in the monthly
revenue totals by service technician. I did not know if the variance
was due to missing paperwork or some of the technicians were not
billing for all their time.

Darren told me he would follow up on the missing paperwork
for December. I also asked him to run the report for each month
for the past year. Darren guessed that the missing paperwork was

because the technicians were late turning in their timesheets to Gina, who does the billing for the department. He planned to call each technician immediately to track down the missing timesheets and have them processed by the following day.

Darren ran the reports for the past eleven months and followed up on missing paperwork for the whole year. He shared with me later that he had tracked down $86,000 of missing timesheets going back as far as January. He also told me that of the twenty technicians employed during the year, fifteen had all their paperwork processed and the other five were responsible for all the missing timesheets.

> **Profit Improvement:** Darren tracked down all the missing timesheets based upon the serial numbers. He processed all the paperwork with some of the timesheets being eleven months old. **$86,000 was invoiced in one day, representing 100 percent profit for the month.** December's financials suddenly looked much better than any prior month that year.

I developed the agenda for the following day's management meeting. We would discuss the existing customers without an assigned salesperson, the new hires in the service department, and next year's budgets, in addition to several other topics. Once I had completed the list of issues on the agenda, I printed copies and distributed one to each manager.

Later that day, Darren handed me a binder with the twelve monthly reports. He told me that all the missing invoices were recovered, processed, and now the reports were accurate. Behind the monthly reports, Darren produced graphs showing the monthly production of each technician along with a chart showing the top to the lowest revenue producers in the department.

It occurred to me that Darren had created a beautifully useful tool.

My first instinct was to get involved and fix the problem technicians on the bottom of the report, but I decided Chris should handle the issue now. I gave Chris the report and asked him to review the information, speak to the technicians, and then let me know how he planned to deal with the issues. Later on, Chris and I met to discuss his opinion on the status of his service department. First, he told me that he had created a department policy in which all timesheets must be turned in each morning for the prior day. He had used this rule at his old company and simply modified it to be our policy now. His assistant, Gina, was going to account for all the serial numbers and let him know if there were any not received. Second, he planned to meet with the bottom revenue producers and discuss their issues with them. I was satisfied with Chris's plan. When it came to dealing with problems, he and I had much in common.

Chris gave me his revenue projections by month for the first six months of the new year, something I did not ask for but appreciated receiving. The sales forecast showed a steady increase, and by the sixth month, the expected revenue almost doubled. I told Chris if he could accomplish this, he would be confirming that I had hired the best service manager in the state.

> A good manager does not stick his head in the sand when he must deal with an issue. He acknowledges the problem, gathers all the facts, develops a plan to resolve the problem, and then executes the plan and solves the issue quickly.

Chris smiled and said, "Bob, I would never give you revenue projections I could not achieve." He also added, "I am not the best service manager in the state—I am the best in the country!"

With a shake of my head, I left "Mr. Best in the Country" and headed back to my office. Tom saw me as I passed his office and called out, "Bob, if you have a minute, I have something that I need to show you."

I swung back around and entered his office. "Sure, Tom, what's that?"

"I had Darren run a sales report for me showing every company that ABC Computer Distributors invoiced over the past two years. He sorted the data from the highest sales volume customer to the lowest. Then he organized the customers by salesperson from the highest volume sales total to the smallest. What this report shows is we have fifty-two customers who have purchased at least fifty thousand dollars of products or services from us in the past two years that either doesn't have a salesperson assigned to the account or had one who is no longer working for the company. About half of the clients have either Craig's or Trish's sales number on the report.

"There are several more customers assigned to the two sales-people who we just fired last week and the one that we transferred to the sales support department. Bob, I owe you a thank-you for bringing this issue to my attention yesterday. When I start digging into the details, the problem always seems to get larger! Before you ask, I am ready to assign these problem accounts to seven different salespeople who must commit to me that they will visit each of these customers this week. Not only do they have to call on these neglected customers, but they must do a sales call with every account assigned before Christmas.

"There may be a lot of purchase orders out there to use up their capital budgets, just like the customer you visited yesterday. I have a checklist of every salesperson's accounts. I am meeting each morning with every salesperson to ask them which accounts they visited the prior day so I can check it off the list. Bob, I believe December is going to be a record month for this company in sales and profits since I joined the company."

> Our goal was to generate every sales opportunity that we could to reduce the year to date losses. Creating sales calls with all our customers to inquire if they had any funds in their capital budget was a great strategy and worked very well creating millions of dollars of computer orders.

"Tom, how many customers purchased less than fifty thousand dollars but more than ten thousand dollars in the past two years?"

"Roughly a hundred more customers, Bob."

"Here is what I would suggest you do. Right now, we have

fourteen salespeople. I don't want to bring Nancy into the project because she has enough work to do with her client base, do you agree?"

"Yes, Bob, I do."

"But, Tom, please give her a call anyway and give her the option."

"Okay, I will do that."

"I do not want to make assumptions that she is too busy to be assigned more customers, and I do not want her to be upset that we did not offer her this newly discovered opportunity."

Tom agreed and went on to say that if Nancy did not want to be assigned more customers, we were left with thirteen salespeople to assign to these accounts. He suggested breaking up the customers into groups: one group with more than $50,000 in sales will be called the "A" accounts. The second group with less than $50,000 but more than $10,000 in sales, we will call them the "B" accounts, and the third group with less than $10,000 in sales are the "C" accounts. He suggested assigning the thirteen salespeople four customers each from the "A" accounts. Each salesperson would be responsible for calling the customer to set up an appointment and visit the customer within the next two weeks. The "B" accounts would be similarly divided and would need to be visited by the salesperson assigned before the end of December. The customers on the "C" list must have a sales call by the salesperson in January."

I was very impressed by Tom's plan, but he was concerned that this would be too heavy a workload for the salespeople and added, "We cannot forget about the ten target customers recently assigned to each salesperson."

"I realize that all these salespeople have target customers and have been working on them for the past week plus. What is the average number of customers each salesperson has assigned to them?"

"The highest is twenty, and the smallest amount is fifteen," he replied.

"And how many customers does Nancy call on?" I asked.

"Fifty-nine."

"According to Nancy's customer base, we have a feel for how

many customers a salesperson is capable of handling. If these thirteen salespeople each currently have fifteen to twenty customers and have recently been assigned ten more target customers, and now we are giving them thirteen to fourteen more unassigned customers, they are still at only at seventy-five percent the number of customers that Nancy is calling on."

If Tom was not already impressed by his wife's extraordinary selling ability, this had laid it out for him very clearly.

"Tom, we have the target customers we assigned to the salespeople listed on the whiteboard in the sales conference room. The goal in doing that is to put pressure on the salespeople to produce. We are reporting to the whole sales team how well each salesperson is doing their job by getting appointments with these possible future customers and selling hardware, software, and service. We are rewarding them extra over their regular sales commissions for doing this.

"Now, these A and B customers are a different story. These customers have purchased product and services from us. They know our company, and we are neglecting them by not having a salesperson assigned to their account. That is different than the target customers. Those target customers may not even know that our company exists. The target customers are a tougher sell than the As and Bs customers. The salespeople should thank you profusely for assigning them these accounts. These customers are truly 'low hanging fruit' just waiting to see a salesperson.

"Tom, what I am concerned about that is that if our salespeople do their jobs properly and call on all these customers in the next two weeks, sales support and the purchasing departments are going to be swamped with work—more than they can handle."

"That is a very valid concern," Tom agreed.

I had a good idea. "Let's get Darren and Patrick in on this meeting. I want them to help track and report the sales of the target customers, as well as the A and B customers for the next three months. I also want to keep track of each salesperson's customer visits during this period. Chris and I visited four clients and received three requests to meet a salesperson for the acquisition of computers and service contracts, so I know there is business out there. I want you to hold the salespeople in your department accountable for visiting their customers a minimum of three times in two months. Do you think that is reasonable, to visit every customer once every three weeks?"

"Nancy is on such a schedule, and that is why she is so successful."

"Tom, let's help these other thirteen salespeople to be as successful as Nancy. Please call Darren and ask him and Patrick to meet us in the conference room."

Tom called Darren, and ten minutes later, the four of us met in the conference room.

"Gentlemen, Tom and I need the help of your department."

"Sure Bob, how can we help?" Darren asked.

"I discovered from my visits to four customers yesterday afternoon with Chris that we have customers without a salesperson assignment. Tom confirmed the problem with the sales reports you gave him. We have over one hundred fifty customers who have purchased product or services from our company in the past two years who do not have a salesperson assigned to call on their accounts. Obviously, that is a problem. It is an easily resolved problem with your help.

"As you know, I am a strong believer in policies, procedures, reporting, and accountability. We have an excellent opportunity to assign these customers to our salespeople and have our sales team call on them immediately. To support Tom with his sales manager responsibilities, please create a report that will help him accomplish this task. First, I would like you to run a report that shows sales by salesperson by customer for this total year. I would like the sales broken down into three buckets: 1) hardware/software, 2) service and 3) the total sales.

"Next, Tom is going to ask each salesperson to call on every one of their customers at least three times every two months. We are going to give each salesperson a Sales Call Report to complete every time they meet with a customer (see page 363). We need an Excel spreadsheet to log those sales calls to ensure that our salespeople are accomplishing their responsibility of meeting face to face with every one of their assigned customers at least once every three weeks. My third request is for you to capture the future customer sales in three new categories. All the salespeople, except for Nancy, have between fifteen and twenty existing accounts assigned to them right now. That is the first sales category: existing accounts. The second category is the ten target customers that the salespeople were all assigned at our last sales meeting. The third category is the unassigned customers. I would also like this report broken down into hardware/software, service, and total sales. Darren, is this reporting doable with our sales system?"

Darren gave me a confident nod. "I thought you were going to give us something tough to accomplish. Our system can handle this without a problem. So, bottom line, you need these reports and an Excel spreadsheet to track the sales departments sales calls. When do you need them by?"

"When can you have them done?"

Darren looked at Patrick and asked, "Do you want to do the Excel spreadsheet, and I will do the sales reports?"

Patrick answered, "Yes, I know what he is looking for, no problem."

Darren said, "Bob, how about one o'clock today?"

I laughed. "I was going to ask if you could get it done by next Monday, but since you offered, today is okay. Thank you, you two are the best! Gentlemen, you are making my job so much easier, and I appreciate it!"

"I am glad we can help! It is exciting watching you make these great changes."

"I am not changing anything. All I am doing is trying to increase sales by making our sales team accountable to visit our customers. What a novel idea: ask your salespeople to call on their assigned customers to sell our products. Is that magic or what? I think I am going to write up this idea and send it to the *Harvard Business Review* to get their opinion on the concept. I can see it now, 'We are asking our sales team to visit our customers to sell them our products and services!' Maybe they should publish that idea in their magazine, so other people reading the article will make their sales force do the same, call on their customers."

The men in attendance laughed, and Patrick remarked, "I am only an accountant, Bob, but I don't think your idea is going to get published."

"And I thought I had such an original idea," I joked.

Tom spoke up and said, "Bob, since you joined the company, I have been working hard, but I am enjoying every minute. Prior to these past ten days, I was going through the motions. But now I am pumped, motivated, excited, and producing. I feel like I am twenty-five years old again. Nancy is energized too, as am I. After you helped her close that big deal, she is flying high. I would not be surprised if she doubles her sales volume next year."

"Tom, you are giving me goosebumps!"

Tom laughed. "By the way, I have those evaluations for each of the salespeople I traveled with on sales calls. Do you want to see the ones I have done?"

"Yes, I do, but give me a recap before I review your paperwork," I requested.

"I think we have a pretty good team. Most of the salespeople dress very nice, are polished, and seem to have some motivation now. The sales calls I attended went very well. I believe that when I am there, they have confidence that if they screw up something, I will save them. I think that is the biggest issue, a lack of confidence when they go on sales calls alone."

"That makes sense to me. How do you suggest we resolve this issue?"

"I am going to go on at least two sales calls every day for the next month to do what I can to build up the confidence of the whole department. Bob, all the salespeople have asked me if they can bring Chris on some sales calls so he can help them close some service deals."

"Talk to him, Tom. I am sure he will be on board with that. His success here depends on building up his department. To accomplish that, he needs a bunch more service contracts signed soon."

"I will do that," Tom said. "I like Chris. He is easy to talk to about anything. Friday night, after the happy hour, we were hanging out with him until ten."

"Wow, Tom, were either of you sober?"

"We switched over to iced tea early on," he assured me.

"Chris is a good guy with a great personality and knows service extremely well. He will be great to take on sales calls to close service contracts, but we should find a salesperson who knows service so we can get more service deals closed quickly."

"How do we go about finding that person, Bob?"

"I found Chris, so maybe I can find a good service department salesperson also. I will check with Chris to see if he knows anyone. Okay, gentlemen, thank you for your time."

I strolled over to Chris's service area to see if he was available. He was in his office, so I gently knocked on his door to get his attention.

Chris said, "Yes sir, what can I do for you?"

"Do you know any salesmen who can sell service for us?"

"Yes, Bob, me!"

"I already know that you can sell. You have an awesome personality and people like you. It is so much easier to sell when the customer likes you. But do we need to add a salesperson to build up your department quicker?"

"Bob, I rather travel with the salespeople and meet the IT managers in each company. The more customers I know, the more service I can sell. I have a great closing rate when I get in front of the customers."

"Okay, I will trust you that this is the best way to do this."

"Bob, once the new techs are on our payroll, I have ten more candidates when we are ready."

"You are going to be the one who needs someone to start your car in the parking lot. The owner of your old company is surely going to be angry at you for stealing all his people and customers."

"That is where he would be wrong. They are not his people to steal; they are my people. You heard Greg's comments last night. Since we met those guys in Duffy's, I have received calls from twelve more techs today asking me if they can come to ABC Computer Distributors, too."

"I know that they are loyal to you, but I guarantee your former employer is going be one hurting entrepreneur if we steal fifteen service technicians who were billing 100 percent of their time from his payroll. He is going to lose a ton of cash flow and profits."

"Maybe he will learn a lesson to treat people right, to avoid anything like this happening to him and his business in the future."

"Maybe," I said. "Please keep me updated on how things go with the new techs after they put in their two weeks' notice."

* * *

Chris called me later to say that the techs handed in their letter of resignation. According to Greg, who had given him the news, their employer first asked them to stay on his payroll for two weeks to a month to give him time to replace them. They all tentatively agreed, that is until he started trashing me for stealing his people. Although they would not tell him who their new employer was, he figured it out and cut them loose. That guy is not very smart! They are all ready to start immediately."

"Okay, Chris. You need to get out to their customers and get a new service contract signed as soon as possible."

"I will get that done this afternoon. By tomorrow morning, our company is going to have five new customers. Exciting, huh, Bob?"

"Don't forget to look under your car," I said, perpetuating our running joke. "Here's a good idea: ask Tom to join you, so he can meet the customers and see if they need hardware. He can also drive and save your car from getting blown up."

Chris laughed. "I will ask Tom to go, but I am not worried about that 'worm' I used to work for causing me any physical harm, and he does not have a legal leg to stand on."

"Well, with him being a worm, I can see why. Anyway, get out into the field and close some deals."

"Will do, and by the way, will I receive a commission for bringing on these techs?" he asked.

"Yes, Chris, if they are here for six months, you will receive one thousand dollars per new hire. And each tech is going to receive a commission for the sales to the new customer for one year starting immediately."

"That is awesome. It is going to be even easier to recruit these guys when I explain that there is some icing on the cake in addition to their salary."

"Chris, I am a firm believer that if you take care of your people, your people take care of you. I am not greedy. My goal is to treat every employee as an entrepreneur. The more money the company makes, the more money every employee takes home in their paychecks and bonuses."

"This company is going to be so profitable; it is going to be ridiculous," Chris said.

"That is the attitude I want to spread out through the whole company. I want everyone to know that the harder they work, the more money the company makes. And the more money the company makes, the more money they make."

"I will be your biggest cheerleader," Chris promised. "Your philosophy is my philosophy."

"Hey, why don't you put on a cheerleader outfit for our Monday night basketball games. You really would be the "BIGGEST CHEERLEADER!"

He laughed at the absurdity. "You know that need me on the court to rebound *all* your missed shots!"

"Speaking of missed shots, get your other ten techs lined up before your old company tries to stop them from leaving. Like the first five guys, make sure they send in their resume to the advertisement in the Philadelphia Inquirer. As soon as we get the first five on the payroll and their customers signed up with new service contracts, I want to meet the others and, if all checks out, get them on the payroll too."

"How about I tell them to meet us at Duffy's Monday night after our basketball game?"

"Make it happen!"

"You know that at one thousand per man, I am looking at making fifteen thousand."

"You are going to get paid a lot more than that when we make this company amazingly profitable. Just wait until you see your bonus check!"

> If you take care of your people, your people take care of you. My goal is to treat every employee as an entrepreneur. The more money the company makes, the more money the employees take home in their paychecks and bonuses.

"My wife is going to love you! Maybe she will even hire a housekeeper!"

Ready to see the profits come rolling in, I urged, "Chris, get with Tom and get those contracts signed!"

"I will see you in the morning, Bob, with five new service contracts signed," Chris promised.

* * *

Before I went home for the evening, I decided that I should also spend some time out in the field with one of the salespeople before and after the management meeting the following day, so I headed to Tom's office.

When he invited me in, I said, "Tom, I would like to go on a couple of sales calls tomorrow. Can you hook me up with some salespeople?"

"Sure, Bob. I was going to ride with Alice tomorrow for a nine o'clock and eleven o'clock appointment. How about you take those two sales calls, and I will find someone else to ride with?"

"Okay, I assume that she will be leaving from here in the morning?"

"Yes, I will text her and let her know you are taking my spot."

"Could you also find another sales call for me after our management meeting?"

"Monica is visiting one of the target customers tomorrow at three o'clock, so you can ride with her. Monica lacks confidence. Maybe you can help her in that regard."

"Tom, I will try my best, but you just named my weakness: confidence."

Tom let out a big guffaw. "You, Bob Curry, will never be short of confidence, not in a million years."

Chapter 13

LIFE IS GOOD!

"Rule #1—Never lose money. Rule #2—Never forget Rule #1."

—WARREN BUFFETT, AMERICAN BUSINESS MAGNATE,
INVESTOR, AND PHILANTHROPIST

WEDNESDAY, DECEMBER 13—DAY 10 OF WEEK 2

AT 8:30 A.M., ALICE KNOCKED ON MY DOOR AND WALKED INTO my office. She said, "Good morning, Mr. Curry."

"Good morning, Alice." Alice was about 30 years old and had long blond hair that she wore in a ponytail. She was only about five feet three inches tall, always dressed very professionally, and looked about ten years younger than her actual age. The beautiful thing about Alice, she was always smiling and appeared happy.

"Tom told me that you are going to be coming with me for my two sales appointments this morning."

"That's right, Alice. Tom told me you could teach me a lot about sales if I just sat back at the sales call and watched a good salesperson do her job. And please, Alice, call me Bob."

"Did Tom honestly say that?"

"No, he didn't, but making a joke is how I break the ice with a person. I have always been a little nervous when I first meet people."

"Is that true?"

"No, I was just kidding about that, too. So, Alice, tell me about the customers we are going to meet today, so I don't have any surprises when we get there. I don't want to get caught saying something stupid to your client."

"Okay, Bob, the nine o'clock appointment is with one of my existing clients. I have been calling on them for a year and a half now. The purchasing manager is Ted. Ted seems like a good guy. When we first met, there was good chemistry, and he immediately gave me the opportunity to bid on a couple of orders. There were three orders, one was two hundred fifty thousand, one was three hundred thousand, and the third was ninety thousand. I won the second and third orders. That was at the beginning of this year. They have not bought anything from us since then."

"Why not?"

"That is one of the questions I plan to ask Ted today."

"Alice, tell me about Ted. What does he like to do? Is he married? Have children? Anything you know."

"I don't know anything personal about him. Why do you ask?"

"I always try to create friendly relationships with customers. If Ted was your friend as well as your customer, your sales success with him would be better. Do we have a service contract with this company?"

"No, we do not."

"Have we presented them a proposal to do their service for the company?"

"No, we have not."

"Why not?"

"I don't have a valid answer to your question, Mr. Curry, I mean, Bob. I should have talked to the IT manager about our company handling their service."

"Do you have a checklist of questions you ask your clients on a sales call?"

"I have never thought about that, but I suppose a list of questions would be valuable."

"Do you know what Ted's annual budget is for capital purchases in IT?"

"No, I don't."

"Do you have a notebook with you?"

"No, I don't."

"Okay, I will wait for you here while you go get one."

*   *   *

Tom came into my office door and asked, "Bob, have you seen Alice yet this morning?"

"Yes, she just left to go to get a notebook to take some notes."

"Notes about what?"

"I asked her some questions about the customer we are going to see. I asked her about the purchasing manager. She has called on this company for a year and a half and knows very little about the company. Tom, I believe your salespeople should know as much about their customers as they know about our company. It is what I call 'relationship selling.'"

"Bob, I could not agree with you more. I knew there would be benefits to our sales team if you rode with some of the salespeople on sales calls. Please give Alice all your best advice."

"After this morning, based on our conversation so far, Alice is going to have the opportunity to grow into a sales career. But my conversation with Alice makes me worry that we have twelve other problems on the sales team. Everyone but Nancy needs to learn how to be a more effective salesperson."

"Bob, I was going to surprise you, but since we are talking about it now, I will share my plans with you. Starting in January, we are going to have mandatory sales training classes with all the salespeople and the sales assistants. I am in the process of putting together the syllabi for the classes. I plan on doing sales training every morning from seven thirty until nine for the first two weeks of the new year. If we are going to do one hundred twenty million dollars in sales next year, we are going to have all the salespeople and the sales assistants firing on all cylinders! My goal is to understand the weakness of each of the salespeople individually and address it through sales training."

"That is a great surprise, Tom! Once you have everything put together, let's sit down and review it together. I am sure that it is going to be great and exactly what the sales team needs. Thank you for being proactive with this training idea."

"I am just trying to do my job as well as I can. I now catch myself thinking, *What would Bob do in this circumstance?* Asking myself that question helps me come up with good solutions."

"Thank you, Tom. Keep up the good work and get your team motivated!"

* * *

When Alice and I arrived at the customer's location and escorted to their conference room with the purchase manager, Alice introduced me. "Ted, I would like to introduce you to the new company president of ABC Computer Distributors, Bob Curry. Bob, Ted is the purchasing manager here, and as I told you earlier, Ted has been one of our customers for almost two years."

"Bob, I am pleased to meet you. How long have you been at ABC?"

"For quite a while, I think that it has been … ten days now."

Ted smiled and sat back in his seat. "Well, if you have only been with the company for a week and a half and decided to come visit our company, I am honored."

"Ted, thank you. How long have you worked here?"

"I have been here for ten years, ten long years!"

"You work for a great company," I said, although, in reality, I knew very little about it. "Please tell me about your company."

Ted stated that the company had thirteen hundred employees, and even added that they were going to finish the year with sales of $950 million. He seemed proud of how well their company was doing. After he had given me a good idea of what this company was all about, I turned to personal matters. "Where are you from originally?" I asked.

"Pittsburgh, born and raised in Pittsburgh, Pennsylvania."

"I thought I recognized that accent. I am from Pittsburgh also. Are you still a Steelers fan?"

"My brothers would disown me if I rooted for another team."

"I was at all four of the Steelers Super Bowls! The first one in seventy-five against the Vikings, in seventy-six and seventy-nine versus the Dallas Cowboys, and in eighty when they beat the LA Rams. What a great team they had back in those days!"

"Do you remember the 'Steel Curtain'? Their defensive front line may have been the best in the history of the NFL, Ernie Holmes, LC Greenwood, Dwight White, and "Mean Joe" Green. Those Steelers teams from seventy-five to eighty had very few weaknesses on either side of the ball."

I looked over at Alice, realizing she was probably not a football fan and had no idea about any of these references we were making. She kept a pleasant expression on her face nonetheless. Not wanting to make her uncomfortable, I said, "Ted, I don't want to waste your time right now talking about the good old days. Maybe we could meet some evening after work to share our Steeler stories."

"I would enjoy that!" he agreed.

"Are you a golfer?" I asked then.

"Yes, I am, but I could be better if I had time to practice."

"Have you ever played at Pine Valley?"

"No, I have not, but I would give my right arm to play Pine Valley!"

"Are you available this Saturday?"

"Are you asking me if I am available to play a round of golf this Saturday at Pine Valley Country Club? Of course, I am. If my wife has any plans for us, I will cancel them for a round of golf at Pine Valley."

"Let me make a phone call and see if we can get a tee time. A wonderful friend of mine is a member and has invited me to play there many times. Let me see if he is in town and available."

I called my buddy, and he said that he was not in town right now but will be back on Saturday. He put me on hold and three minutes later, he came back on the line and told me that we have a nine thirty tee time for a foursome. I shared this news with my new friend Ted.

"Ted, is your IT Manager here a golfer too?"

"Bob, he is, will there be room for him to join us?"

"Sure, if that is okay with you. Can we meet your IT manager now?"

"I will give him a call and see if he is available to come over to meet you and Alice."

Ted called Scott, and within two minutes, he walked into Ted's office.

"Scott, this is Bob Curry and Alice. Bob is the president of ABC Computer Distributors, and Alice is our sales rep. Have you ever met Alice, Scott?"

Scott said, "I have not. It is very nice to meet you both. Bob, are you a member of Pine Valley?"

"No, Scott, but I wish that I was. Their price tag to join there is way above my budget for golfing. But I have the second-best option at the country club, a close friend of mine is a member and can get me on the course with a phone call."

"Now that is what I call an excellent friend!"

"Scott, are you available Saturday morning to join Ted and me to play?"

"There are very few things that would cause me to turn down an invitation to play Pine Valley. Yes, I am available."

"Great, so now we have a foursome. I would suggest that you get there between eight and eight thirty to hit some balls before we tee off. The weather is supposed to unseasonably warm, and there is no rain expected for the weekend. If anyone asks you who you are with, you tell them that you are a guest of R. Jay Sigel."

"Jay Sigel, the pro golfer who played on the Champion Tour, *that* Jay Sigel?"

"Yes, Jay and I have been friends for almost thirty years. He is the best. An amazing golfer and an upstanding gentleman!"

"I followed him when he was an amateur. I know that he won

the British Amateur, the U.S. Amateur twice, and was the only golfer ever to win the U.S. Amateur and the Mid-Amateur in the same year."

"He was the low amateur in the 1980 Open Championship, the 1984 U.S. Open, and the Masters Tournament three times. He invited me to stay at his rental home when he played at Augusta National in the Masters twice. Yes, Mr. Sigel is the person who made the phone call for you to play Pine Valley."

"Bob, please tell him that Ted and I said thank you for the opportunity."

"Scott, you can tell him Saturday when you meet him on the number-one golf course in the nation and the world as determined by *Golf Digest Magazine*."

After the discussion about football had turned to golf, I realized that Alice was probably becoming increasingly uncomfortable. "Alice, I owe you an apology. You came here to talk about business with these gentlemen, and I have monopolized the conversation. I am very sorry."

"Bob, Scott and I are happy to have you join Alice on every sales call. What a pleasant surprise this has been!"

Alice smiled gracefully and took the lead. "Ted, several of my customers have money in their capital budget for the year and placed orders recently so they would not lose the opportunity to upgrade before they started buying against their next year's budget. Do you have any need to purchase computers or software before the end of the year?"

"I have about two hundred sixty thousand dollars available. How about I review my needs and send you the order tomorrow morning?"

"Ted, that would be great. Do you want me to call you in the morning to follow-up?"

"Yes, that would be perfect, Alice."

"And, Scott, when is your service contract for all your computers end?"

"In a month and a half, at the end of January."

Alice wrote that down in her notebook, and I asked, "Would it be okay if we quoted on your next year's contract?"

"Yes, please do."

Then I asked, "Do you have a list of all the hardware covered by the contract?"

"Give me three minutes. I will run and get you a copy of last year's contract and a list of our purchases for this year."

Scott left and returned a few minutes later with the prior year's contract and purchases orders for the additions for this year.

"Is there any hardware that we should delete from this list as retirements?" I asked.

"Good question. Everything that we purchased this year was an upgrade for hardware we retired and deleted from our asset schedules. We donated all the old hardware to the local computer tech college in Philadelphia."

"Ted, I see that only two of these purchase orders are from our company last year. Can we improve that this year?"

Possibly thinking of our golf game on Saturday, Ted replied, "I am sure I can make that commitment to you and Alice."

"Thank you, sir. We sincerely appreciate your business. And, Scott, I will get with our service manager, Chris, and get this contract quote back to you by Friday. Would that timing be okay with you?"

Scott asked if I meant the same Chris who had signed their present service contract, and when I confirmed that it was indeed the same person, he told me that they had the highest trust in Chris and was glad that he was now working for ABC Computer Distributors.

"Chris and I have played on the same basketball team over at the Y for many years," I shared. "I finally had the opportunity to work with him. And since he reports to me, he is going to have to pass me the ball on the basketball court more often. Other good news is that we hired five of Chris's best techs from his old company."

The two men seemed pleased by this news. Wanting to see Alice in action, I asked her to recap the meeting for us. She straightened up and said, "Scott will send me a purchase order by tomorrow morning, and if I have not received the PO, I will give Ted a follow-up call. Bob, you will be giving Chris this inventory of hardware for the service contract so he can draw up a quote by Friday morning. Does that cover everything?" she asked.

"Just about," I said and added, "Gentlemen, I will meet you two gentlemen at Pine Valley this Saturday between eight and eight-thirty."

"Bob, Scott and I will be riding together. We will be there by no later than eight o'clock. Plus, there is not a problem if we take a bunch of pictures of every hole while we are there, is there?"

"Pictures are not a problem!"

We stood up, and I said, "Alice and I sincerely appreciate your business. Here is my business card. If you ever have a problem, Alice is your sales contact. I promise you that you are in great hands with one of ABC Computer Distributors' top salespersons. But, please feel free to call me directly if there is anything that I can do to help either of you two gentlemen."

"How about the two of us meet you at Pine Valley to resolve any problems," Ted joked.

"Hmm, that does not sound like a bad idea," I replied. "Thank you again, and have a great day, gentlemen!"

* * *

"Alice, where are we headed next?" I asked when we got back in the car.

"Bob, before we go to the next client, could we talk for a few minutes?" she asked.

"If we have enough time before our next meeting, of course."

"Bob, you just closed two orders, and you never once tried to sell those guys. That was amazing. You were so comfortable talking to Ted and Scott. You traded a round of golf for two large orders, and they had no clue what you were doing. That was so smooth. I loved watching you in action. I learned so much. That was awesome."

"Thank you, Alice, I appreciate that. I have found over the years that it is so much easier to sell when you are not selling. Also, people do not want to buy anything from a salesperson. They much rather buy from their friends. If you become their friend, they will buy from you much more than if you are just another salesperson. Alice, I am not a salesperson. I have never held a sales position in my career nor do I look forward to it. You have probably noticed that I don't have a salesman type of personality. I enjoy meeting new people and having fun. There was an opportunity, I saw it and turned my new relationship with Ted and Scott into a friendly one. After four hours on the golf course together, they will never purchase any computer hardware from another computer distributor as long as I work for this company."

"Bob, I completely understand. I have always struggled with being a good salesperson. I cannot talk about the Steelers or invite my customers to play golf at Pine Valley, but I can become my clients' friend. I think that I can do that and do it well. My new plan is that I am going to try to be a good friend to my customers, and while I am there, I will sell them some hardware and service."

"Alice, since you are probably not a golfer or followed the Pittsburgh Steelers back in the late 70's and early eighties, I would not suggest that you bring up those topics in the future with Ted and Scott. But I would suggest that you do some research on those two gentlemen on Facebook and all the social media platforms and learn about their wives and children. Guys love to talk about their kids. If you get them talking about their families, they will let their guard down and start treating you like a friend rather than a salesperson."

Alice made some notes and thanked me for the sales relationship ideas.

"Alice, you are going to be a superstar. I can feel it in my bones."

After that bit about my bones, Alice and I headed to her second sales call. This company was a large manufacturer of medical equipment. We were on time for our appointment with the purchasing manager, Phil. I decided to greet Phil and sit back, observe Alice, and see what she had learned from our conversation.

Alice asked all the right questions and was much friendlier with this guy then she had been with Ted, even though she had been calling on Ted for a couple of years. When she had the opportunity, she asked Phil some personal questions, and he was open to talking about the company, his family, and the computer distributors that were our competition. She questioned Phil about his budget amount for capital purchases for the next year and asked if he had any money left in the current year's budget.

That question worked again. Phil committed to Alice that he would write up a purchase order and get it to her that afternoon. This PO was significant to her because this customer was on her target list and she could potentially receive a sizable bonus on the order if it was large enough. Alice asked if we could meet with the IT manager, but unfortunately, he was offsite. Phil agreed to have him call her right away. Alice's face lit up. This sales call was going exceptionally well, and the more Alice talked, the more confident she sounded. When the meeting ended, and we were in the car heading back to the office, Alice could hardly contain her excitement.

"Bob, we just closed two hardware deals, one service contract with the opportunity to close a second as soon as I hear from their IT manager. That is amazing! Your suggestions worked like a charm. The more I treated Phil like a friend and not like a customer, the more open he was to work with me. That felt so good. These two customers are going to make my month, maybe the best month of sales I have ever had since I joined the company."

"Alice, when we get back to the office, send these guys a thank-you note. Get with Chris to have him put the quote together for Scott. It will not take him very long since Scott was his customer last year. Then, post on your calendar to call Ted and Phil late in the morning if you have not received their purchase orders by noon. If Chris can finish the quote by tomorrow morning, I suggest you call Scott and ask him if you can hand deliver the quote, so he has it before noon. That will show him that you are a service-oriented 'friend' who sells computer hardware, software, and service. When you get the PO's from Ted and Phil, meet with Alan in purchasing, give him the orders, and ask him when he thinks he can ship the product."

"Do you mind if I pull the car over and take some notes?" she asked.

"I do not mind at all, Alice. It is better than taking notes while you are driving. I want to get back to the office in one piece!"

* * *

Our scheduled management meeting was at 1:00 p.m. I walked past the conference room at noon, and the whole management team was there. I went in to see what was going on. When I entered the room, the conversation suddenly stopped.

Although they obviously did not want me to hear what they were talking about, I did not expect that anything underhanded had been going on. I had come to know each manager pretty well at that point, but I had to ask, "What is going on in here? You all look as guilty as a kid with his hand in the cookie jar!"

"You caught us," Tom admitted. "We were just discussing what we are going to get you for Christmas!"

"Hmm. I am not sure if I believe that, but I do trust the people in this room, so I will not ask any more questions. Wait, I take that back. Here is one: do you want to have the management meeting now since everyone is already here?"

They all agreed. I went to get a copy of the agenda and my notebook and returned a few minutes later. When I arrived back at the conference room, someone from the local Panera Bread was setting up lunch.

Tom explained that they had all agreed to meet at noon for lunch in the conference room so that they would be there for the management when it started at 1:00. "We have plenty for you too!" he added.

"Works for me, let's eat!" I said. I was impressed that the management team had taken it upon themselves to meet up as a group for lunch prior to our weekly meeting.

We had several important issues on the agenda, so I started the meeting between bites. We first talked about all the unassigned customer accounts. Tom assured me that he assigned each account and that Darren and Patrick were going to have a weekly report to track the sales to these customers.

Next on the agenda was the hiring of five new technicians from Chris's old company. Both Donna and Chris confirmed that all five have gone through the hiring process and would be starting soon. Donna told me that she had received my comments back from the non-compete and non-solicitation agreements and made the changes. She also had the five new technicians sign both agreements, and they were now in their personnel files.

Donna then distributed copies of employee manuals to each manager, enough for each of their direct reports. She explained that the last page in the manual contained a tear-out signature page that each employee would need to sign and return to their manager. The page stated that the employee had read the employee manual, and would comply with all the policies from that day forward. Each manager was responsible for turning in the signed sheets from their team to Donna no later than Monday afternoon. Donna would file them in each employee's personnel file.

When Donna finished, Chris and Tom talked about having visited several customer accounts with the salespeople and how well those visits were going. I wanted to interrupt them so that I could talk about how Alice did that morning, but I kept quiet to keep Tom and Chris in the spotlight.

Chris next talked about all the missing service invoices that had been found and processed in the past few days because the service techs had not been turning in their paperwork timely. Chris assured the management team that the problem was solved, or we would never have this problem again! The good news was Darren processed the $86,000 of sales that went straight to profit for the month.

Finally, Darren talked about the status of the preparation of next year's budget to update everyone to make sure that everyone understood the deadlines. Darren shared with everyone that missing the deadline is not a good thing to do. The management meeting went very well and ended in fewer than thirty minutes, which included the time to finish our lunches.

* * *

At 2:00 p.m., it was time for our accounts receivable meeting. When I got back to the conference room, Darren was there with a copy of the accounts receivables listing for each of us.

"Darren, how are the receivables, buddy?" I asked.

"Bob, we are doing well with the AR."

"Where are the problems here?"

"I have good news for you," he said cheerfully. "The problems we discussed last week have been cleaned up. I talked to the three salespeople, and they all went to visit the customers and got checks for the delinquent invoices."

"That is great! Are there any invoices that are going to be delinquent by the end of the week?"

"Yes, Bob, but we are all over them right now. I expect to have several checks coming in the mail, based on the customers' commitments on the phone yesterday and this morning."

"Are there currently any problems with our payables?"

"No, sir, we are paid up current with every one of our vendors. This is the best cash position this company has been in for the past three years."

"Okay, I am done here. Darren, you are doing a great job. When our meeting ends as quickly as this one, my confidence in you and your department's work builds. But I just want to make sure that you are not getting too bored. Am I giving you enough work?"

"Bob being bored is not a problem right now. Patrick and I are very busy with all your requests. I am sure that your demands in the future are going to keep me busy as well. At some time in the future, I may come ask for help."

"If you need help right now, you have my permission to find another person for your department. Remember, I have already mentioned that once."

"Bob, things are going well right now because the more we accomplish, the easier the department is to manage," he said.

"Accurate and timely information is a great tool to get this company back to the point of profitability. Thank you for your and Patrick's help. The two of you have been superb. It is much appreciated!"

Darren gave me a big smile. "Okay, Bob, thank you for your time. I am willing to help fix any problems or roadblocks that get in the way of this company's success, so keep me in the loop if anything comes up. I know we need to establish a 'corporate culture' for this company where we all work together as a team and care for our customers, employees, stakeholders, and vendors."

*   *   *

It was time to ride along to the sales call that Monica had scheduled.

"Mr. Curry, may I call you Bob?" she asked.

"Yes, of course, Monica. Mr. Curry was my father, and he is much older than I am. If you call me Bob, I feel so much younger!"

Monica laughed. "Bob, we need to leave right now to make the sales call on time."

"I am ready to leave when you are."

Monica was a beautiful woman in her mid-thirties with short brown hair. She was average height and had a very athletic build. Monica had a very aggressive personality and was very easy to talk to anytime. Much like Nancy, I thought that she could be a top salesperson for the company.

In the car, Monica said, "I had a long conversation with Alice earlier. I have never seen her so excited about her future with this company. Did you give her a magic pill to get her this excited?"

"Of course, I did," I said, playing along. "No one can get that excited without the help of a magic pill!"

"I want one of those magic pills too."

"My magic pill turns a *salesperson* into a *friend* to the customer."

"Alice said she learned from you not to be a salesperson but to be a friend, but I did not believe it could be that easy. She told me that with your assistance, she closed two big computer orders, sold a very high-dollar service contract, and had another service contract ready to close tomorrow morning. Is that true?"

"It is quite true! Monica, let me ask you a question. Let's say you go to a car dealership to buy a new car. A salesman walks up to you and does his best to sell you a car, displaying his absolute best sales tactics. Then, one of your friends who works at the dealership walks over and asks what you are doing there. 'I am trying to purchase a new car here,' you answer. So, my question is, who do you purchase the car from—the salesman who is *trying* to sell you the car or your friend who works at the dealership?"

"My friend!" she replied without hesitation.

"Of course, you would! Today, Alice changed her sales approach from being a sales rep to become a friend to the purchasing and IT managers. She has a great future at this company if she stays with this method. I call it 'relationship selling.' Do you want a magic pill for this sales call?"

> All top salespeople build relationships with their clients through relationship selling. Salespeople that have strong relationships with their clients rarely loose an order for price. If their prices are too high, the customer will give you the final look at the order to adjust your prices, so you don't lose the order.

Monica gave me a shrewd smile. "Bob, this is not a sales call. We are going to see some of my friends. While I am there, I might ask them if they need some hardware or service from our company."

"I wish I would have thought of that!" I said, pretending to toss my magic pills out the window.

As we approached the building, Monica said, "Bob, sit back and watch, you will learn from me!"

"Ah, I forget to mention the other magic pill that I keep in my briefcase. It is called confidence. People love to see their friends acting with confidence. Add those two qualities together, friendliness and confidence, and you will *always* do well!"

And she did—very well.

On our way back from the sales call, Monica turned to me and said, "Bob, life is good!"

Chapter 14

I NEED TO INVEST IN THE EMPLOYEES!

*"Profits are better than wages. Wages make you
a living. Profits make you a fortune."*

—JIM ROHN, AMERICAN ENTREPRENEUR,
AUTHOR, AND MOTIVATIONAL SPEAKER

THURSDAY, DECEMBER 14—DAY 11 OF WEEK 2

WHEN I ARRIVED AT WORK, THERE WERE TWO LARGE SEALED white envelopes on my desk with the sales and service department's meeting agendas on top. The sales meeting was at 2:00 p.m. the following day, and the service department meeting was at 3:00 p.m. I reviewed the details of each meeting, made a few notes and filed each in my desk file drawer.

I opened the first envelope, and there were performance review forms for every employee in the company except the management team, which was my responsibility. I read each review in detail. I initialed each performance evaluation on the bottom of the page. Since Chris did not know the details of all the service techs, both he and Roger did the reviews together and signed the review forms for the service department. I was very impressed with how all the managers took their time and meticulously completed these evaluations. At the front of each department's review forms, there was a summary sheet recapping all the suggested raises. As instructed, they stayed within the 4 percent maximum increase for the department total. I saw that Donna's initials were on each of the employee reviews, indicating that she had also reviewed the information and agreed with the manager's reviews and recommendations.

I then got up out of my chair and closed my office door. I pulled out a half-dozen performance review forms and completed one for Tom, Donna, Tim, Roger, Darren, and Alan. I was in such a good mood about the performance of each manager that it was hard for me to be critical. I had only been with the company for a couple of weeks, so most of the information I wrote was very general. This group has done an excellent transition of working under Craig's rules, then following my leadership and direction. Once I finished the evaluations, I completed the recap form for my direct reports. Since I was the one making the rules, I decided I could break them and give raises that were higher than my original instructions. I gave Tom, Darren, Donna, and Alan each a 7.5 percent raise. I gave Roger and Tim each a 5 percent increase. After I posted the raises on the recap sheet, I changed my mind and gave Tim and Roger each a 7.5 percent raise also.

I then typed a memo to Donna and Darren requesting them to process these raises in the next pay period. I also stated in the note that I wanted them to cut bonus checks for the six managers (Darren, Donna, Tim, Alan, Roger, and Tom) for $1,000 each. I included Roger in the bonus checks because I thought that he deserved a reward for his positive attitude while he was managing the service department. I also asked Donna and Darren to cut a check for Chris for $2,500 because I owned him the signing bonus as per his offer letter. Then finally, I wanted a $250 bonus check for each of the other thirty-one employees. I checked my math, and I had just spent $16,250 of the company's money on year-end bonuses for all the employees. I decided that if I was going to depend on this management team and all the employees to turn this company around, I needed to invest money in the employees to motivate everyone to help me accomplish my goal.

Once I finished the memo, I put all the paperwork back in the envelope and took it over to Donna's office. I handed her the evaluations with my memorandum and asked her to meet with Darren and get these all processed for the next payroll. I also asked her to write all the bonus checks first and put each in a separate envelope and give them to me once they were all done.

Donna read the memo. She looked up at me without saying a word. Then she opened the envelope and saw that I had given the managers each a 7.5 percent raise. "Bob," she said, "this is *not* what you told me to tell the managers."

"I know, but I have been doing some soul searching and decided to invest some money in these people if I am going to expect them to give an extra effort to make this company successful."

"There is no doubt that you have everyone on the management team trusting and believing in you and your mission for this company. You do not need to do this."

"This is what I *want* to do, not what I *need* to do. I trust and believe in each member of the management team, too. I never want to do the minimum required. I always want to do what is right. I want to do what these people truly deserve or better."

Donna has a hard time containing her appreciation, and she burst out, "Every day I work with you, I learn more and more why you are in the president's chair at this company."

"My job is fairly easy when you have a great management team. Please get me the bonus checks as quickly as possible because I would like to hand them out tomorrow at the sales and service department meetings."

"You will have the checks early this afternoon," she promised.

"Thank you, Donna. You are a treasured member of this team. I appreciate your commitment to this company!"

I went back to my office and opened the envelope marked "Goals." Inside was a list of the goals for next year for each member of the management team. As I started to read them, I thought that it would be a better idea if I had each person explain their goals to me. I walked around the office and asked everyone for the best time to review their individual goals with me. Chris was the last manager I approached; he was also the most aggressive.

He said, "Bob if you have time right now, I can go over them with you immediately."

I pulled out his goals sheet form the stack I was holding and said, "Okay, Chris, let's do it. Tell me about your goals for next year."

I closed his office door, and we talked for nearly forty-five minutes. He did most of the talking, and I listened. Chris's written goals were:

- *Hire another fifteen technicians from my old company and have them all fully billable by the end of January.*

- *Implement the customer survey program with each technician, so I know precisely how each tech is performing their assignments at the customer's locations.*

- *Have a complete inventory of each tech's skills and weaknesses done by the end of January to assist in scheduling service calls as well as implementing training classes to eliminate the tech's and the department weaknesses.*

- *Spend at least two days a week out of the office meeting potential customers on sales calls with the salespeople or visiting the IT managers of existing customers to ensure that our techs are doing a good job.*

- *Work with Darren to improve the weekly and monthly productivity reporting. I want to be able to tell Bob, at any point in time, that we have processed 100 percent of every technician's invoices, thereby maximizing our monthly sales totals. My goal is to meet or exceed my budgeted sales and gross profit goals for my team every month next year.*

"Chris, thank you for your time," I said. "Your work here is excellent. You are right on with these goals. I could not have written them any better myself!"

"Bob, just like I told you before, I am the best service manager in the country."

"You probably are the best, but certainly not the humblest!"

*   *   *

During the afternoon, I met with each of the other members on the management team to discuss the first draft of their goals to have them all finalize the details of each and have them submitted to me by Monday before 5:00 p.m.

One issue Chris made in our discussion about his goals was excellent. It is Chris's goal to spend at least two days a week out in the field with our salespeople to help sell service contracts and meet with our existing customers to ensure that the service department is delivering excellent service from service technicians. I decided that I would talk to Tom about spending a minimum of three days a week out on the field with his sales team to assist them in closing deals with our existing customers and potential new customers. Since I thought that it was such a great idea for those two gentlemen, I also decided that I should follow suit and do the same.

Chapter 15

I CAN SEE
THE FINISH LINE!

*"Always treat your employees exactly as you
want them to treat your best customer."*

—STEPHEN R. COVEY, AMERICAN EDUCATOR, AUTHOR,
BUSINESSMAN, AND KEYNOTE SPEAKER

FRIDAY, DECEMBER 15—DAY 12 OF WEEK 2

FRIDAY MORNING, I DECIDED TO HAVE BREAKFAST AT THE
local diner before I went to the office. When I arrived, Tom, Darren,
Alan, Chris, Tim, and Donna were all sitting at the big corner table
having coffee. They were all reading a document and making notes
on the page. I walked up and said, "I caught you again! What are
you all doing here?"

Tom said, "Bob, our boss, who is a slave driver, wants each of
us to submit the final draft our goals for next year. We all decided
to meet here for breakfast and review and comment on each other's
goals. That way, we know what each other is trying to accomplish
so we can help each other when possible."

"Do you mind if I join you for breakfast?"

Tom said, "I don't mind, but Chris is probably going to object.
He said something about you never pass him the basketball!"

"Did Chris tell you that he is getting foul-shot lessons from Shaquille O'Neal? Shaq's career foul-shot percentage was fifty-three percent, which is much better than Chris's. That is one of the current goals Chris is attempting to accomplish."

Chris chimed in, "Tom, why are you trying to get me into trouble? Now Bob will *never* pass me the ball! Here, Bob, sit next to me, I saved you this seat just in case you showed up."

"I don't believe you, but I will sit there anyway."

Then Tim looked at Chris and asked, "Chris, is Bob kidding, or can't you make a foul shot?"

Chris said, "Don't embarrass me with your questions, and the answer is that I can, three or four times out of ten. Ever since I threw up that airball from the foul line a couple of weeks ago, I have a mental block when I am shooting a foul shot now."

"Chris, if you need my help with foul shots, all you need to do is ask," Tim said.

Chris gave him a sideways look. "Have you ever been on a basketball court in your life?"

"I have never played in an organized game, but when I was in high school, they had a foul-shooting contest in our gym class, and I won the competition. I made eighty-five foul shots in a row, and the reason it was only eighty-five was that the period ended, and I had to go to my next class."

"Are you serious, I don't believe you!"

"If you want, I will come some Monday night to your YMCA and show you that I am serious."

Chris said, "Bob, do you believe this guy?"

"Chris, don't get me involved. I don't have a problem making my foul shots. If I were you, as bad as you are, I would take foul shot lessons from anyone."

"Bob, you know that I am not that bad!"

"Chris, let's start working on these goals and worry about your foul-shooting problems later."

"I am just saying . . ." Tim said but didn't say anything more when Chris gave him a threatening stare.

Entirely by accident, we ended up having a management team meeting at the diner with eggs and bacon. We passed around everyone's goals and marked them up with each of our suggestions. After we all had breakfast and three or four cups of coffee, I hit the men's room. That was a lot of coffee.

Before everyone left the breakfast table to go back to work, I handed out the bonus envelopes to every manager as well as their direct reports bonuses. "I decided to distribute a little Christmas bonus to every employee since everything was going so well with our company. This bonus will help every with their credit card bills from all the gift shopping!"

> The management team and I agreed that we would meet at the same diner for breakfast once a month with the specific mission to review as a group each manager's goals. I loved the idea because not only would they all be accountable to me for their accomplishments, but they would also be accountable to each other. Peer pressure from each other to stay focused and accomplish their goals would be a great tool to get this turnaround accomplished.

The surprised looks on their faces indicated that they were not expecting this. Sometimes a surprise bonus can make a big difference in the morale of the company, and this was one of those occasions. Everyone on the management team shook my hand or hugged me, or both. They all said they could not thank me enough. Tom added that the rest of the employees would be as surprised and appreciative of my generosity.

"Guys, just get your team working hard so we can give out large bonuses on a regular basis!" I said.

By noon, the whole group had their final copies of the goals on my desk. By the time I was done reviewing the goals and filed the forms away, it was 1:45, and I missed lunch.

* * *

At 2:00 p.m., everyone who was supposed to attend the weekly sales meeting was sitting in the conference room. Each person had a copy of the agenda and a notebook in front of them.

> My management style when working with a sales team had always been to hold the salespeople accountable. My goal was to ensure that their focus was on what I wanted them to accomplish, rather than on what was easy for them to do well within their comfort zone.

I knew that this was not an easy task for them, to go after ten new "Fortune 1000" customers in addition to handling their sales responsibilities with their existing customers and the new unassigned group of customers.

When managing a sales team, if you do not demand production, you will not get production. The more you push them, the more they will produce. I am not saying that all salespeople are lazy. I believe that the more the sales manager sets sales quotas, motivates, rewards, challenges, monitors, reports the weekly/monthly/quarterly results of their efforts, the more the sales team will accomplish. At this company, Nancy was the exception. She did not need anyone pushing her; she was genuinely self-motivated. The rest of the sales department needs carefully managed, or their results would be average, at best.

> It has been my professional experience when working with salespeople that they will accomplish as much as you demand and only at the level you demand it.

There are several ways to motivate salespeople to become more productive. One is to publicly reward the sales team in front of their peers and management team. Another way to use a well-written sales commission program. Sales reporting can also be very motivational for a sales department. Providing each salesperson their weekly/monthly sales results versus their quota and their department ranking compared to the other salespeople generates improved sales production. The top-performing salesperson with the highest sales total for the month is motivated as is the bottom ranked performers on the list. The salesperson on the top of the list is proud to be there, rewarded accordingly, and wants to stay there. That person works hard to maintain the top position. The salesperson at the bottom of the list is also motivated. They realize that everyone else is doing much better than they are and their effort level must be raised to do much better to get off the bottom. They want to do better, make more monthly commissions, and most important, to save their job.

> I believe that a "tiered" commission compensation program is the best. The more a salesperson sells, the higher the percentage of the gross profit they are paid in commission. Every time they move to the next commission tier, they earn a more significant portion of the sale.

Monthly sales contests are also motivational for a sales department. Most good salespeople like winning and equally, if not more, hate losing. The cost of the reward for a sales contest is minimal compared to the benefit of getting the whole sales team excited and motivated to raise the bar for their results to win the competition.

At ABC Computer Distributors, the goal of assigning each salesperson the ten (Fortune 1000 corporations) target customers was to get the whole sales department out of their comfort zone of calling on small, easy-to-sell customers to companies that issue purchase orders that can be as much as several millions of dollars of computers per year. If the sales department is not pushed to grow out of their comfort zone, they would never improve their skills.

In my opinion, there are few things worse than a salesperson who is very comfortable with their sales results from the past five years. The salesperson who sells the same amount in the current year as they did the prior year and is comfortable with those results is not someone I want on my sales staff. I want a salesperson who sets their own goals to be 25 to 50 percent higher than the prior year and is very unhappy with themselves if they do not achieve the goal. I want salespeople who are aggressive. I look to hire salespeople who are creative and have imagination on how to be more productive with their time to grow their sales totals.

In the case of this turnaround, I wanted more sales people like Nancy, someone who produces more sales herself than the sum of the other thirteen salespeople in the department and then looks for new ways to improve her production.

The first salesperson on my list was Olivia. I asked, "Olivia, please come up to the front of the group and tell all of us how you have done during this past week. Tell us how you did with contacting the companies on your target list to schedule appointments and sell them computer hardware, software, and service to those corporations."

"Bob, I have only been able to reach two purchasing managers on my target list. I left a voicemail for each to call me back, but I have not heard back from them yet. I am in the process of researching the other companies on my list, but I have had little success in finding the names of the right people who are responsible for purchasing computers and service."

I decided rather than make any negative comment about Olivia's results; I would move on to the next person to see if the results were any different. My goal was to help make these salespeople more successful, not put them in fear of losing their jobs.

"Lisa, you are next on my list. Please come up and tell the group how you have done with your target list."

"Bob, I have been swamped this past week with my existing customers. I have not had any time to devote to this target list."

"Nancy, you are next, it is your turn to tell us all about your success with your target list."

"Okay, Bob, do you want the short version, or do you want me to tell all the details?"

"Give us the details because it appears that there has not been a great deal of progress with some of the other members of the sales team. Your details may help the rest of the salespeople in the future."

Nancy looked pleased to share the long version. "Well, okay, the first thing I did when you gave me the list last week was create a profile in Outlook for each of these companies' purchasing managers. To accomplish that quickly, I took Amanda, Traci, Charlene, and Vicki to lunch and asked them for their help with this project. Buying people lunch makes them more agreeable to help. No, just kidding, I love these four women. Each of them volunteered to research each of the companies on my target list. When they agreed to help, I told them that any bonus I received for getting orders from these target companies would be distributed evenly among the four of them. If they do the work, they will earn the bonus. We all agreed that the best thing for them to do was first to go to the target company's website to see what they could learn about the management team of the organization and who was responsible for the purchasing department. Next, they each signed on to LinkedIn to do searches by entering the company's name to see what all employees for that company had LinkedIn profiles. Nine of the ten target companies' purchasing managers had profiles. We entered all the information about the purchasing managers into their Outlook profile. If their picture was not on their LinkedIn account, we googled their name and the company, then went to images section of Google to find their pictures to add to their Outlook profile. We found eight out of ten pictures on LinkedIn, and the last two on their company's website.

"Next, we researched to see if they had profiles on Facebook and Twitter. Our goal was to find more information about each purchasing manager such as their birthdays, their anniversary dates, whether they belonged to a Rotary Club, Chamber of Commerce, networking group, or mastermind group.

"After we had complete profiles built for each of the ten purchasing managers, I next called three of my larger customer's purchasing managers, whom I call on regularly. I knew these three gentlemen all belonged to the Association of Purchasing Managers or APM. I scheduled a meeting with each—one for breakfast, one for coffee at Starbucks later in the morning, and the third for lunch at Seasons 52, which was his favorite restaurant. I showed each my list of the purchasing managers on my target list to see if they knew any of these people. Between the three purchasing managers, they knew all but one of the guys who worked for companies on my target list. I asked them if they would write an introductory email to introduce me to the purchasing managers I needed to meet."

"All these purchasing managers from the larger companies know each other from the APM. Plus, they meet regularly and talk about which of their suppliers are doing well and which ones are struggling. I asked my buddy that I took to lunch at Seasons 52 for a copy of the membership list of APM. After lunch, we went back to his office. He gave me a copy of the list and told me not to tell anyone where I got it. Traci made copies of the list and is about to distribute one to each of you now. When you review the list, you will find that there are hundreds of purchasing managers that belong to the APM. Good luck, and I hope the list helps everyone in the department."

"Later that afternoon, I received nine 'introductory emails' introducing me to the purchasing managers on my target list. That evening, I stayed late after work to write handwritten thank-you notes to each of the referring purchasing managers. On the way home that evening, I dropped off the thank-you notes at the post office to get them mailed the same day. I have personally found that sending a thank-you card is a fantastic tool for me to continue to build relationships with my customers. I regularly get complimented by many of my customers for taking the time to write them a hand-written thank-you note for something very nice that they did that benefitted me."

"I checked my calendar for open dates/times and responded to each of the introductory emails suggesting three possible dates and times for us to schedule an appointment to meet. I suggested that we meet for only fifteen to thirty minutes so that they could squeeze me into one of my three proposed times. The next morning before noon, I received calls back from all nine of the managers. I had eight scheduled appointments, and one purchasing manager was traveling during the dates I had suggested. He emailed me back and offered three other dates and times for us to meet. I did not hear from the tenth manager, so I called to see if I could get him on the phone. It turned out that, per his administrative assistant, he was on vacation and will be back on Monday morning. I left myself a reminder in the 'tasks' section in Microsoft Outlook to follow-up with him on Monday. I went to two appointments, one on Wednesday and one yesterday. I have seven scheduled appointments for next week."

I was incredibly impressed with Nancy's go-get-'em attitude, and I was so glad I had asked her for the long version. I hoped she had more insight to share with the rest of the sales staff and asked her to tell us all how those first two appointments turned out.

"The first appointment was Wednesday. I had Traci call on Tuesday to the purchasing manager's assistant—her name is Kim—to confirm Wednesday's appointment. Traci's mission on that call was much more than just confirming the appointment, though. Traci needed to find out if ABC Computer Distributors needs to apply to become an 'approved vendor' of their company. As it turned out, we did, so Traci asked to have an application emailed to her so that we could complete the form before the meeting with the purchasing manager. Once the form was received, Traci and I completed it and emailed it back immediately. I also wanted Traci to get to know Kim better. After Traci's phone call, we also set up a profile in Outlook for Kim. We found her profile on LinkedIn. Kim also had a Facebook account. I have learned over the years that having a relationship with the purchasing manager's assistants can be equally as valuable as the relationship with the purchasing manager himself or herself."

"On Wednesday, I took Traci with me to the appointment. We left thirty minutes early to ensure that we were not late for the meeting due to traffic or any other reason. We had no problem with the trip. We found the company and arrived twenty-five minutes early. We sat in the car for twenty minutes and discussed strategy, and then walked into the offices five minutes before we were to meet the purchasing manager. Arriving too early or late for an appointment can irritate the executive, so I do not do either."

"Traci and I were walked back to the purchasing department by Mark's administrative assistant, Kim. It was funny, Traci and Kim looked like sisters. When they met in person after they had talked on the phone several times for business calls, they hit it off immediately. Kim walked me into Mark's office and introduced me, while Traci stayed out in the reception area with her goal of building a relationship with Kim."

"One important point I would like to make is concerning how I dress for sales appointments. I dress differently when my appointment is with a man than I do when I am meeting with a woman. I know this sounds very stereotypical, but I am not afraid of stereotypes. When my appointment is with a male executive, I dress in outfits that are feminine but not flashy or seductive. When my meeting is with a woman, I dress in a conservative business suit, which indicates that I am not in any fashion competition with her. I want the customer to like me. If the customer likes me, it is easier to close a sale. If the customer does not like me, they will never give me the opportunity to win their business. I try to do the right things to get the customer to like me. When I am meeting with a man, I wear a bit of perfume, but when I am meeting with a woman, I don't because I do not want my perfume clashing with hers. These are all minor issues, but they all work."

"The meeting with Mark went very well. I gave him the application we had to complete to be an approved vendor. He was a little surprised, in a good way, that we had that accomplished already. Mark told me that David, who referred me to him, said that I was a real fireball salesperson and there are none better. I just smiled and said, 'David was probably right.' I wrote myself a note to give David a call and thank him again. It never hurts to say thank you to someone who has done something helpful for you. Mark told me that they were going to bid out a purchase of computer hardware before the end of the year because they had some capital money left over in the budget that they are going to spend. He said that with his company, it is a 'use to or lose it' rule and the IT department did not want to lose the opportunity to do some upgrading of systems before the new year. I asked him if we may have the chance to participate and deliver a quote for all the products. He said, 'Nancy, absolutely!

Our existing computer distributor has not done a good job for our company lately, so David's introduction came at the perfect time.' I told him I also would like to talk to him about computer service. I mentioned that we have a great service department, and at the right time, I would like to introduce him to Chris. As it turns out, he knows Chris—it is a small world, isn't it?— so I said I would schedule an appointment to bring Chris in soon to meet his group."

"Then Mark called their IT manager and asked him to come over to his office immediately; he wanted to introduce him to me. Two minutes later, Steven walked in and introduced himself. As it turns out, Mark and Steven play in a basketball league with Chris. Steven said, 'Chris is a good basketball player. He is like bumping up against a stone wall when he under the basket.' Steven added that he did not know that Chris left his old firm to join ABC. I told him that we were very excited to have Chris managing our service team. When Mark told Steven that Chris and I would like to bid on their service contract for next year, Steven asked how soon he could meet with Chris. They were about to decide on their service contract next week. I said I would have Chris there the next day. Steven then agreed to get me a list of the computers they planned on purchasing before the year's end."

"After the meeting was over with Mark and Steven, Traci and I drove back to the office. As I drove, Traci made notes in her notebook about everything she had learned about Kim, Mark, and Steven. Kim had told Traci that she knows well in advance if the company goes out to bid for purchasing computers. Kim also told her that neither Mark nor Steven like the company they are dealing with now. When Traci and I got back to the office, Traci updated Mark's and Kim's Outlook profile and started one for Steven. Traci researched Steven on LinkedIn. We now know a lot about these three people we knew nothing about one week ago. I gave the list computers to Alan to have him research the pricing of the hardware they would soon be purchasing. I asked Traci to email Kim to tell her that it was wonderful to meet her today and maybe the three of us could have a 'girl's night out' sometime soon. I then went to see Chris and asked him if he could come with me tomorrow early afternoon to meet with Mark and Steven. Chris had a one-on-one meeting scheduled with one of his technicians, but he said that he would gladly postpone that meeting and be available to join me to visit my new customers."

"My meeting with my second target customer was Thursday at eleven o'clock, so I just dragged Chris with me to that meeting also. Chris did much better talking to the IT manager than I did with the purchasing manager. The purchasing manager told me that they were not going to do any IT purchasing until later in the first quarter of next year. But Chris was asked to bid on the service contract for this customer for next year. Traci did a great job with meeting the purchasing manager's assistant, as well as the IT manager's administrative assistant. This morning, Traci updated the profiles for all three people for the second target customer."

"Chris might be the service department manager, but he is a good salesperson for this company. He knows many people in the IT industry, plus he has the most jovial personality. He has that big smile that makes everyone like him. After our first meeting, I took Chris and Traci to lunch, and we discussed our strategy for the second meeting with Steven and Mark. Before we went to the second meeting after lunch, we stopped off to get a nice bouquet of flowers for Traci's new friend, Kim. When we arrived at the second appointment, Traci gave Kim the flowers. Traci told her she had gotten her the flowers as an apology for taking up all her time the previous morning. Kim was very thankful for the beautiful flower arrangement."

"At the meeting with Mark and Steven, we hit a home run. Chris knew both of the guys from playing basketball together. Chris also told them that you, Bob, are the new president of our company. Chris said that he would get you and we could all meet Monday night after the basketball game. We left the meeting with a purchase order for two hundred eighty thousand from Mark and Steven for servers and laptops. Chris had a complete list of all their computers to develop the quote for the service contract. Steven was nice enough to tell Chris the amount that the other company had bid for the contract.

Steven told Chris if he can match the number or beat it, we will have their business. Chris told Steven that he would get back to him by this morning."

"Bob, I am pleased to tell you that Chris just landed our first service contract for one of my ten target customers plus the gross profit on the hardware purchase order is going to be over forty-three thousand dollars. I do not know the profit on the service contract yet, but I do know that Chris was pleased with the two sales appointments. And, Bob, I would like to acknowledge Traci, Amanda, Charlene, and Vicki for doing an amazing job helping me build these profiles. And Traci was great with Kim at the first target customer. I know that Kim will be whispering in Traci's ear if she hears that her company is about to purchase new computers."

"And, as I agreed with these four hard-working women, when it is time to distribute any bonuses for sales to my target companies, they should be called up to the front of the sales department and paid. This morning, Traci, Vicki, Charlene, Amanda, and I met again. We discussed what Traci did on the sales call so that Vicki, Charlene, and Amanda could follow the same procedure on the sales calls for the following week. I also want everyone in this room to know that if you want to sell computers and make some big commission checks in the future, take Chris with you on your sales calls. Not only is he great with the customers, but he also knows a lot of people in the IT industry. This morning, Traci and I wrote thank-you cards to Mark, Steven, and Kim, in addition to the purchasing and IT managers from my second target customer. I entered a reminder on my calendar in Outlook to contact my second customer in mid-January to see when they may be purchasing computers."

"Bob, I must share with the group that the key to this business is to stay organized with everything that is going on. Outlook calendar, Tasks, and the Contacts are invaluable tools for keeping me in touch with all my customers. If every salesperson in the room is not using those programs like I am, you are missing out. I am twice as efficient because of Outlook, which means twice the sales and double the amount of my monthly commissions."

Nancy had certainly said a lot, and I noted that while she was talking, most of the salespeople were taking notes.

> There are many electronic sales programs out there for salespeople to use to maintain their data base of customers and information about each customer. But, for the money, Microsoft Outlook, (contacts, calendar, email, and tasks) is excellent and a very valuable tool to salespeople and executives.

It was finally my turn to speak again. "Nancy, thank you for all that information and advice. I agree with you; Outlook is a lifesaver for me also. And, thank you, Traci, Amanda, Charlene, and Vicki for being such as valuable help to Nancy with her target customers. Nancy, I have a question for you. But first I must thank you for everyone in this room for sharing the list of purchasing managers belonging to the APM. My question is, is there an organization like the APM for IT managers?"

"Oh, my gosh, Bob. I did not think about that an organization for the IT managers," Nancy said. "I bet there is one. I will be on that immediately after this meeting, and I will let you know what I find out."

I thanked her and said, "My plan for the meeting today was to try to have every one of the salespeople review their results regarding your successes with ten target customers. Tom, I have a feeling that if I did continue with the rest of the salespeople in this room to report your results, there would be more stories like Olivia's and Lisa's rather than Nancy's. I want everyone to know in this room that next week, I will be calling each one of you to report your results regarding your target customers. I am hoping that your accomplishments will be much more like Nancy's rather than . . . well, I think that you all understand. You should all know that Nancy averages over two million dollars per month in sales. There is no one else in this department that is close to her year-to-date total. Even though she is very busy with her existing customer base, she made time to work on her target list and, as you all heard, was effective. I honestly did not expect everyone in the room to have success at Nancy's level, but I did expect much better results than were communicated today. I look at this meeting, and I point the finger at myself because the results were not better. I feel like I failed. I feel like Tom, and I failed. Would anyone here like to help me out on how I can help all of you to be more successful this week than you were these past seven days?"

The room was silent.

"Tom, I am going to ask you to get more 'hands-on' with each of these salespeople next week to help them get motivated. Everyone should set up a sales system like Nancy's and be able to talk about their better results with their time this week. I am going to end this meeting on a very positive note. I want you all to be successful. I want you all to earn big monthly commission checks. I would like you all to be very proud of what you have accomplished and know that you are the best salesperson in the world. I want to provide you with the tools to do a better job. Tom and I want you to get more customers, close more deals, and be happy here at ABC Computer Distributors. Tom, do you have anything that you would like to add?"

"Yes, Bob, thank you. I want every salesperson to stay here after this meeting to have a little chat. Amanda, Vicki. Charlene, and Traci, I would like you to stay after also."

"Okay, Tom, thank you. The meeting is over. GO WITH CONFIDENCE!"

I asked to see Tom outside the conference room.

Once outside, I asked, "Do you think the other salesperson we terminated last week would be a valuable addition to the sales support team? I think we need to build that department. If we grow that department enough to support the whole sales team the way Traci helped Nancy this week, we can materially grow our sales very quickly."

"I agree. I guess you are not referring to Frank, right?"

"Not in this lifetime. Frank is not the type of employee I want to invest this company's money in. Please have Donna contact that ex-salesperson to see if she wants to come back on board in a support position . . . and, Tom, I am done leading the sales meetings. Next week, it is your turn, but I will be there observing and available for questions."

"Thank you, sir!" he said, sounding glad to be taking the reins.

Tom went back into the conference room to meet with his team, while I headed to the service department meeting.

It was 1:50 p.m. and the service department meeting is at 2:00 p.m. When I walked back to the service department conference room, I saw that all the technicians in addition to Chris and Gina were already inside. The door was closed. I waited a few minutes because I did not want to interrupt Chris. Then I heard Chris say, "Thank you, everyone. I am going to go get Bob to start the meeting."

When Chris opened the door, there I was.

Chris looked a little startled to see me there but said, "Your timing is perfect. This fine group of highly skilled computer technicians and I had a little mini-meeting. Some of them have questions and suggestions for you."

"Who would like to start?" I asked as I took my seat.

Troy raised his hand and said, "Mr. Curry, I have a suggestion about our department meetings."

"Okay, Troy, let's have it."

"Well, sir, I am going to suggest that we either have the meeting first thing in the morning at seven o'clock or noon. When I am at one of our clients in the middle of a job, I hate to pack up my tools, leave to come back to the office for this department meeting, and not be able to finish the job. I also think that it looks bad to the customer if we leave for lunch at noon, come back to the customer's location at one o'clock, work for fifteen minutes, then pack up my tools and leave again to get to the office for the two o'clock department meeting. My suggestion is if we have the meeting at seven in the morning, then I can be at the customer's location and have a full eight hours of billing time of Fridays."

When Troy finished, I looked at Chris and said, "Troy is a smart man. I am the dummy for scheduling the department meetings at two o'clock. Troy, your suggestion is spot-on. That is a much better time for the meetings. By having the meetings on Friday mornings, we can increase our billable hours per technician by an hour for the meeting, an average of forty-five minutes for each technician to get to the meeting and forty-five minutes to drive back to the customer's location. That is two and a half hours of nonbillable time for eleven technicians per week times an average billing rate of one hundred dollars per hour times fifty weeks for the year equals one hundred thirty-seven thousand dollars in increased revenue."

I had done all that math in my head, but no one seemed surprised. "Chris, what do you think that we should do about this, change the meeting times for the department meeting or not?"

"Bob, yes, sir, we should change the meeting time to seven a.m. on Friday mornings."

"Troy, let me ask you a question. Is there a favorite place to take your family for an incredible dinner?"

"Ruth Chris Steakhouse, sir."

"Okay, Troy, you let me know when you want to take your family out for dinner and I will call the restaurant and give them my credit card to pay for your and your family's dinner."

"Wow, Mr. Curry, that is more than generous of you. My wife and kids are going to love this, thank you, sir!"

"No, Troy, you just increased this company's revenue by a possible one hundred thirty thousand dollars with your suggestion. When we build up this department again to twenty or thirty technicians, the increased revenue is going to be almost four hundred thousand dollars. Troy, it is me who should be thanking you, sir!"

"So, Chris, does anyone else have any questions?"

"Yes, I have a question. How soon can we hire some more technicians? The techs that we hired from my old company will be stationed full time at a client, and they will not be available for the day to day service calls. We terminated ten employees last Friday, and this week, it appears that Nancy and I have closed two big service contracts. I believe we will sign new contracts early next week and the work on those two will start on January first. We probably need to hire at least three new techs immediately. It would even be better if we had five new technicians ready to be at customers locations billable on January first. Bob, as we have discussed before, I have several techs in the 'on deck' circle from my old company ready to jump over here on a phone call."

"Chris, did you tell these computer technicians to send their resumes to the address on the advertisement for computer technicians in the Philadelphia Inquirer?"

"Yes, Bob, I called everyone and told them what to do as soon as you told me. I don't want to be fighting a lawsuit either."

I looked at the rest of the group and asked, "Are the rest of you okay with having five new faces here very soon?"

Roger said, "Bob, terminating those technicians last week was a good business decision. Because of their weak skills, someone should have fired them a long time ago. I am sorry that they were terminated right before Christmas, but as I said, most of them should have been fired thirty days after they started with our company. None of them had the skills or ability to do service calls. If we had more qualified technicians working for this company, like the people in this room, this department would be very profitable for this company."

"Does everyone agree with Roger?"

All eleven techs said yes.

"Chris, get with Donna about scheduling interviews, background checks, and drug tests for the candidates."

"Do we have to go through all that background and drug testing crap with these guys?" Chris asked, surprising me because I thought he knew the deal.

"No, we don't, Chris, but we do if you would like to hire them. This is the hiring process. If they are not going to pass the background checks and drug tests, they can stay right where they are."

"But, Bob, what if the guy is a great technician and smokes a little marijuana on occasion?"

"Tell him to get cleaned up for a month and then come talk to us about a job," I said. "Chris, you went through all the tests, so why should anyone else be exempt? For the eleven other gentlemen in the room, please know that there will be random drug testing for all our employees starting next year. If any of you have a drug problem right now, you need to talk to Chris or me so that we can help you. We are going to be very strict about this issue. If one person in this company has a problem, it puts every employee in this organization at risk. If an employee comes to me before getting tested positive for an illegal drug in his or her system, I can help that person before it is too late. But if that person fails the drug test without saying anything to me first, that employee will be fired."

Chris said, "Bob, you just gave Troy and his family a dinner at an expensive restaurant. Now you are stressing them all out with random drug testing?"

> In the first turnaround that I did as a consultant, a hurricane shutter company, I was told by the management team of the company that if the company did a random drug tests of the installation group, not one of the installers would have passed. For me, that was a business nightmare. I decided from that point on, if I was managing the company, drug tests would be performed on 100% of candidates interested in joining our company. In addition, we would be doing random drug tests for all existing employees.

"What I said, Chris is that this is going to be a drug-free company. If any employees in this department or this company have a problem, see me now before you get caught. I will commit to everyone here that the company will support any employee to get off the drugs. I cannot let any employee with a drug problem visit our customer's locations. If that employee does something bad because he or she was strung out on drugs, that will put this company and every employee in jeopardy. By the show of hands, who in this room disagrees with my policy?"

No one in the room raised their hand.

"Good, and thank you, gentlemen. Please imagine if I was not strict with this drug issue and one of our employees was high at one of our customer's locations, or arrested for buying or selling drugs. That would be the end of the company within weeks. We would lose every customer that this company currently has and rightfully so."

"Bob, I will talk to these guys and deliver the message. Better yet, how about, I invite them all to meet at Duffy's Monday night after our basketball game? Then you can tell them all and be the bad guy."

"Chris, I am not the bad guy for having rules for the employees that will protect your job. Can you imagine if one day you go home and must tell your wife, 'Honey, I must find a new job because one of the employees at one of our customer's locations was selling drugs to one of the customer's employees and got caught.'"

"Bob, when you put it that way, I understand. If someone does something to screw up my job, he will have to answer to my wife— and boy is she is scary when she gets mad!"

"Okay Chris, Monday night is good and if anyone in the room would like to join us, you are welcome. I will even pick up the tab. And by the way, there is a maximum of two beers Monday night if you are eating and only one if you do not have any food in your stomach. I am not bailing anyone out of jail Monday night for driving under the influence."

"Next item on the agenda, I have started receiving the customer surveys in the mail from our customers regarding the quality of our service calls. Chris, have you reviewed the ones I forwarded on to Gina for the monthly reporting?"

"Yes, Bob, I have. That was one of the topics of our mini-meeting before this meeting."

"Gentlemen, the scores were awesome. I am very proud of this group. I am going to share the results of those surveys with the sales department weekly, so they can see that selling service again is a good thing. Can I ask this group what has changed about our service calls to go from being rated poor to excellent so quickly?"

Troy stood up and said, "Bob, the answer is straightforward if you think about it. Two weeks ago, the company hired a new president, a guy by the name of Bob Curry. A few days later, he hires a new service department manager. Five days after Bob joined the company, he terminated ten technicians, two salespeople, a training department manager, and the owner of the company. What a wakeup call for every employee working here. We all believed that you were a 'hatchet man.' Sir, you sent a direct message to every employee here that they better improve their skills with their job performance and deliver excellent service to our customers or find a new job. I know that several of the techs in the room were dusting off their resumes. Seeing that many people, including the owner of the company, fired all in one day was very intimidating. I think that I speak for the whole department that we now understand what you are doing. You have cleaned out the deadwood that was dragging this company down. You brought in a super-qualified service manager. Now you are going to build the department back up with more highly skilled technicians to take care of our customers. You have installed systems for our customers to report the quality of our service calls. You are rewarding those techs who are doing their job and taking care of our customers. You are now motivating the salespeople to sell more service contracts. Giving me and my family dinner at Ruth's Chris Steakhouse for a simple suggestion that is going to save the company money was over the top. I am on your team, Mr. President."

Roger chimed in, "How does everyone else here feel about working for a department that Chris is leading and a company that Bob is president?"

I started to get a little emotional. This group of techs could not have turned around any quicker. Now, they all got it. They understood that when they do good work, the whole company does well. When the company does well, it gives me the opportunity to give out an expensive dinner for his family at a five-star restaurant to one of the hard-working techs who deserved a reward for his money-saving suggestion.

After the meeting ended, I hung around the conference room to get to know the guys a little better. I felt their loyalty. I did not have any other obligations for the rest of the day, so life was good.

* * *

When I got back to my office, there was a note on my desk:

Happy Hour at Carrabba's at 5:30. Don't be late!
Tom and Nancy

I was exhausted at this point, but I knew that I better socialize with my team.

When I walked into Carrabba's, the whole group was there again at the big table in the middle of the bar area. Nancy and Donna stood up when they saw me at the door, and both came over to escort me to their table. There was an empty chair between where they were sitting with a vodka tonic with limes waiting for me.

Nancy said, "Bob, we were not sure if you were going to show up, but we are glad that you did. We want you to have some fun. You are working your tail off making our company successful, and we don't want you to stress out."

"You can't imagine how much fun I am having working with this group. You have all been fantastic. In fact, you are turning into a dream team. I would only be stressed out if we did not see significant results. You all are golden, and I appreciate your hard work. I can see the finish line! Next year is going to be amazing!

Chapter 16

IS NANCY COOKING?

*"I don't know where we should take this company, but
I do know that if I start with the right people, ask them
the right questions, and engage them in vigorous debate;
we will find a way to make this company great."*

—JAMES C. COLLINS, AMERICAN BUSINESS
CONSULTANT, AUTHOR, AND LECTURER

SUNDAY, DECEMBER 17—DAY 13 OF WEEK 2

MY CELL PHONE RANG, AND IT WAS TOM CALLING ME ON A
Sunday morning. I wondered what Tom could want on a Sunday
morning.

He quickly explained, "Nancy and I are having a little get-together at our home this evening, and we would like to invite you if
you are not too busy."

"I am not busy, and I would love to come over, what time?"

"How about you plan to get here at six-ish and bring a healthy
appetite because there is going to be plenty of food."

I knew that if Tom said there was going to be plenty of food,
there was going to be *plenty* of food!

"Is Nancy cooking?" I asked, keeping the humor out of my voice.

"Bob, it's me, *Tom*, your sales manager!"

"I had to ask!" I said with a laugh.

"Were you going to decline if Nancy was cooking?"

"No, just the opposite, I would not miss this little party for anything, I would love to taste Nancy's cooking."

"Bob, no you don't, trust me."

"See you at six," I said and thanked him again for the invitation. I grabbed a bottle of red wine off my wine rack and put it by the door. I did not want to forget it and arrive at Tom and Nancy's home empty-handed.

Later that evening, when I drove into Tom and Nancy's development, there were several cars parked up and down both sides of the street close to their property. Although Tom had said he was having a "little get-together" at his house, I suspected it was more than a little gathering.

I parked my car, went up to the front door, and rang the doorbell. Nancy answered, gave me a big hug, and thanked me for the wine when I handed it to her.

"Nancy, I expected to see you wearing an apron from cooking all day."

"Bob, I did prepare the food by calling and ordering it from the caterer. Besides, I did not want to give anyone food poisoning. Everyone would call in sick tomorrow!"

I looked around the living room and saw that the whole management team was there, as well as every salesperson. I was a little surprised. I did not expect to see so many employees at this gathering. I poured myself a glass of red wine and then walked around to say hello.

Tom came over and shook my hand. "Bob, thanks for coming on such short notice. How has your weekend been so far?"

"I relaxed all weekend and did not think about work once, Tom."

"Hmm . . . let me think, do I believe that? . . . NO!" He gave me a little pat on the back.

"Well, you are right. Most of the morning, I planned what I needed to do this week at work with the holidays just a few days away. I don't want to lose the momentum we have going here. Tom, this is a lot bigger than just a little get- together."

"I will tell you how this all happened after we get everyone together in the other room."

Tom picked up a spoon and started pinging it against his wine glass to get everyone's attention. "Everyone, please get a plate of food. I would like you all to go into the great room. We are going to have an informal meeting so I can write off the cost of this party on my income taxes." Tom turned to me and said, "I'm kidding!"

I went to the dining room where all the food was set up and lifted some barbecued chicken, baked beans, and coleslaw. I then went to the great room, found an empty chair, and started eating my Duffy's barbecue chicken.

Tom and Nancy came into the great room a few minutes later.

Tom stood in the middle of the room. "Bob, he began, "on Thursday, Darren and Patrick distributed the worksheets and schedules for next year's budget to everyone on the management team. Later that afternoon, Darren, Patrick, Donna, Tim, Chris, Nancy, and I all met in the conference room to review the numbers. Darren first told everyone in the meeting that you were planning on doing one hundred twenty million dollars in sales next year, up from the fifty million dollars for the current year. Everyone looked around when they heard that number for next year with a look that said Bob Curry is nuts. Darren told us all to settle down until the group heard the rest of the budget information. He said that you were planning to have six people in the sales support department, three in purchasing, and at least thirty technicians by the end of the year. Darren said that the budget for sales salaries and commission was four million six hundred thousand dollars. He told us that you were planning to keep the sales team at the current number of employees in the department, and you were not going to be hiring anyone new. Is that right, Bob?"

I nodded. "That *is* what I shared with Darren."

"Well, Bob, I did a little math with those numbers. That means that the average salary and commission in the sales department is going to be *two hundred seventy thousand dollars*. Are you aware of that?"

"Yes, Tom, I believe that is accurate."

"So, what you are saying to this sales team sitting in this room today is that you are budgeting two hundred seventy thousand dollars compensation per person for next year."

"Tom, if we do the one hundred twenty million dollars in sales, yes, the average salesperson for this company will be making *a lot* of money next year."

"Bob, that is amazing. You joined this company two weeks ago. I believed at that time that we were not going to make it to the end of this year before the company had to file for bankruptcy protection. One week later, we have fourteen fewer employees. Two weeks later, your budget for next year is to grow this company's sales by two hundred forty percent in the next twelve months."

"Yes, Tom, that sounds about right," I confirmed.

"Darren also told us that you are going to distribute a certain percentage of the profits back to the management team starting after the first quarter."

"Yes, I don't mind telling this group, I plan to bonus for thirty-three percent of the profits next year to the management team. I would like the number to be fifty percent, but we first need to build up the balance sheet. If we had a strong balance sheet right now, the number would be fifty percent. I am hoping that this year the bonus be thirty-three percent of profits, and if everything goes well in the next twelve months, the following year will be fifty percent."

"Darren said that you had added a one hundred twenty thousand expense to the budget for a scholarship fund."

"Yes, that is true also. But I have not finished my plan yet to announce the details right now. I will be ready to discuss my scholarship idea by the date of the holiday party."

"Bob, it appears to me and others in this room that when Rick and Kevin hired you and announced that you were the new president and CEO of the company, you ignored the fact that this company was in a very distressed financial position."

"No, Tom, I knew about this company's financial problems. Think about it, one of the first things I did when hired was to get rid of the Mercedes."

"Bob, I know. I must tell you, that amazed me. When you did that, it sent a message to me and the others on this management team that this guy has some 'big ones' and does not mess around."

"I can see where you are going with this conversation, Tom. I was not prepared to come here tonight and talk about business. But since you invited most of the key players from the company and me here tonight, I will share with everyone some of my thoughts about the status of the company and my plan for the future of ABC Computer Distributors."

I put my plate down and joined Tom in the center of the room.

"We all work for a great company," I said. "I am very pleased and proud of this management team right now. You all have made a huge transition from working for a guy who had given up on the business to a manager who would like to lead this company to do an enormous increase in sales next year. Just for your information, the following year, I would like sales to hit three hundred million dollars. I know that it is not an easy transition to work for Craig then one day be told that I am your new president. I compliment you all for handling the change so well."

"The day I started at ABC, Craig brought the management team into the conference room to make introductions. You all should have seen the looks on your faces when you entered that conference room: sorrow and defeat. It was as if you had just returned from a funeral. I knew I had a huge challenge in the immediate future if I was going to turn this company around."

"Then over the next two days, I met with each of you, one on one, to talk and understand your strengths and weaknesses. At the end of those interviews, I knew what the problems were and immediately began to attack each issue, one by one. Craig's car was low-hanging fruit, so Darren and Patrick returned it to the dealership. Darren and I met with the company's bank and improved our cash management policies, which will reduce our interest expense this coming year by fifty-two thousand dollars. After interviewing Alan, we decided to get rid of our inventory on hand in the warehouse and drop ship all our sales to our customers directly from the master distributors.

This policy change will reduce our loan balance by four million dollars, thereby lowering our interest expense by one hundred eighty thousand dollars next year.

"Half of the service team was not qualified to do computer service for our customers, so, unfortunately, we terminated their employment at the end of my first week here. I hired an excellent manager to oversee the service department, who I am expecting great things from this next year. Unfortunately, we needed to fire Craig as an employee of the company, even though he is still the owner. And we had to let Trish go because the company had not sold a training contract in a very long time."

"When Darren developed a monthly and year-to-date sales report for me, there were a few salespeople who did not sell enough product during the past year to cover their salaries. I included them in the group that had to go. That 'Black Friday' reduction in staff reduced our operating expenses by a little over one million dollars, which instantly made this company cash flow breakeven. By accomplishing that, I satisfied my promise to Rick and Kevin. I had told them that I would have the company stop bleeding cash before the end of December. They hired me to make some tough decisions that would improve the financial results of this business. Business is tough; you cannot have a bunch of deadwood employed by the company and be profitable. I believe that I owe it to everyone in this room to make those tough decisions and get rid of the non-productive employees. My job was to weed them out so the rest of you can be working for a profitable company again. Then, my good friend, Nancy, brought a big customer order into my office and was ready to kick my butt if I did not get the order financed by our bank."

"Bob, I would have kicked your butt hard too!" Nancy chimed in with her strong internal passion.

"Believe me; I knew that. I saw the look in your eyes, and it was scary!"

"Bob, I gave you a big hug before I left your office that day!"

"Yes, you did after Rick and Kevin agreed to give us a

ten-million-dollar increase in our line of credit. So, Nancy's order was an insurance policy for me ensuring that this company was going to start the year off strong. Plus, Nancy provided me with the model of the sales volume that a good salesperson in this industry can do for a year."

Nancy shouted, "A great salesperson!"

"I stand corrected, a *great* salesperson is a more accurate statement! That is what motivated me to give everyone in the sales department ten new target customers and to plan to average ten million dollars in sales a month for next year's budget. That is why I am very nice to salespeople. Their sales pay for my salary. It is because of that, and many other reasons, that I work hard to support their ability to be successful."

"A month ago, I worked for a very successful company that had two great owners. They created an excellent corporate culture for their company. While I worked there, the owners taught me valuable lessons. Hal told me, 'The way you make money in business is to hire the best people for the job. You must treat them with respect, provide the employees the tools to accomplish their job responsibilities, then monitor, measure, report, and reward their accomplishments. He said you must also give them a pleasant work environment and compensate everyone in the company appropriately. I plan to copy the corporate culture from my old company at ABC Computer Distributors.

"People, I do not want next year's budget to be my plan. I want it to be my management team's budget. I sat with Darren and Patrick this past week to give them some suggestions I believed we could accomplish next year as a team. I asked Darren and Patrick to put together the schedules and worksheets, so the management team would have a minimal amount of work to do with planning for next year. Because I have the experience of working for larger companies throughout my career, I have seen what a good leader with a strong management team can accomplish.

"There is no doubt in my mind that we can achieve those budgeted sales and profits. But please know that this is not my budget;

it is yours, the management team's budget. Once you sign off on the numbers that you are responsible for accomplishing, I am going to hold you accountable. Don't get me wrong; I am also accountable. I will be supporting each manager and helping you to be successful in growing this company's sales and profits. But each manager has employees reporting to you also who you are accountable for every day. For this company to sell one hundred twenty million dollars; it is going to require *everyone* in this room and everyone else who works for this company to work hard and stay focused.

"Last year, several non-productive people on the payroll are gone now. The people in this room are the employees I believe are going to work hard and watch the other employees who receive bi-weekly paychecks from ABC Computer Distributors to ensure that they are also working hard and are therefore productive. We cannot be successful if there is deadwood working from this company. So, Tom, let's get back to your point. Do you, the balance of the management team, and every salesperson who works for this company agree with the sales goal for next year?

"Bob, I don't know about the rest of the team, but I believe we can do much better."

"Great, then let's ask the rest of the management team. Chris, what do you think?"

"Bob, you know me. Give me a goal, and I will either accomplish it or exceed it."

"Donna?"

"My position has nothing to do with sales, but I will commit to you and everyone in this room that I will work very hard and support every employee in this organization."

"Tim?"

"If you recall our one-on-one meeting, I told you that I am fully committed to the long-term success of this company. I love this company."

"Alan, how about you, my friend?"

"Bob, a number is just a number. We have a sales team here that should be able to accomplish it with no problem in my opinion. I will commit to you that the purchasing department will never hold our sales team back from accomplishing their goals."

"Darren, what does our controller have to say about the sales plan for next year?"

"Bob, you know that when you suggested that kind of sales growth, I started looking at it from a very conservative point of view. Alan and I struggled to get our master distributors paid current on a regular basis, so our vendors would ship the products for the customer's next order. After Patrick and I put together the budget numbers, I better understood the foundation of your business plan. It is clear to me that you have assembled a team of people here who can and *will* accomplish any goal that you set for next year. I understand your philosophy to reward those employees who accomplish their goals, or in the case of a salesperson, meet their sales quotas. Bob, I wish I could be part of the sales team and make more than next year's projected salaries for that department."

"Darren," I assured him, "once we distribute a percentage of the profits for next year, you will make that kind of income and hopefully more. I want everyone here to know that I want everyone in the company to make a ton of money, plus work here for the rest of our careers. The company I worked for just a few weeks ago would still be there today if the owners did not sell the business. As I said earlier, they had an amazing business philosophy. Since I am not bright enough to come up with a better way to manage this business, I am going to copy theirs. '*Hire the best people, treat them with respect, provide them the tools to do their job, monitor, measure, report, and reward their excellent work, give them a good environment to work, and pay everyone appropriately.*'"

"People, if you think that I am not doing this, please bring it to my attention. Please challenge me if I stray from this path because I don't want to vary even a little bit from this business plan. People, the budget is just a bunch of numbers. Hiring the right people, treating them with respect, and so on, is what is going to make this company successful. If I strongly follow these business philosophies and the management team does the same, we will be able to accomplish the budgeted sales for the year by the end of September."

I started to get a little emotional, so I stopped talking.

Tom stood back up and said, "The reason for this little party tonight was that I wanted everyone in this room to see and feel your passion for this company." Tom looked around the room. "It is my impression that Bob cares about everyone who works for this organization, more than anyone could believe. As you all know, that has been the material change from the president who used to run this company. I am fortunate. I get to see and feel Bob's management style and passion every day. It is crucial for me to let the sales team observe who they are working for and how much our leader cares about us. I know that there are people on the sales team who were harassed by the former management or just treated poorly. You are now working for someone who will help and support you every day. It has taken me two weeks to see and finally believe that what I have seen from Bob is real, and it is not going to change. Bob is on my team, and he is on the team of everyone who works for ABC. If you want to work hard and be successful in your career, you are working for the right company now. If you do not want to put in the extra effort to be successful, chances are, maybe you should find a new job. But I never want to have another Black Friday at this company ever again."

"I thought that next year's projections seemed like a big challenge when I first saw the number, but it does not now. Let me ask the sales team. By the show of hands, who thinks that our team here can do one hundred twenty million dollars next year?" Every hand went high into the air. "Who thinks that we can do more than that?" Every hand again went up. "Bob, the management team will all review the budgeted numbers tomorrow morning with Darren and Patrick. You will have the finalized plan by noon. Does that work for you?"

"Tomorrow by noon is fine with me. And Tom and everyone here, thank you for giving me the opportunity again to work with great people, I sincerely appreciate it!" I started to get emotional again, so I stopped talking and sat back down.

Before the evening was over, I got hugs from every salesperson. The first one was from Nancy. She had been the first to recognize that I was on her team.

When I got back into my car after the "little" get-together, my first thought was that Tom was a crafty executive. He knew that if he had his sales team in a room with me in a casual setting and asked me a few questions about the company, he would get my passion up. He probably also knew that if I got a little emotional and started talking from my heart, he would have more success managing his sales team in the future. I drove home that evening knowing that next year was going to be a record-setting year for the company and every employee on the sales and service teams.

Chapter 17

HAPPY WIFE, HAPPY LIFE!

"Management is focusing on getting someone to get a result. Leadership is producing a standard in someone that when you're gone, they will live by to produce higher level results consistently."

—TONY ROBBINS, AMERICAN AUTHOR, ENTREPRENEUR, PHILANTHROPIST, AND LIFE COACH

MONDAY, DECEMBER 18—DAY 14 OF WEEK 3

THE VERY FIRST ITEM ON MY AGENDA FOR WEEK THREE WAS to finish up the budget. When I got to my office in the morning, there was a white binder sitting on my desk labeled BUDGETS. I did not expect to see this binder until noon. The first page was a signature page signed and dated that morning by Tom, Nancy, Chris, Donna, Tim, Darren, and Patrick. There was a yellow sticky note from Tom on the first page saying, "The management team did not need additional time to adjust the budget. We are going with these 'conservative' numbers. We all knew that we could beat our goals in this plan!"

All I could do was smile and think that these people really do get it! I went to get a cup of coffee. When I returned to my office, I closed the door and sat down to review each schedule, one by one. Darren and Patrick did a beautiful job developing the budget package for next year. There were dividers between each section, marked SALES, COST OF SALES, OPERATING EXPENSES, FOOTNOTES, and then finally INCOME STATEMENTS AND BALANCE SHEET. At the bottom corner of each page were the signed initials of who developed the schedule and which manager approved the numbers. Behind the reports were charts and graphs of each significant budget item showing the comparison between last year's actuals and this year's budget. Because we increased our sales plan from $50 million to the budgeted sales of $120 million, several of the graphs almost looked silly. In reviewing the operating expenses, the payroll expense was down compared to last year in the early months, but by the end of the year, the monthly payroll was much higher due to the planned increase in hiring additional employees.

The sales commission expense was up by 250 percent compared to the prior year, which was ballpark accurate based on the planned sales increase. We had not negotiated the insurance premiums yet, but we did anticipate a 25 percent decrease in annual expense. We were getting rid of all inventory on hand and bidding out the policies to three new agencies. Our conservative estimate was that we would reduce our insurance costs mostly because we were going to use another agency rather than the "we are like family" agency owned by Matthew, Craig's cousin.

I reviewed every schedule and could not find one number that I would change. I decided that I must give Darren and Patrick a reward for taking over this budget project. They together developed the first budget ever for this company. They did such a professional job with all the schedules and the whole presentation of the package. Before I went over to their offices to pat them on the back, I decided that I wanted to talk to Tom, Chris, and Alan just to confirm that they feel comfortable with next year's plan. I walked over to Tom's office, and he had all the sales schedules spread out on his desk.

"Good morning, Tom."

"Good morning, Bob."

"Nice *little get-together* last night, my friend!"

"Thanks!"

"Tom, you used me last night. You knew that if you could get me in front of your team and ask me a few questions, I would get fired up, didn't you?"

"Yes, of course, I did. That was the whole reason to get the management and sales team to my house. It was to let them all see the Bob Curry I know and am growing to love! My job becomes easy when you pump the people up, and you do it so well!"

"Tom, the barbecue chicken was good!"

"Thanks, Bob."

"You are completely on board with this budget?"

"Yes, sir!"

"If I go ask Chris and Alan the same question, are they going to respond the same?"

"Yes, sir."

"Thanks, I am going to expect you to make it happen!"

"I know."

"Have a good day, Tom."

"You too, Mr. Curry!"

I smiled when he called me Mr. Curry.

I went over to see Darren and Patrick, and both were in Darren's office. "Gentlemen, an amazing job you did with this budget package. My compliments! I could not have done it any better if I did it myself."

"Bob, we understand the quality of the work that you are demanding from this department, and we will never let you down," Darren said.

I felt lucky to have these two quality employees as part of my team. "Darren, let me ask you a question. What is your wife's favorite restaurant in the area when you go out to celebrate something like a wedding anniversary or your wife's birthday?"

"Bob, Morton's The Steakhouse—my wife loves that place."

"Patrick, same question!"

"Bob, same answer."

"Okay, dinner and drinks are on me as a thank-you for doing

such a great job with the budget. This budget is a much better package than I ever expected. Thank you, gentlemen, for a job well done! Let me know when you want to take your wives out to dinner, and I will call the restaurant and give them my credit card to pay for night out."

"Thank you, it is sincerely appreciated, but I have a question," Patrick said.

"Which is?" I responded.

"What if my favorite restaurant is different than my wife's. Why didn't you ask me about my favorite restaurant? My wife did not do this budget."

I laughed and said, "Patrick, happy wife, happy life!"

* * *

After a long day at the office, I was excited to go home, change clothes, and head to the Y for a run-and-gun basketball game. When I first entered the gym, I saw Tim and Chris over in the far end at one of the side baskets. Tim was showing Chris how to hold the ball before shooting a foul shot. I could see from Chris's body language that he did not want Tim teaching him anything. Chris was about eight inches taller than Tim. Tim then started showing Chris the shooting motion for shooting fouls. I stood there and watched Tim make twenty straight foul shots. He did not even hit the rim on any of the shots—*every* shot was all net.

I went and warmed up by shooting some jump shots. Chris walked over with Tim at his side. "Bob, this guy is an expert. He has not missed a foul shot probably in thirty-five tries. He is amazing!"

"Chris, it is obvious. Tim is the man!"

"Bob, it is unbelievable, he throws the ball up, and it goes in every time. He cannot dribble a basketball, and he also cannot miss a foul shot."

"Chris, did you learn anything?"

"Yes, that guy is a crazy good shooter!"

Luckily for me, our whole team showed up this week, so I did not have to be on the floor the entire game. Chris got to the foul line four times during the game and did not miss a shot. Not only did he not miss, but not one foul shot even hit the rim. Each shot had the perfect arch and fell in the basket right over the front of the rim. After Chris made his fourth foul shot in a row, he gave Tim a "thumbs up" as he ran down the court.

Immediately after the game, Chris, Tim and I headed to Duffy's to meet his whole department and many of the service guys from his old company that he wanted me to meet. Chris asked Tim to stay for our game and join us at Duffy's after. Chris had gained a new respect for Tim.

When we arrived at Duffy's, the parking lot was full, so finding a parking spot was difficult. When we went in, the room was full of computer technicians. They were all socializing and having fun. All sixteen techs of our service department were there along with a dozen service techs from Chris's former company. Because we were such a large group, we were able to move to a separate meeting room at the restaurant. When we all got settled, there were thirty of us sitting at five large tables. The waitresses brought in platters of chicken wings and pitchers of beer for each table.

Chris stood up and thanked everyone for coming. Chris talked for a while about his new company and all the exciting things that were going on. Then he introduced me and asked the group if they have any questions to ask the new president of ABC Computer Distributors.

Roger stood up and talked a little bit to the potential new hires that if they did join the company, it would be one of the best career moves they could ever make. He told them that ABC was the company to work for if you wanted to make a lot of money and grow your career. Chris added that I met the whole service department at Duffy's every Monday night and paid the tab for the beers and wings every week. I smiled and shook my head. I never knew what was going to come out of Chris's mouth.

There were a few questions, which we each took turns answering until only one question remained: "Can we get more beer and wings at our table?"

Bottom line, the meeting went very well. Chris asked the twelve new potential hires if they passed the background checks and drug tests would they be ready to come over to ABC. They all said they were prepared to join our organization as soon as we could make it happen. We also talked about meeting with their customers to get the service contracts signed over as quickly as possible. The group of us left Duffy's agreeing that they would give notice between Christmas and New Years and start with our organization the first Monday in January.

We had just potentially doubled the size of the service department with 100 percent billable techs in the first three weeks of my employment with this company.

Life was good.

Chapter 18

TOM THREATENED TO BRING CRAIG BACK

"Great vision without great people is irrelevant."

—JAMES C. COLLINS, AMERICAN BUSINESS
CONSULTANT, AUTHOR, AND LECTURER

FRIDAY, DECEMBER 22—DAY 18 OF WEEK 3

FRIDAY MORNING, AT 7:00 A.M., CHRIS HELD THE FIRST EARLY morning service meeting with a whole room full of technicians. I got there on time to attend the meeting, but there was not a chair available for me to sit at the table. I told Chris that this was his meeting, and I had some other issues that needed my immediate attention."

At 8:00 a.m., Darren called me to ask if I could join him in the conference room to meet with some insurance agents. I did have some time, so I got a cup of coffee and went to the conference room. Darren and Patrick were there with three other gentlemen all dressed in expensive suits. They all stood up as I entered the room and were holding their professional cards to give me. I set down my coffee, shook their hands, and sat down at the table to listen.

Darren and Patrick handled the meeting entirely. I did not have to say a word the whole time. When Darren was done telling them the rules for bidding on our business insurance as he and I had discussed earlier, he asked me if I had anything to add. I said, "No, I think that you covered everything much better than I could have, so I will continue to remain silent."

The gentleman, Stanley, who owned the agency spoke up and said, "Bob, before we quote your insurance, I have a few questions. We like to get to know the client before we go out to the market to ask our carriers to bid on each of the coverages that your company needs."

I replied, "Stanley, that certainly makes sense to me. Is there anything I can help you with that Darren and Patrick did not share with you about this company?"

"Bob, Darren, and Patrick were kind enough to put together a fact sheet about your company as well as the details about each of the policies we are going to quote, but that does not tell us much about the company."

"Okay, Stanley, what would you like to know that will give you all the information you need to quote our insurance?"

"How long has your current insurance agent been selling insurance to your company?"

"Nine years."

"Why did you decide to bid out the insurance this year?"

"Because it is my feeling that our premiums are too high, so we are going to check the market by asking your firm and two others to bid on the insurance."

"I see that you want to meet with us at the end of January when the policies end in February, why is that?

"Because I want Darren and Patrick to have enough time to review all the information and pick the firm that is going to give us the best prices and service for our premium dollars."

"Are you going to give the incumbent the last chance to match the lowest bid after you see all the numbers from the other agencies?"

"Good question, Stanley. I can see that you are attempting to determine what your chances are of landing our account, and I appreciate that. It makes good business sense to me. The current insurance agent is not bidding on the insurance this year. He has no chance to keep our business. He recently displayed an attitude that we should not be bidding our insurance coverages because he has sold us insurance for nine years and he was *entitled* to maintain our account without us checking his numbers. His entitlement attitude cost him this account. Stanley, we have many customers who we sell computers, software, and service to every day. We treat those customers with the ultimate respect. Our sales and service people know that we must earn our right to serve our customers with every sale and service call. We take nothing for granted. We show our customers that we appreciate their business with every transaction. If I have a sales or service employee who displays an attitude as our last insurance agent did, I will fire him. We have no room in this company for people like that. So, Stanley, you are welcome to bid on our insurance coverages, but you will be asked to treat us the same way I demand our employees treat our customers. They earn the next sale by how well they treat the customer with pricing and the level of service with the current transaction. I hope that I have answered your question."

"You have, and I appreciate you sharing with us about your corporate culture. How you have so adequately stated your demands on how your employees treat your customers, I have attempted to do the same. Unfortunately, I believe that I have fallen short at times. Could you share with me what I need to do to get my team in the same place as your sales and service departments are with your customers?"

It has been my experience over the years with insurance agents and brokers that they have many sales tricks to close a new or existing account. The incumbent agent will inflate his pricing hoping that the client did not get other bids for the coverage. They attempt to show up at the very last minute before the current insurance policies expire. The insurance agent knows that the client cannot go without coverage for one day. If the client has other bids for the coverage that are priced lower, the incumbent has pricing room to lower his bid if necessary to get the business.

Darren asked, "Bob if you don't mind, may I answer Stanley's question?"

"Sure, you probably can answer it better than I can anyway."

"Stanley, Bob is a different kind of leader. He is open, he listens, and he lets his managers make their own decisions. Bob leads by example. He does his job, and we do ours. Bob does not want puppets working for him. He hires the best people. When he joined the organization, he explained how he wanted to manage this company and was very clear with his message."

"Darren, what was his message?"

"We treat our customers, employees, stakeholders, and vendors with respect. We all work hard and work smart. We are all accountable for our actions. Patrick and I are responsible for operational and financial reporting to show the management team how everyone is doing. We ask our customers how we are doing using a customer survey with each service transaction. If there are employees here who do not have the proper attitude and work ethic, they are not here very long. The management team here is pulling the rope in the same direction, and the results are showing the success already. This company rewards success and terminates employees with bad attitudes. Success is contagious, and unfortunately, so are bad attitudes. There is no room in this company for someone with a bad attitude."

"Thank you, Darren. Bob, I have always been afraid to get rid of people, the people who are not doing their job."

"Stanley, if you stick your head in the sand and ignore those people, you are hurting the employees who are doing a great job for the company. You are sending a message to your employees that it is okay to be a D player and still work for your firm. Can you imagine if you took the payroll dollars that you are wasting on those employees and used them to reward your A players? What would your firm's financial statements look like?"

Stanley let out a breath. "Mr. Curry, I can promise you, beginning in March, we are going to be your insurance agency for all your insurance needs."

"Stanley, that is quite a promise, I will leave you in the hands of my two best employees, Darren and Patrick."

I shook their hands and returned to my office to get some work done.

At noon, Darren tapped on my office door to get my attention and asked me if I would like to join him for lunch. At lunch, I was expecting Darren to talk about something that was on his mind about the meeting with the insurance guys, but I was wrong. I asked him how the other two insurance meetings went after the meeting with Stanley. He said the meetings went well and we should have all three firms' quotes soon. We only had a quick lunch together and then went back to the office. I was heartened that Darren just wanted to have company for lunch, which further drove home my opinion that he was one of the good guys.

At 1:55 p.m., I walked into the sales conference room and looked around at all the salespeople. Everyone in the room had smiles on their faces, and the whole atmosphere felt charged. I had no idea what was going on, but it felt good.

I sat down next to Nancy because I needed to talk to her. I told Nancy that I had just received notice ten minutes earlier from our three suppliers that the full shipment of all the computers for her big customer order would be at our warehouse doors Monday morning.

Nancy's face lit up with a big smile. "Bob, that is great news, thank you."

I asked her to contact her customer after the meeting to notify them so that we could get the second installment of $4.5 million.

"Bob, I already told the purchasing manager about the schedule. He has the check already sitting on his desk waiting for my call."

"I should have known that you were on top of this whole transaction," I said with a hint of awe.

Tom stood up and said, "Okay everyone, may I have your attention? We have a considerable amount of information to cover in this meeting, so let's get started. I would like to ask everyone to be very brief with what they must say in this meeting because we are going to be in this room for only one hour, and we probably have three hours of stuff to cover. First, I will start the meeting by letting everyone know that we rehired Barbara earlier this week to join the sales support department. She will be starting on the first workday of the new year. We need to have her desk, computer, and phone ready for her so she can hit the ground running."

I told Tom I would talk to Darren and make that happen this week.

Traci raised her hand. When Tom motioned for her to speak, she said, "Tom, on behalf of Vicki, Amanda, Charlene, and myself, thank you in a major way. We sincerely appreciate the help, and we certainly need it. This past week, the activity in our department has been intense!"

"Well, Traci, you are welcome. Bob and I are looking forward to great things out of your department. We knew you needed the help. Bob and I both thought that Barbara would be able to fit in well since she knows the company, the products, the processes, and the paperwork your department handles."

Tom then started passing out a sheet of paper with each salesperson's sales quota for next year. After he finished, he explained that sales quota begins this January. Tom said, "I wanted to make the quotas substantially higher, but Bob made me reduce them down."

That was not accurate, but if it worked for Tom, I was okay with his story. I knew that Tom was a salesperson at heart and this was his way of selling the sales quota totals to each salesperson.

I have always believed in setting sales quotas for a sales team. I think that it is crucial and motivational to let every person in the sales department know the total sales that are expected from each of them every month, quarter, and for the whole year. I thought it was critical to set quotas for two categories: hardware and software sales as one category and service as the second. Once we determined everyone's sales quota for the year, we broke down the total as 90 percent for hardware and software sales and 10 percent of service sales. We also increased the sales quotas by 10 percent each quarter. My goal was to push these salespeople hard.

Darren also received a copy of the sales quotas so that he could create a monthly report with every salesperson's actual sales totals versus both for the current month and year-to-date (see page 367). Darren would distribute the results to each salesperson and the consolidated report of all salespeople to Tom and myself. Our consolidated sales report sorted the salespeople's totals from the highest dollar amount to the lowest year-to-date sales.

Typically, when I had set sales quotas in the past, I increased the prior year's actual sales by one-third. If the salesperson was not with the company for the whole year, I took their average sales for the last three months and annualized it. With Nancy, since her sales volume was so high, and she was starting January with the $18 million-plus sale, Tom and I agreed to set her sales quota equal to last year's total plus her recent huge pharma company sale set to ship in January. That made her sales quota at $35 million, which was a sizable goal. With Nancy's success with the new target companies assigned to her, I had a feeling that she was going to sell a lot more than her quota, and that was okay with me!

I looked up on the whiteboard on the wall, and under Nancy's list of customers, there were magnetic markers over the squares of two customers indicating PO RECEIVED and seven customers marked APPTS. MADE. There was a stack of the magnetic markers next to Tom ready to be posted on the board as each salesperson reported their results.

At the last meeting, Nancy was the only person with excellent results with her target customers. I was excited to see the progress the rest of the department had made. The previous week, Tom had kept the sales team in the conference room after our last sales meeting. Earlier this week, I asked Tom what had happened that day after I had left. He told me he would explain at this week's sales meeting, and I was curious to find out.

Tom asked, "Who would like to start the meeting by reporting their results with their target list?"

Every person in the room, including Nancy, raised their hand.

That got my attention, and I wondered what was going on.

Tom said, "Okay, let's start with Karla and then just go right around the table."

Karla stood up and grabbed a handful of the magnetic markers to post on the whiteboard. She started at the top of the customer list under her name. She placed one of the makers over the first five customers and wrote on each "Appt. made." Then she told the group what happened with each of the five customers. The next customer, she placed a marker and wrote on it, "PO Received" and showed a copy of the $290,000 order from the customer. She told the group that Alan had processed the purchase order, and it would ship before the end of the month.

Every person in the room applauded to congratulate Karla.

Karla said, "I have thoroughly researched the other four potential customers and will be calling each before the end of the day to introduce myself to the purchasing and IT managers. I plan to schedule a meeting with them next week with each company. I followed the process that the whole sales department set up last week, thanks to Nancy. And, Nancy, it works very well! Everyone in this room owes you a big thank-you!"

Every one of the other salespeople and sales support department stood up and applauded for Nancy. I noticed that Nancy did not blush.

As each salesperson stood up to talk about their successes with their target list, it just kept getting better. Most of them had at least five appointments scheduled, plus everyone in the room received at least one order more than $150,000 from the target list customers.

Tom must have lit some big fires under their butts after the poor results from last week's meeting. December was going to be a strong sales month for this company because the sales team had finally woken up. Unfortunately, there were only three sales of service contracts other than Nancy's during the prior week. I liked the hardware/software sales, but I loved the service sales more because the profit margin on the service sales was materially higher.

After the final salesperson finished reporting her results, I stood up and clapped for the whole group, including Tom. I walked over to the whiteboard and told the sales team they should be very proud of their results. These were the results I had expected last week. *What had Tom done to motivate them?* I wondered, so I asked the question aloud.

Rachael gladly offered the answer: "Tom threatened that if we ever had another sales meeting like that one last week, he would bring Craig back as the sales manager for the bottom ten salespeople! Obviously, that threat was enough to get us all motivated to upgrade our results. None of us would ever want to see Craig walking around this office ever again!"

"I could not agree more," I said, not bothering to tell anyone that Craig would never be allowed to set foot in this building as an employee ever again. But I think they all knew that. I did want to bring up the issue with the service sales, so I said, "Tom, the sales results by this group were good this week, but please tell me your idea of how we can get this team to sell more service. As you know, the new sales commission plan introduced last week doubled the commission rate on the sale of service contracts."

"Bob, I will deal with that immediately. These people react to incentives. Last week the incentive was to bring Craig back if there were not better results, and it obviously worked well."

I smiled at him, but I was serious now. "Tom, I will talk to Chris to make himself

Nancy
ALC, Inc.
Appt. made Dec XX—9:00
All Good, Co.
Appt. made Dec XX—11:00
Best Company
Appt. made Dec XX—1:00
CDF Company
CRR, Inc.
Appt. made Dec XX—2:00
DDR, Inc.
PO Received $415,000
East Co.
Appt. made Dec XX—12:00
Farmer, Inc.
PO Received $365,000
The Red Co.
Appt. made Dec XX—8:30
Uncle, Inc.
Appt. made Dec XX—1:30

available to attend more sales calls with your salespeople. He can close service contract deals when he gets in front of the customer's IT managers."

"He *is* easy to like and too big to say no to when he does a sales pitch," Tom said, and he was only half-joking.

"Tom, I meant to ask you, how did it go last week when you attended the sales calls with your people?"

"It went very well for two reasons. First, I was able to evaluate the individual salesperson's approach with customers, and second, I was able to help close several of the deals. Look at that whiteboard . . . pretty good, huh?"

"Yes, I agree, but my only comment is that I want to see more service contracts sold."

"Come to our next sales meeting, Bob. I promise you will see better results."

"I will be there, I promised."

Chapter 19

THE PARTY

"Your most unhappy customers are your greatest source of learning."

—BILL GATES, AMERICAN BUSINESS MAGNATE, INVESTOR,
AUTHOR, PHILANTHROPIST, AND CO-FOUNDER OF MICROSOFT

SATURDAY, DECEMBER 22—DAY 19 OF WEEK 3

THE HOLIDAY PARTY WAS SUPPOSED TO BEGIN AT 6:00 P.M.
and end at 10:00 p.m. I planned to visit the venue an hour or two
early just in case the planning committee needed my help with any
last-minute setup or decisions. The party was at Whitford Country
Club, which was less than two miles from our office and a mile
away from my home.

Tom told me earlier that they bartered a deal with the country
club to exchange an old network server that was in our warehouse
with outdated technology in exchange for the use of the banquet
room. Tom also agreed to give the country club a year of free computer service for all their computers in exchange for the open bar for
one hour before the dinner plus bottles of either red or white wine
for each couple attending.

The only thing that we had to write a check for was the dinners
for forty-four couples. We also invited Kevin and Rick and their
wives. A friend of Donna's owned a flower shop, and again Tom
bartered a deal for all the flower arrangements on the tables for

a year-old laptop out of our inventory, which was only worth 40 percent of what ABC had paid for it.

Without Donna, Nancy, Darren, or Tom knowing, I had Tina, our receptionist, purchase forty-one gift cards for dinners at Ruth's Chris Steak House for $100 each and wrapped each card in a little box with beautiful red wrapping paper and pink bows. Then, I purchased three seven-day, six-night cruise certificates and had Tina wrap them up in the same boxes as the gift cards.

I had asked Chris to rent a Santa Claus outfit for the evening. With Chris's gregarious personality, he was the perfect candidate for the job. He had to go to three different costume stores before he found a suit large enough to fit his big frame. My plan was for him to eat dinner with everyone and when the wait staff started serving the desserts, he would sneak off and change into the Santa suit. He was then supposed to bring all the gifts in a big bag over his shoulder, walk around to all the tables, and let each person pick out a gift from Santa's sack. There would be forty-one couples receiving a $100 gift card, and three lucky couples would find a certificate for a one-week cruise to the Caribbean Islands. No one was permitted to open the gifts until they were all distributed. I probably could have swapped some of our old computers in our warehouse inventory for the cruise certificates, but I did not think of bartering as Tom had, and I felt kind of foolish.

I arrived at the country club at 4:00 p.m., and there were two college-age students out front in the parking lot to valet park the cars. I walked through the festively decorated entrance, and I just had to stop and stare at the beautiful decorations before going into the party room. When I got to our banquet room, I was equally as impressed. Tom, Nancy, Donna, and Darren had set up the room like expert designers and the flower arrangements added an elegant touch. Considering the minimal amount of money we spent on this first ever holiday party for ABC Computer Distributors, this management team had done an incredible job.

I knew the whole company, and their families were going to appreciate this party. Everyone in the organization had been working very hard for the past three weeks. They had each raised the bar for their contribution.

Although I had only started working for this company a short time ago, I noticed a distinct change in everyone's attitudes, efforts, and accomplishments. I wanted every employee who worked for this company to have the same feeling I had when I worked for H&N Construction Company. I tried to make everyone feel proud and fortunate to work for ABC. I believed that most, if not all the employees, were sensing a positive change in the corporate culture. This party would enable the employees to feel the difference and also give their families an opportunity to get to know the kind of company their loved ones were working for now.

When I walked into the banquet room, Tom, Nancy, Darren, and Donna immediately came over to give me a big Christmas hug and wished me Merry Christmas.

I asked, "How can I help?"

"Bob, we have this covered!" Donna said, and the rest agreed.

I looked around, smiled, and said, "Okay, I guess I am not needed here." It delighted me that these managers worked together as a team and did a fantastic job. Then I said, "I have one concern about the party."

"What's the concern?" Tom asked.

"Tom, this is a company-sponsored event, and if we are serving alcohol, we need to make sure that no one at the party gets drunk and makes a fool out of themselves. And more importantly, no one drinks too much and gets into an accident or a DUI on their way home tonight."

"No need to worry, Bob, we talked about that already. We are giving everyone two drink tickets when they arrive. We also told the club to use the small glasses for the mixed drinks. The bartender is also going to fill each of the glasses full of ice before pouring any alcohol. Everyone attending tonight is going to be served drinks with a very minimal amount of alcohol. I already told the sales team, and Chris has instructed his service guys that if anyone starts looking like they have had too much to drink, Darren and Chris, the two biggest guys in the company, are going to take that person outside and kick their butt. I am just kidding. Darren and Chris have agreed to stand at the front door on the way out to the parking lot at the end of the evening. If they see anyone looking like they may have had too much to drink, they are going to call Lyft."

The management team's forethought impressed me. It seemed like they had thought of everything. I had no worries tonight!

Later, when my wife and I arrived at the country club for the party, she admired all the beautiful decorations and the red rose centerpieces. The country club had even set up a beautiful Christmas tree in front of the banquet room. Each table had seat assignments, and my wife and I shared a table with Darren, Kevin, Rick, and their wives. There was a bottle of wine for each couple at the table to take home as a holiday gift.

My wife and I walked around the hall greeting people, and after a short while, she turned to me and said, "Wow, Bob, they love you!" I could only smile. After a while, she went to sit at our table to chat with the other wives seated there, and I continued to circulate to make sure that I greet every employee and their plus-ones.

When Chris and his wife entered, I immediately walked over to introduce myself to Chris's wife, Mandy. "I have been looking forward to meeting you forever," I said, exaggerating just a bit. "I have known Chris for several years, so I am surprised we have not met before tonight."

Mandy said, "Chris has been keeping you and your basketball games a secret, I guess, but he had told me so much about you these past couple of weeks. I am so glad he decided to join your team. I have not seen him this happy for many years. He comes home from work each night, energized and excited."

"Hmm. I don't think it was only Chris' decision alone! Chris told me that you encourage him to jump over to our company."

"Chris and I are a team," she explained. "We talk about every important decision in our marriage, so we can always make the right decision that works for us both. Chris is a good guy; I dearly love him."

"I am also a huge fan of your husband! I am so glad I have him to manage our service team. No one on earth could handle that position better."

"I know, he is very good at his job, always has been!"

"Now, Mandy, if you could teach Chris to shoot a foul shot!"

"I would rather teach him how to make a bed, Bob! I am always cleaning up after him. Besides, he told me that one of his new coworkers helped him with those foul shots!"

Chris interjected, "Come on, Bob, why did you have to bring up my foul shot shooting skills? I was having such a wonderful time listening to your conversation about how great I am until you mentioned that. And, besides, my buddy Tim made that problem go away."

"Come to my table and meet my wife later. We should make dinner plans," I suggested.

"Bob, that is only going to happen if you promise not to talk about my foul shot issue."

I said, "I promise, Chris," and stepped aside so they could mingle with the others. "Merry Christmas, both of you and to your little ones at home!"

"Thank you, Bob, Merry Christmas to you and your family also."

As I was walking away, I heard Mandy say, "Chris, which one is Tim? You must introduce me to him. I did not think there was a person alive who could teach you anything."

After forty-five minutes, Tom tapped his wine glass with his spoon to get everyone's attention. He asked everyone to find their table and have a seat. I rejoined my wife at our table. The door to the room opened, and a regiment of servers entered carrying trays over their heads to serve the salads. Next came the entree, a choice of prime rib, filet mignon, or lobster tails. After dinner, the waiters served dessert—cherry pie and ice cream. I looked over, and Chris was still sitting in his chair eating his dessert rather than hustling off to change into the Santa suit. I started to get up to go over and remind him when I felt Tom's hand on my shoulders.

He whispered in my ear, "Did you think that we were not going to have Santa come to the party tonight?"

I looked at Tom, and he had a big smile on his face. I sat back down to see what they planned. I finished my cherry pie and ice cream. It was good; I mean really good!

> It was important to me that everyone in the company had a wonderful time at this holiday party. I wanted every employee in the company to know that I was just a very normal person that was hired to turnaround this company. I did not want them to have an image of me that I was an "ivory tower" type of manager. I wanted every employee to know me as a regular guy who was going to support each hard-working employee who worked for ABC Computer Distributers.

As the waiters were clearing the tables, the doors to the room busted open. Santa, who I immediately recognized as Tom, entered the room and Nancy followed behind, appropriately dressed as Mrs. Claus. The Santa suit fit Tom perfect, with no stuffing needed. He did indeed look like the real Santa.

Tom let out a big hearty "Ho, ho, ho, Merry Christmas" and carried a big bag full of Christmas presents over his shoulder. There were two chairs next to the Christmas tree where Santa and Mrs. Claus sat to pass out the gifts. Tom pulled a list from his bag, and one by one called each employee and significant other to the front of the room to sit on Santa's lap. Tom and Nancy seemed really into this part of the evening, and it occurred to me that if they were not on my sales team, they could get a full-time job doing this skit.

As each couple came up, Tom said something funny and handed them their gifts. I just sat back and watched the fun.

After Santa handed out all the gifts, including one to Kevin and Rick and their wives, Santa called my wife and me to the front of the room. I hesitated. Being the center of attention in a situation like this was not in my comfort zone. When we got up there, Tom pulled out a sheet of paper from his Santa suit pocket. He stood up, took off the fake beard and cap. He called Alan, Donna, Chris, Tim, and Darren to the front of the room.

Tom spoke into the microphone and said thank you for the past three weeks. He said that my leadership, direction, friendship, and confidence had pulled this company out of the grave and pushed it right up into the stars. It was now the brightest star in the sky. He pointed to the star atop the Christmas tree. Then he said that he loves working for ABC Computer Distributors. Next, he handed the mic to Alan.

Alan said that he had learned more about buying product and inventory management in three weeks than he had learned in his whole career. Alan handed the microphone to Donna.

Donna was too emotional to say a word, so she just gave my wife and me a hug. Donna handed the microphone to Chris.

Chris thanked me for recruiting and hiring him and said that he was very excited about the future of the company.

When Tim got the mic next, he pulled out a tightly folded sheet of paper from his pocket. Once he had it all unfolded, he said, "I am not great at giving speeches, so I wrote mine down." Tim turned the sheet of paper over and showed it to everyone in the room. The paper said, "THANK YOU, BOB!" Everyone laughed.

Darren was last. He told everyone about how he had given his notice to the owner of ABC several times for various reasons. He said, "With Bob leading this organization, reasons like that no longer exist. To tell you the truth, I have forgotten most of what happened because the last three weeks have been the best three weeks of my career. Every day I learn more about how to be a better controller for this company. If I could make a wish to the real Santa Claus, my wish would be to work with this group of people for the rest of my career."

Darren handed the microphone to Nancy.

Nancy's face broke out into a huge smile and said, "I would like to introduce this guy next to me. Some of you may know him as Bob Curry, the new president and CEO of ABC Computer Distributors. That is his name and title, but my name for him is 'Bob, the Go to Guy!' No matter what problem you bring to this guy, either he will solve it immediately with a good business decision or, like he did for me, made a five-minute phone call to Kevin, who is sitting right over there and helped me close an eighteen-million-dollar deal."

Nancy kissed my wife and me on our cheeks and handed the microphone back to Tom. My wife squeezed my hand. Her eyes told me how proud she was of me.

Tom put the Santa hat and beard back on and said, "So, Mr. Curry, Santa has a little Christmas gift for you tonight too.

Chris and Darren went to the far corner of the room, pulled the white sheet off two brand-new sets of TaylorMade golf clubs, one for me and one for my wife. I could not wait to see them up close. They carried them to the front of the room, as Kevin and Rick stood up and joined the management team upfront.

Kevin took the microphone from Tom and said, "Bob, these clubs are from Rick and me. We know that before you joined this company, you were planning a year-long trip to play the best golf courses all around the country with your wife. Well, we would like you to play those courses with these golf clubs as our gift to both of you. In three weeks, you have done magic with this company, and we want you to know that we appreciate everything that you have done for this company and every person in this room. Thank you, Bob!"

Kevin handed me the microphone, and he, Rick, and the whole management team took their seats as did my wife. I was now stuck up in the front of the room with a microphone, two brand-new sets of golf clubs, and eighty-seven people staring at me.

"First, I want you all to know that I have not prepared to stand in front of this group tonight with a microphone in my hand. I also want everyone to know that Donna, Santa, Mrs. Claus, and Darren worked very hard to make this night possible. They all did an awesome job, and I want to sincerely thank them for their hard work to make this night special for everyone in this room."

Everyone in the room stood up and applauded them for their efforts.

"Thank you, Kevin, Rick, and your lovely wives for coming tonight and celebrating Christmas with our team of forty-two hard-working employees at ABC Computer Distributors. And thank you also for the golf clubs. I promise you that they will go to good use. I also want to thank the wonderful servers and everyone at Whitford Country Club who made this night special for our company. This room and food are first class!"

"This has been an incredible evening, and I want everyone in the room to know that I care about all of you. When Kevin came to me and asked if I would get involved with this company, I knew it was going to be a huge challenge to make this company successful again. I only knew after I sat down with each member of this management team that the turnaround was possible. I am a fortunate man to be surrounded by these people. These six managers are lucky to have a great staff reporting to them. We have made some great strides toward improving our business. We have a strong foundation of good people in this room who believes in this company. Unfortunately, a couple of weeks ago, I had to reduce the staff, but that reduction made this company stronger. Making those types of decisions was very difficult for me, but I did it because it was the right thing to do for all of you. I hired Chris to lead our service team . . . because, again, it was the right thing to do to make this company successful."

"I wanted to share with everyone that this month was the first profitable month in a year and a half at this company. Congratulations to everyone in the room for doing such a wonderful job during the first three weeks of December. As you are all aware, businesses are always slow this time of year—that is, the week between Christmas and New Year's. But I challenge all of you *not* to slow down. Keep striving and improving your respective departments. If you are on the sales team, go out, visit your customers, and close some sales. If you are on the service team, continue to handle those service calls and make our customers happy with your work. I am asking you to keep this great momentum going. Let's close this year with the best month ever in the history of this company!"

Everyone in the room cheered. Any nerves I had about speaking into the microphone at this gathering were gone. So, I continued, "All the rest of us are in a support role for our sales and service teams. It is those employees, the sales and service departments, who generates all the revenue to pay for the rest of our salaries. I want each of you to know that I appreciate your hard work. I will be working hard every day to support each of you so that you can be successful. I want you to be successful for yourself, for your families, and for the company."

Everyone cheered again.

"I have an announcement to make," I said when the cheering died down.

"My announcement is that this company is going to start a new scholarship fund. We will deposit the scholarship funds into a separate bank account, and those funds will be used to provide college scholarships for underprivileged students who do not have the funds to afford college. Every month our sales team hits their monthly sales budget, we are going to add $10,000 to the scholarship fund.

"I am going to ask the six members of the management team and Nancy to form a committee to oversee this scholarship fund. Can I ask Nancy and my management team to let me know if you are willing to accept this responsibility?"

All seven-people called out that they were on board. The room roared again.

"Well, I am taking that response as they are willing to handle this important task," I said above the noise. "If the management team do as well as with the scholarship fund as they did with this holiday party, there are going to be some happy high school kids going to college soon. This scholarship program is one of the ways I would like to spend some of our hard-earned profits by giving some bright kids a chance."

"I have taken up too much of your time tonight. Now it is time to open your Christmas gifts."

Everyone in the room had two boxes in front of them. Please go ahead and open your gifts and Merry Christmas to all of you!"

I knew what was in one of the boxes, but not in the second. I sat back down at my table and watched everyone open the packages.

One box contained a gift card for dinner out and the second

package had a gift certificate for every couple to go on an all-expense paid seven-day, six-night cruise to the Caribbean Islands. I looked around, having no idea who had made this generous donation. I had only purchased three cruises.

Tom pulled up his chair next to me and whispered in my ear, "Bob, we did not want to tell you, but Nancy and I donated the money to purchase the cruises for the balance of the employees. I did barter part of the deal, but the cruise line gave us the certificates at cost and discounted them all by fifty percent. I gave them five old laptops out of the inventory and a check for ten thousand. Nancy thought that was the least we could do for your help getting Nancy's a big deal done. And by the way, the cruise line is now our newest customer. They have already given Nancy her first purchase order for two hundred computers. On Monday, she is meeting the head of their IT department to quote on the service contract for all their computers in their headquarters offices and on each cruise ship."

I honestly did not know what to say. This couple had exceeded my expectations. I croaked out, "Thank you, you guys are the best." Had I said any more, I would have found myself crying.

"Bob, at our first lunch together, I told you that Nancy and I are on your team, and that is where we plan to stay."

The evening did not end until 11:30, an hour and a half longer than we had booked the room for, but I decided to pay the club and the wait staff for the extra time. Everyone shared stories, laughed, and had fun. When people were leaving, they shook my hand in appreciation and thanked my wife for supporting me in my decision to undertake the turnaround at ABC.

I decided that I was going to start the scholarship fund to give back some of our successes to the community, to poor, underprivileged high school students. I knew that it would be a little risky when spending some of the company's money for a party and scholarship fund, but I believed that the reward would be much more valuable than the risk. I felt that the party and Christmas gifts would strengthen the corporate culture and the relationships between all the employees. It would bond all the employees together to make

this company more successful. I also believed that granting scholarships to kids would make everyone proud of our organization.
Everyone would be motivated to work harder to grow sales and
profits, so we could continually increase the number and amount
of scholarships granted to kids that could not afford to pay their
college tuition.

My wife and I sat with Tom, Nancy, Kevin, Rick, and their wives
in the party room after everyone else had left. The wait staff had
cleaned all the tables, and the room was quiet. We chatted for a bit
until Rick, Kevin, and their wives stood up to leave. Kevin shook
Tom's hand and hugged Nancy. Then he turned to me and said,
"Bob, it was worth it!"

"What was worth it? I asked.

"All those rounds of golf I let you win to get you to feel sorry
for me so that you would take on this turnaround and save my butt
from getting fired!"

"You are a good friend, Kevin, but that is a bizarre recruiting
method! I am not buying it!"

"Are you telling me you do not believe I let you win?"

I said not a word other than "Merry Christmas to you all! Be safe
with your drive home tonight!"

I gave Tom and Nancy a big Christmas hug and took the new
golf clubs and my wife home.

Chapter 20

"THEY ARE HERE"

"The smartest business decision you can make is to hire qualified people. Bringing the right people on board saves you thousands, and your business will run smoothly and efficiently."

—BRIAN TRACY, CANADIAN-AMERICAN MOTIVATIONAL
PUBLIC SPEAKER, AND SELF-DEVELOPMENT AUTHOR

WEDNESDAY, DECEMBER 26—DAY 20 OF WEEK 4

AT 9:00 A.M., WEDNESDAY MORNING, THE DAY AFTER CHRISTMAS, three 48-foot trailer trucks were parked at the loading dock of our warehouse, waiting to unload the laptops and network servers worth over $15 million. I was in my office unaware.

Tim excitedly rushed into my office and said, "Bob, they are here!"

Not sure exactly what he was talking about or what had gotten him so excited, I looked at him expectantly.

"Bob, the computers for Nancy's big order are here!"

I found Tim's excitement mildly humorous, but I did not laugh. He was the company's best cheerleader and was genuinely committed to making this business profitable any way that he could, even if that meant cheerleading.

On the way to the warehouse, we stopped by Darren's and Alan's offices because I wanted them to participate in receiving the inventory. While in Darren's office, I took the opportunity to ask him to make arrangements to set up Tom's re-hire, Barbara, with everything she would need in her new sales support position as of the first week in January. Then, when the three of us reached Alan's office, he joined our group after retrieving a copy of the PO for Nancy's order from his filing cabinet to match up against the driver's manifest.

The four of us headed to the warehouse to meet the truck drivers. Each driver gave Alan their driver's manifest to match up with his PO's. The paperwork was in order. I asked Darren and Alan to help Tim receive all the computers because I wanted them to be very careful with the counts and to make sure none of the boxes were damaged.

"Gentlemen, please count every laptop when unloaded, then count the complete order a second time once everything is off the truck. Don't let the drivers leave until you are confident that we have everything listed in our PO's and driver's manifests. I have had stuff stolen off trailer trucks in route to our warehouse, and then the driver tries to unload the cargo quickly, so the receiver may not catch the shortage. Because we purchased all the ThinkPad inventory that the three suppliers had of these laptops, I asked them to be very meticulous with their receiving counts."

I reminded Darren, Tim, and Alan that I did not want to broadcast that we have almost $18 million of inventory in the warehouse (the amount of this shipment plus the existing stock).

I asked Darren if he had received the endorsement for the increase in insurance to cover all this product. He assured me that we had proper insurance coverage for this computer inventory. Then I asked Tim to show me his plan for storing the computers in the warehouse. He and I walked over to the warehouse racking, and he pointed out where he intended to warehouse the inventory. He told me that he had three college students arriving at noon to help him run the diagnostics on all the machines and load and test the client's software.

I also asked about his plan and process for staging all these laptops. I knew Tim had his plan developed for a while now, but I wanted to make sure that nothing would go wrong. A lot was riding on this, but especially our good standing with Nancy! The plan was to get all the computers staged during this last week of December and delivered them all to the customer in the first week of January. January was going to be a record-setting sales month for this company, and we were all very excited.

By noon, Alan, Tim, and Darren had received all the laptops, servers, and had them stored in the warehouse racks. Alan and Darren came to my office to let me know that the receiving of the shipment went very well. There were no exceptions, shortages, or damages. I thanked them for giving Tim a hand. Tim was a capable employee, but receiving this valuable order was a two or three-person job. They also informed me that the college students had just shown up and Tim was getting them started doing the diagnostics and loading the programs.

I left myself a reminder on my Outlook calendar to check the number of the laptops Tim's team staged by the end of the day to estimate when all the machines would be ready for delivery.

While in my office, Darren told me he had meetings set up with three insurance agents to bid our property and casualty insurance policies. The first one was at 1:00. He asked if I had the time to sit in the meetings.

"I will attend the first meeting and see how it goes," I agreed. "But honestly, I enjoy meeting with insurance guys about as much as I enjoy meeting with bankers—and you know what I think about bankers . . . Rick and Kevin excluded, of course!"

Darren chuckled, as Nancy made her grand entrance wearing a big smile. I figured she had the $4.5 million-plus check from the customer for the second installment of her order. So that she could enjoy the moment of surprising me with the check, I played dumb. She reached into her briefcase and pulled out an envelope and gave it to me.

"Nancy, I have to give you credit, you always are on top of everything. You are an excellent salesperson!"

Nancy laughed. "Bob, if you smell the envelope, it also smells like a big commission check for your favorite salesperson!"

I handed the check to Darren and asked him to get the funds deposited as quickly as possible to pay down the outstanding loan balance that day or at least no later than the following day.

Darren agreed and left to call Kevin, saying that if Kevin was in, he would give Patrick the check and ask him to deliver it to the bank and have them transfer the money immediately to Kevin. I knew that this check would pay our loan balance down close to zero. Getting the loan paid down this quickly would save us $23,000 per month in interest.

My office line rang, and I picked it up on the second ring.

"Bob, this is Kevin."

"What's up?"

"I wanted to call you to congratulate you. Paying down the loan balance to zero this fast is a miracle, plus you have saved my job. My company had written off five million dollars of the loan balance for ABC Computer Distributors before you started managing the business. Rick just told me that the company reversed the write-off and now I am being paid a bonus rather than getting fired," he said with joy in his voice.

"Good for you, buddy! What a great Christmas present. Thank you for giving me the news. Kevin, the only reason I agreed to take this engagement was to help you. I did not want to see you get hurt by losing your job."

"Well, Bob, I owe you one, my friend."

"Kevin, you owe me nothing, other than dropping one of your big banana drives in the water at the first hole on the next couple rounds of golf," I kidded.

Kevin chuckled. "Bob, don't ever expect me to lose another round of golf against you."

"Hmm. That bonus check you just received is giving you some false hope . . . which is good."

Kevin did not bother to keep the joke running, but truthfully, I expected to continue beating him.

"Bob, if I don't talk to you again, happy New Year to you and your family."

"Same to you and yours. Send my regards to Rick for a happy New Year also. And thank you both again for the new clubs. That was a total surprise!"

"You deserved them . . . and more!"

* * *

It was 5:00 p.m., and I decided to visit the warehouse to see how Tim was doing with the staging. When I got there, the door was locked, which I was glad to see. Tim answered my knock. The less the company knew about having all this inventory in the building, the better.

Tim had set up an efficient assembly line for this staging process. One of the three college students was speedily opening the boxes and placing the laptop on the long line of four-by-eight tables that Tim had rented from a local party rental store. The second student was plugging the computer into a series of power strips and booting up the machines. The third was running the diagnostic programs and loading the customer's software from jump drives.

Once the software was loaded and checked to make sure the download was successful, the first student would unplug the machine, repack it in the original box, and stack it on the "finished" skid.

I watched the whole process and noted that Tim had this system "tweaked" to the peak of efficiency. With Tim and the three students, the process was going very quickly. I asked Tim if he was keeping count of how many machines he had completed so far.

"Bob, we have three hundred machines done. We can do about seven hundred machines in an eight-hour day. We will have all these computers finished by Wednesday at the end of the day ready to deliver."

Tim's calculations seemed to be accurate. If he had all the staging done by next Wednesday, that gave us two extra days (Thursday and Friday) to get all the machines delivered by the end of the first week of January, which was perfect. I crossed my fingers, hoping that nothing would go wrong with Tim's plans.

Chapter 21

AND NOW, THE REST
OF THE STORY

*"If you talk about it, it's a dream, if you envision it,
it's possible, but if you schedule it, it's real."*

—TONY ROBBINS, AMERICAN AUTHOR, ENTREPRENEUR,
PHILANTHROPIST, AND LIFE COACH

THE MONTH OF DECEMBER HAD RECORD SALES AND PROFITS
for the company, which was an excellent start for the new year. The
sales and service department sold a total of $5.2 million in sales,
which resulted in a $300,000 profit for the month. The prior month,
November, reported $3.9 million in sales and a loss of ($104,000).
The final year-to-date sales were $48.3 million with loss of ($852,000).
This loss was very intimidating but reporting a profit for December
was encouraging.

Our outside accounting firm came in during the week between
Christmas and New Years and did most of the year-end work to
confirm all the financial information through the end of November
and was present for the physical inventory. They returned during
the third week of January and finished the review within one week.

The first sales meeting of the new year was the best meeting with
the sales team to date. I had the opportunity to hand out bonuses
to seven salespeople for orders each received from their ten target
customers. Nancy's bonus total was $5,000 (fifty $100 bills) for the
shipments to her two new target customers. When Nancy received

the money, she immediately called Amanda, Traci, Charlene, and Vicki to the front of the room and divided the bonus between the four of them. The smiles on the salespeople's faces as I was stacking the $100 bills in their hands as they were standing in front of the whole sales team was fantastic. Each of the salespeople who received the cash motivated everyone in the room to get to work and be the next in line to receive their new target customer bonuses.

Alice won the sales contest for the overall sales for the last three weeks of December. She received an iPod as her prize plus a big commission check at the end of the month.

I paid a total of $9,000 in sales spiffs to almost every salesperson in the sales department for selling the inventory in the warehouse. At the end of January, the inventory balance was down from $4 million to $1.5 million. I was very pleased. I figured that by the end of February we would sell all the inventory in the warehouse.

Tom started doing sales training the first week of January for the whole sales team. The training began each morning at 7:30 a.m. and ended at 9:00 a.m. He created a list of topics to be taught each morning for Monday through Friday for the first weeks of the new year. He was the instructor for most of the classes, and Nancy was the instructor for three or four. The results of the training started showing up immediately based on the January monthly reporting.

Darren distributed a weekly report that showed each salesperson's month-to-date actual sales versus same period prior year and their monthly quota. Every single salesperson, all thirteen, met or exceeded their sales quota for both hardware/software and service contract sales.

Tim's team delivered Nancy's order to all seven divisions of her pharma customer. Nancy rode on the delivery truck for four of the deliveries just to make sure everything went according to her plan. There was not one hiccup in the whole process of ordering the product, receiving it into the warehouse, staging each computer with the software, and delivering 3,500 laptops and 30 servers. There were still 100 laptops in the warehouse stored for the customer as per our agreement. After transporting all the machines to the seven divisions and all seven sign-off sheets had been signed, Nancy got the third $4.5 million-plus installment.

That following morning, I called a company-wide meeting to congratulate the employees. I prepared my notes to run down each accomplishment as follows:

- *We delivered an $18,210,000 order to our customer flawlessly.*

- *Our loan balance with the bank has been fully paid down to zero.*

- *As of the first week of January, we have record sales for the month in the history of the company.*

At the meeting, Nancy gave both Tim and Alan an envelope with twenty-five brand-new $100 bills for their part in handling her customer's order so perfectly.

Tim also received the first "Employee of the Month" award for December. He had received, warehoused, staged, and delivered Nancy's customer order three days early. Once we had received the laptops in the warehouse, Tim and his three-man crew worked from 6:00 a.m. until 12:00 a.m. four days straight to get all the work done. (Because Charlie had installed the security system app on my cell-phone, I was able to look in occasionally and see Tim and the college students working each evening.) For January, Tim would get to park his car in Craig's old parking spot with the sign labeled: EMPLOYEE OF THE MONTH. Tim's name would also be the first on the "Employee of the Month" trophy located in the company's reception area. He also received a gift card for dinner for two at the Ruth's Chris Steak House. When the management team handed Tim the award in front of every employee in the company, a round of applause followed. ABC's biggest cheerleader became teary-eyed and said thank you to everyone a record number of times.

The most significant surprise in January was that Tom had lost twenty-four pounds; he had been on a strict diet, which was unbe-knownst to me. At first, I did not notice his weight-loss efforts until his clothes started looking a little baggy. I was so proud of Tom because he had some terrible eating habits that would put him in an early grave if he didn't change them.

January sales were $26.4 million. I was extremely pleased because even without Nancy's record order, the sales were $8.2 million, which was materially higher than the company's best sales month ever. The bottom line for ABC Computer Distributors for January was a few thousand dollars less than $4 million profit. The large order did distort the numbers but in a very positive way. January's successes excited every employee at the company.

I asked Darren to schedule a meeting with our bankers to work with the bank on investing our idle finds in our checking account for the maximum return. Darren met with them and came up with a new cash management system to have the bank sweep our funds daily at the end of the day and invest them overnight. We opened an investment account, and now we had a new line item on our financial statements called "Interest Income"! What a significant change from a month earlier: $23,625 expense versus $535 income.

We met with three insurance agents in late January. All three quotes were between 25 percent and 35 percent less than what we were paying for our existing policies. Darren had been right. Matthew had indeed been robbing our company, and Craig had been letting him get away with it each year.

As it turned out, Stanley's quote was the lowest, and both Darren and I believed that his firm would provide us the best service. Darren planned to do some research on the insurance agency because we still had thirty days before Matthew's policies were set to terminate. Matthew had called Darren in an attempt to save our account, but Darren told him that even if his comments on the golf course had not turned off the president and CEO of ABC Computer Distributors, his prices were materially over the market price. He quietly went away.

At the end of January, the service department had thirty technicians in the field. The service department had exploded under Chris's leadership in workforce and profitability. At the end of the month, Chris and I mutually agreed that the department was too big for one person to manage at this point, and we decided to look for a manager, who would still report to Chris but would supervise half of the service techs. We also wanted this new position to be an excellent salesman to go on sales calls with the salespeople.

We presented the opportunity to the existing team, but as it turned out, another person from Chris's old company was perfect for the position. He was young, polished, personable, and quite knowledgeable in the computer service industry.

Each month, after Darren and Patrick completed the financial statements, I scheduled a meeting with Craig to review the progress of the company's profitability mission. I usually met Craig at Whitford Country Club for the financial review and update. I never invited him back to the company because I knew it would have a negative impact on every employee if they saw him walking around the offices. Once we had the loan paid off with the bank, he knew that his legal exposure was over. Each month as the company became more profitable, I could tell that Craig was anxious to sell the company and reap the financial benefits of the financial turnaround.

Fast forward now to June: On June 30, the company's year-to-date sales were slightly more than $80 million, which was much higher than I had anticipated. When I planned to distribute 33 percent of the profits to the management team, the managers decided that they wanted to pay 15 percent of the profits to their employees which reduced their share to 18%. I was very impressed by their loyalty to their teams. No one in the company could believe the size of their paychecks—all because they were working hard and pulling on the same side of the rope. The sales and service departments were working like one big team, and the relationships between the members of the management team were warm, respectful, and friendly.

Tom continued to lose weight. In six months, he had lost seventy-two pounds and said that he had thirty pounds to go. Nancy started taking cooking classes and was cooking healthy dinners at home every night for her and Tom.

By June, the service department was up to thirty-five techs. When I started back in November, no one wanted to work for Craig and Roger, but the success of the service department attracted more successful, quality people. At the end of June, Chris received a $31,000 bonus—that is, $1,000 per technician he recruited and hired.

When we distributed the June bonus checks to the management team, we decided to have another "little" get-together at Tom's house with all the managers and their spouses to celebrate the first six months of the year.

On July 1, Craig contacted one of the master distributors about selling his very successful company. By August 30, the attorneys had completed the transaction, and I was out of a job once again. I had successfully turned the company around, and my services were no longer required.

At the settlement date, the company recorded more than $121 million in annual sales. I did receive my share of the proceeds per my agreement. Happily, the acquiring company kept every employee at ABC Computer Distributors, and they finished the year as strong as they had started.

During the eight months I was at ABC Computer Distributors, our number-one achievement was awarding three high school seniors a four-year scholarship to the University of their choice. Alan, the purchasing manager, did an excellent job at raising money from our vendors for the scholarship program. ABC contributed $120,000 and our vendors matched our contribution dollar for dollar. I always stayed in touch with the three scholarship students even though the company was sold. The management team did a great job with picking the students because all three graduated with high honors with bachelor's degrees in four years.

Unfortunately, I never was able to go my golf trip as planned back in November because Kevin and Rick offered me another turn-around opportunity with another one of their customers, and I was off to Bristol, Pennsylvania, for my second turnaround.

Appendices

THE FORMS

Management Meeting Agenda (see page 357)—This form is significant because it documents the date, time, and location of the meeting. The document lists the topics to be discussed in the meeting and gives all the attendees at least twenty-four hours to prepare to talk intelligently about the subject matter. It also lists the attendees who are expected to attend the meeting and the amount of time allocated for each topic.

Income Statement and Balance Sheet (see pages 358 and 359)— The format of the company's financial statements is critical. I have always formatted the statements, so it would be easy for a "non-accountant" to read and understand the information on the reports. The income statement should always list the current month and year-to-date financial information compared to the budget and prior year. Unfortunately, ABC Computer Distributors did not have an operating budget for the company and did not list the prior year's financial information. The income statement should be able to be reported on one sheet of paper. Many times, the company's controller lists the expenses in too much detail, making the statements very hard to read and understand for a "non-accountant." The expenses on the income statement should be listed from the highest dollar expense (usually payroll) to the lowest dollar expense. That way, the executive reading the report can quickly focus on the most critical expense categories first since it is on the top of the expense category.

Job Offer Letter (see page 360)—When extending a job offer to a candidate, the job offer letter should state all the terms and conditions of the job offer, so the relationship between the employee and employer does not start off with any confusion or misunderstandings about the position. Essential items include starting salary, commission plan (if applicable), bonus plan (if applicable), the employee's start date, who the employee's supervisor is, a statement that the employee benefits are listed in the employee handbook, relocation benefits (if applicable), signing bonus (if applicable), and the 90-day probationary period.

Sales and Service Department Agenda (see pages 361 and 362)—Much like the management meeting agenda, the departmental agendas for these two revenue-generating departments are significant to keep the meeting on focus and provide a list of topics for every attendee to be prepared to discuss at the meetings. When you calculate the cost of employees attending a meeting (salaries, benefits, etc.), it is costly to waste any time. The meeting agendas' goals are to make the time of the scheduled meetings as efficient as possible to exchange information with all employees attending.

Sales Call Report (see page 363)—This report is a tool used to enforce the salespeople to gather essential information about the customer or potential customer to be added to the company's customer database. This report helps the salesperson report all the data about the sales call and the customer so that nothing may be missed or forgotten.

Customer Satisfaction Report or Survey (see page 364)—This report or survey is used to have the customer report to the executive management of the company the quality and results of the service call by the company's service technicians. When handled correctly, this customer survey procedure is a great tool to help improve the level of service provided to the customers by the technicians in the field.

Monthly Service Log (see page 365)—This report recaps the daily service reports and customer surveys information by each service technician to document the monthly production and quality of service as reported by the customers. This is the service technicians' "monthly report card" to be used by management to evaluate each technician.

Payroll Breakdown by Department (see page 366 to 368)—These reports recap the payroll data by the department to be used by management for several essential functions. The reports list all the critical payroll and performance data by the employee by the department for the administration to use and evaluate each employee properly. The list should rank the employees from the highest sales and service to the lowest.

Sales Pipeline Report (see page 369)—This report lists all the relative data about sales that are in the pipeline and soon to close. Sales and operations management uses this report as a tool to evaluate each salesperson's productivity and with the operations departments to prepare for future sales with inventory, staffing, etc.

Weekly Service Log (see page 370)—This report is a recap of the service department's weekly production to be used by management to determine and understand the level of productivity by the whole department.

Alternate Sales Call Report (see page 371)—This sales report is a very detailed recap of potential large sales to customers. This report would be used by sales management to stay in touch with each salesperson's activity to support them to close each of the deals.

Management, Sales, and Service Department Meeting Rules (see page 372)—This is the list of management meeting rules that everyone should follow to ensure that the meetings are executed as efficiently as possible.

MANAGEMENT MEETING AGENDA

ABC Computer Distributors
Management Meeting Agenda

	Date: Wednesday, December 3
	Time: 1:00 PM
	Location: Conference Room

Meeting called by: Bob Curry

Facilitator: Bob Curry

Attendees: Management team (Craig, Darren, Alan, Donna, Tom, Trish, Roger, and Tim)

Craig and Trish did not show up for the meeting.

AGENDA ITEMS

Topic	Presenter	Time allotted
Management Meeting Rules	Bob	10 Minutes
Chart of Organization	Bob	5 Minutes
Comments about Chris, the company's new service manager	Bob	5 Minutes
Goals for the Organization for the next thirty days	Bob	10 Minutes
Task Lists for the management team	Bob	10 Minutes
Inventory Adjustment Procedure	Tim	10 Minutes
Performance Reviews for all employees	Donna	5 Minutes
Questions or comments	Management team	5 Minutes

Other Information

Handouts: Management Meeting Rules, Existing and Revised Chart of Organizations, Task list for each manager, and Employee Performance Evaluation Policy and Form. Tim's Handouts.

Special notes: Please show up to the meeting on time!

INCOME STATEMENT

ABC Computer Distributors 11 Months Ending November 30				
	November		**Year To Date**	
	Actual		**Actual**	
INCOME	$	%	$	%
Sales	$ 3,916,750		$ 43,084,251	
COST OF GOODS SOLD				
Purchases	3,525,005	90%	38,775,826	90.00%
Direct Labor	121,905	3%	1,330,221	3.09%
Freight-in	55,150	1%	573,373	1.33%
TOTAL COST OF GOODS	3,702,060	95%	40,679,420	94.42%
GROSS PROFIT	214,690	5%	2,404,831	5.58%
SELLING EXPENSES				
Sales Salaries & Comm.	110,110	3%	1,228,352	2.85%
Advertising Expense	13,000	0%	142,954	0.33%
Travel & Meal Exp.	4,595	0%	55,095	0.13%
TOTAL SELLING EXPENSES	127,705	3%	1,426,401	3.31%
GENERAL & ADMIN. EXP.				
Salaries	72,592	2%	797,408	1.85%
Officer's Salary	15,000	0%	165,000	0.38%
Rent	20,000	1%	220,000	0.51%
Professional Services	9,030	0%	115,243	0.27%
Insurance	9,625	0%	105,875	0.25%
Depreciation	4,705	0%	52,542	0.12%
Taxes & Licenses	4,500	0%	60,935	0.14%
Telephone Expense	5,581	0%	60,296	0.14%
Utilities	6,510	0%	42,456	0.10%
Office Supplies	4,521	0%	43,129	0.10%
Auto & Truck Expenses	6,020	0%	56,421	0.13%
Repairs & Maintenance	2,758	0%	29,640	0.07%
Miscellaneous	1,825	0%	20,068	0.05%
Pension, Profit-sharing Plan	230	0%	14,213	0.03%
Collection Fees	-	0%	7,847	0.02%
Bank Charges	990	0%	8,782	0.02%
Dues & Subscriptions	804	0%	8,736	0.02%
Bad Debt Expense	-	0%	33,550	0.08%
Other G & A Expenses	2,635	0%	29,003	0.07%
TOTAL GEN & ADMIN EXP.	167,326	4%	1,871,143	4.34%
TOTAL OPERATING EXP.	295,031	8%	3,297,544	7.65%
Interest Expense	23,625	1%	259,659	0.60%
NET INCOME	$ (103,966)	-3%	$ (1,152,372)	-2.67%

BALANCE SHEET

ABC Computer Distributors Balance Sheet as of November 30	
	November
Assets	**Actual**
Current Assets	
Cash	$ 274,822
Accounts Receivable	4,752,500
Employee Loans	5,724
Inventory	3,123,000
Total Current Assets	**8,156,046**
Property & Equipment	
Office Equipment	251,350
Auto & Trucks	115,388
Leasehold Improvements	159,890
Software & Computers	175,000
Sub Total	701,628
**Less Accumulated Depreciation	(650,500)
Total Property & Equipment	**51,128**
Total Assets	**$ 8,207,174**
Liabilities & Capital	
Current Liabilities	
Accounts Payable	1,366,541
Accrued Expenses	200,500
Bank Line of Credit	6,300,400
Total Current Liabilities	**7,867,441**
Long Term Liabilities	
Note Payable - 2007 Lincoln	42,001
Total Long Term Liabilities	**42,001**
Total Liabilities	**7,909,442**
Capital	
Common Stock	300
Paid In Capital	308,145
Retained Earnings	(10,713)
Total Equity	**297,732**
Total Liabilities & Equity	**$ 8,207,174**

JOB OFFER LETTER

ABC COMPUTER DISTRIBUTORS
123 Main Street
Philadelphia, Pennsylvania 9999

December 7, 20XX

Christopher Last Name
456 Elm Street
Philadelphia, Pennsylvania 99999

Dear Chris:

We are pleased to offer you the position of Service Manager at the salary of eighty-five thousand dollars ($85,000) per year, effective at our agreed upon start date. In your first paycheck, you will receive a signing bonus of two thousand five hundred dollars ($2,500). You will be able to participate in the management bonus program as outlined in the employee manual on page XX.

This job is an exempt management position. The company's paydays are the fifteenth and thirtieth day each month. You will be reporting to me, the president. I will be available to respond to any questions you may have about our company's policies and practices. Your initial work schedule will be Monday through Friday from 8:00 a.m. until 5:00 p.m.

This offer is contingent upon your ability to perform the essential functions of this position, as determined by your performance and meeting any educational, technical, and experience standards as defined by your job description. The offer is further conditioned upon your signed acknowledgment of the employee handbook, your successful passing of a background check, credit check, drug test, and your eligibility to work in the U.S., as determined by the requirements of the Immigration Reform and Control Act. Your employee benefit will be as they are outlined in the employee manual starting on page XX.

Please be aware that you will be in a ninety (90) day probation period once you join the organization. The detail information concerning this probationary time is in the employee manual on page XX. The probation period starts on your date of hire ending in three months. I will work with you regularly to provide performance feedback.

We hope you find this offer satisfactory and that you decide to accept employment with our organization. As with all our team members, your job with the company is on an at-will basis and can be terminated at any time with or without notice by you or the company. If you have any questions, feel free to call me.

Please let us know your decision within seven days of this letter so we may complete our staffing plans. We look forward to hearing from you.

Sincerely yours,

Robert S. Curry
President / CEO

Acknowledgment of receipt: _____ _Date: _____

SALES MEETING AGENDA

ABC Computer Distributors Sales Meeting Agenda	Date: Friday, December 5
	Time: 2:00 PM
	Location: Conference Room

Meeting called by: Bob Curry

Facilitator: Bob Curry

Attendees: Sales Manager, All Salespeople, Sales Support Employees, and Purchasing Manager

Agenda Items

Topic	Presenter	Time allotted
Future Sales Meeting Schedule	Bob	2 Minutes
Sales Meeting Rules	Bob	2 Minutes
Introduction of Chris, the New Service Manager	Bob	5 Minutes
Company Mission	Bob	2 Minutes
Business Goals	Bob	2 Minutes
Add Additional Employee to Sales Support	Bob	2 Minutes
Sales Department Goals	Bob	5 Minutes
Weekly / Monthly Sales Contests	Bob	5 Minutes
Sales Target Lists, Reviews, and Payments	Bob	5 Minutes
New Sales Commission Plan	Bob	5 Minutes
Tom to Ride with Sales Staff	Bob	2 Minutes
Sales Spiffs for Sales of stock Inventory	Bob	1 Minute
Sales Training Classes	Tom	2 Minutes
Christmas Party	Bob	5 Minutes
Questions and Answers	Bob	5 Minutes

Other Information: _____

_____

Special Notes: _____

_____

Service Department Meeting Agenda

ABC Computer Distributors Service Department Meeting Agenda	Date: <u>Friday, December 5</u> Time: <u>2:00 PM</u> Location: <u>Conference Room</u>

Meeting called by: Bob Curry

Facilitator: Bob Curry

Attendees: Chris, All Service Technicians, and Gina

Agenda Items

Topic	Presenter	Time allotted
Future Service Department Meeting Schedule	Bob	1 Minute
Service Department Meeting Rules	Bob	2 Minutes
Introduction of Bob Curry	Bob	3 Minutes
Goals for the Business	Bob	5 Minutes
Service Department Problems	Bob	5 Minutes
New Service Department Productivity Reporting	Bob	3 Minutes
Service Technician Goals	Bob	5 Minutes
Evaluation of Technical Skills	Bob	5 Minutes
Saturday Morning Skills Training	Bob	5 Minutes
Sales Projections for the Service Department	Bob	2 Minutes
Implementing a Customer Survey Program	Bob	2 Minutes
Service Department Rewards for Productivity and Quality Service	Bob	4 Minute
New Employee Referral Fees	Bob	2 Minutes
Questions and Answers	Bob	5 Minutes

Other Information: _____

_____

Special Notes:_____

_____

SALES CALL REPORT

ABC Computer Distributors Sales Call Report		
Account Details		
Account Name	Project or Opportunity	Phone Number
Location	Primary Contact	Call Date
Account Executive	Primary Contact E-Mail	Call Time
Call Purpose & Expected Outcomes		
Customer Participants **(Name, Title, & Position)**		**Our Company Participants** **(Name, Title, & Position)**
Planned Agenda (Include Our Business Value and Client Industry Issues)		
Competitive Issues & Obstacles		**Required Resources & Advance Preparation**

Signature: _____   **Date:** _____

CUSTOMER SATISFACTION REPORT

ABC Computer Distributors
123 Main Street • Philadelphia, PA 19103

Customer Satisfaction Report

Date of Service: _____   Service Order #: 012345

Dear Mr. Customer,

I would like to thank you for purchasing our products and services. For us to improve the quality of our products and the delivery of our services, I would like to ask you to grade us. Our employees and management team are measured and compensated on the quality of their work. I, the president/CEO of the company, use this valuable information to understand better how we are servicing our customers. Thank you in advance for your time and effort of answering these questions and mailing this letter back to me in the envelope provided.

5 = Excellent	4 = Good	3 = Satisfactory	2 = Fair	1 = Poor

_____ **How would you rate the quality of our service to your computer?**

_____ **How would you rate the service technician as being courteous and friendly?**

_____ **How would you rate the responsiveness of our service technician?**

_____ **How would you rate the professionalism of the service technician?**

_____ **How would you rate the service technician regarding the clean-up of the work area once the service was completed?**

_____ **How would you rate the service technician; did he answer all your questions concerning the operation of your computer once he completed his work?**

Comments: _____

_____

_____

Sincerely,

Bob Curry
President/CEO   Service Technician: _____

MONTHLY SERVICE LOG

ABC Computer Distributors Monthly Service Log

Month Ending _____

Service Technician: _____

#	Service #	Date Assigned	Customer #	Customer Name	Customer's Employee Requesting Service	Date Service Completed	Date Survey Received	Total Cust. Survey Rating
1								
2								
3								
4								
5								
6								
7								
8								
9								
10								
11								
12								
13								
14								
15								
16								
17								
18								
19								
20								
21								
22								
23								
					Total Average Customer Survey Rating			

PAYROLL BREAKDOWN

ABC Computer Distributors
Payroll Breakdown by Department
As of December ___

#	Dept.	Employee	Date of Hire	Annual Salary	Commission	Total Compensation	Date of Last Salary Review	Dollar Amount of Salary Review

SALES DEPARTMENT

ABC Computer Distributors
Sales Department
As of December _____

#	Employee	Date of Hire	YTD (Hardware/Software) Sales ($)	Gross Profit ($)	YTD (Service) Sales ($)	Gross Profit ($)	YTD (Total) Sales ($)	Gross Profit ($)

SERVICE DEPARTMENT

ABC Computer Distributors
Service Department
As of December _____

#	Employee	Date of Hire	Billing Rate / Hr.	Hours Billed	YTD (Total) Sales Revenue

SALES PIPELINE REPORT

ABC Computer Distributors
Sales Pipeline Report

Responsibility	Opportunity Name	Project Type	Client Contact Name (Last, First)	Salesperson		Business Opportunities						
				Initial Contact Date (MM/DD/YY)	Lead Source	Forecast Amount ($)	Forecast Close of Deal (MM/DD/YY)	Forecast Project Length (Days)	Pipeline Phase	Date Entered This Pipeline Phase (MM/DD/YY)	Next Step in Processing of Getting Deal Closed

WEEKLY SERVICE LOG

ABC Computer Distributors
Weekly Service Log

Week Ending _____

Service Technician: _____

Service Number	Date	Customer Name	Address	City	Phone Number	Warrantee / Billable	Original Purchase Date	Date of Service Call	Amount Invoiced	Check/ Invoice #	Amount Collected
Monthly Totals											

ALTERNATE SALES CALL REPORT

ABC Computer Distributors
Sales Call Report

As of _____

Salesperson: _____

Responsibility	Opportunity Name	Sales Type	Client Contact Name (Last, First)	Initial Contact Date (MM/DD/YY)	Lead Source	Forecast Amount ($)	Forecast Close of Deal (MM/DD/YY)	Forecast Project Length (Days)	Pipeline Phase	Date Entered This Pipeline Phase (MM/DD/YY)	Next Step in Processing of Getting Deal Closed

Business Opportunities

ABC Computer Distributors
Management, Sales, and Service Department Meeting Rules

- There will be an agenda for the meeting distributed to everyone at least twenty-four hours in advance of the meeting. Whoever is chairing the meeting is responsible for creating the agenda. Everyone should be prepared to intelligently participate with all topics since each of you have a day to prepare for each issue to be discussed.

- Attendance for the complete management team is mandatory for all future meetings.

- Setting all cellphones in silent mode will stop all phone interruptions, with only emergency calls answered.

- The meetings will be set for the same day and time each week, so members of the management team can post the meetings on their calendars for the balance of the year to ensure there are no scheduling conflicts for any of the meetings in the future.

- The meetings will start on time and last a maximum of one hour.

- Meeting minutes will be taken at each meeting and distributed to all attendees.

- The first item on the agendas will be the follow-up on any open tasks from the prior week's meeting.

- Finally, if anyone is late or does not attend the meeting, that person will put twenty dollars in the dish on the conference room table.

ABOUT THE AUTHOR

Robert S. Curry is a seasoned business coach and successful turnaround specialist. Early in his career, he served as a public accountant for two years before taking on the role of assistant controller, controller, and later CFO for a public retail company. Later, Bob served as president and CEO of three different companies—all of which experienced successful turnarounds under his direction. In the late 1990s, he began his turnaround consulting firm, and for the past twenty years, he has worked with more than seventy companies helping each to establish a strong management team and become profitable. Bob is the author of *From Red to Black* and resides in Fort Lauderdale, Florida, with his wife, Esther.

Made in the USA
Las Vegas, NV
07 August 2022

52892144R00210